10

8

9

11

12

15

13

14

16

17

18

19

ALSO BY JOAN RIVERS

Having a Baby Can Be a Scream
The Life and Hard Times of Heidi Abromowitz
Enter Talking

Still Talking

Still Talking

·····

Joan Rivers

with
Richard Meryman

Turtle Bay Books · Random House

New York · 1991

Library of Congress Cataloging-in-Publication Data

Rivers, Joan.
Still talking / Joan Rivers with Richard Meryman
p.   cm.
ISBN 0-394-57991-7
1. Rivers, Joan.   2. Comedians—United States—Biography.
I. Meryman, Richard, 1926– . II. Title.
PN2287.R55A3 1991
792.7'028'092—dc20
[B]   90-53477

Manufactured in the United States of America
2 4 6 8 9 7 5 3
First Edition
Book design by Jo Anne Metsch

To Melissa,
who has shared so much of the pain,
and so little of the glory

Thanks to Susan Kamil,
who was head of the cheerleading team,
and to Dorothy Melvin and Tom Pileggi,
who taught her the steps.

Still Talking

1

○○○○○

The news had already been on the radio, and all hell had broken loose. The phones had been ringing with calls from friends and the press, but my daughter, Melissa, had already taken over. It was she who received the phone call from Philadelphia, and immediately called the house staff together. Her face streaming with tears, she told them, "I want you to know he loved you all very dearly."

Now she was making the important calls to the extended family and organizing the secretaries to notify a long list of friends and acquaintances. My assistant, Dorothy Melvin, had flown to Oklahoma to meet her boyfriend's parents; at the airport they gave her the news, and she took the next plane back.

Flowers began arriving—which pleased and enraged me for my husband's sake. The time when Edgar needed such attention was after the firing from Fox. They were two months late. I sent most of them to an AIDS hospice.

The awful practicalities took over—can Edgar be cremated in time for a service on Sunday? Which temple for the funeral? Who should speak at the service? Who should handle the catering for the reception afterward? How many valet parkers would we need? I think everybody during the first days of a death feels the person is somehow there, knows what is happening, and the buzzwords for the next three days were, "It should be done right. Edgar would have wanted that."

A rabbi arrived with words but no comfort. The press was telephoning. My publicist, Richard Grant, came to write the press release and work up an obituary. Almost nobody knew that I had separated from Edgar, and I was terrified that it would leak out and become a scandal, the press picking us apart again. During this frenetic activity, my Yorkshire terrier, Spike, came into the office and did something he had never done before, never did again. He jumped up on Edgar's chair and onto his desk and sat there.

Throughout the day my support group kept arriving. Coral Browne, wife of Vincent Price, heard the news on the radio, and this elegant British actress, never out of her Chanel suit, jumped into her car wearing a bathrobe and slippers and drove over immediately. She was furious with Edgar for doing this to me, but insisted: "All right, darling, you've got to deal with this. You'll get through it."

From New York came Tommy Corcoran, a loyal friend since before Edgar; from Las Vegas came Mark Tan, a columnist who adored Edgar, their friendship dating back to the nights we roamed the casino showrooms. My dear friend and dresser Ann Pierce came from Vegas and moved in. Dorothy Melvin moved in. Kenneth Battelle, the great hairdresser, who had been wonderful to me for twenty years, called and said, "What can I do?" I said, "Come out." This man who in thirty-four years of business had never missed or broken an appointment, this Calvinist who once worked right through pneumonia, got on the next plane.

Tom Pileggi, though Edgar's closest friend, did not come out, and I completely understood. When Edgar lied to him about his state of mind, saying, "I won't do anything foolish," Tom answered, half joking, "If you do, I won't come to your funeral." Well, Tom lived by the code that a man's word is his bond. That weekend, full of anger and sorrow, he went off by himself on his boat.

When Roddy McDowall arrived, very consoling, a man who

truly loved Edgar, he brought a message from Elizabeth Taylor. She had told him, "If Joan wants to call me, she can." I thought, Call her? Who the hell does she think she is? Gee, if I'm real polite maybe she'll even say something kind to me. That anger was the first emotion to penetrate my numbness.

In my trancelike state, I wanted people around me who were feeling the sharp pain of mourning, who could do my feeling for me, could give Edgar that testimony to his value. I wanted Edgar, who had been so unloved for the last three years, so put down and hurt and publicly humiliated, to have their caring and respect. The only people I wanted around were those who knew the worth of the man. Certain relatives, who would have upset him, we asked not to come.

My inner circle constantly gathered in little groups, talking, talking, talking, often in the kitchen when they came down to get a snack, or in strange places—meeting each other on the stairs and sitting down and talking—searching, searching for the why, searching for the unknowable.

Billy Sammeth, my manager, said, "He had played out all his cards." I repeated to the others something Edgar said to Tom Pileggi—"Pride can kill a man, and that's all I have left." Most of those closest to me in my life believed that Edgar wanted to be found and have his stomach pumped. They argued that he had left his hotel room door unlocked—*very* un-Edgar—so security guards could easily save him. They pointed out that his body was found on the floor, evidence that he had reached too late for the telephone and missed and fallen.

Melissa—and Tom Pileggi talking on the telephone—believed that Edgar thought he had cancer, which ran in his family. They reminded us that he had a growth in his mouth that kept returning. Tom said, "He thought he was going to slowly deteriorate to nothing, and he didn't want his family to see him die that way." For some reason, what gave me the most comfort, what I kept repeating, was somebody's opinion that "Edgar was looking for a door to go through and take his pride with him."

I guess I think that during all those days of mixed messages, he wanted in his head to die and in his heart to live. I think he was throwing out cries for help to bring me back, but people get

enmeshed in their stratagems until they don't know if attempt-
ing suicide is a game or feel, By God, I've got to do it. And then
when Edgar felt the pills taking over, it was, Uh-oh, this is stupid.
I've got to get help.

One thing everybody agreed on, Edgar had needed to go into
therapy. That would have been the only way to save him.

Throughout the morning Melissa was all poise and efficiency,
directing the office. But as the day progressed, she began disintegrating, and the veil would momentarily drop and the pain was
stark in her face.

I was dazed with shock. I could remember, as if it were a
century ago, waiting in the hospital room that morning after
minor surgery—and Melissa suddenly appearing, short of breath
from running. She said, "Sit down." I said, "Tell me." I like my
bad news right away and standing up. She said, "Daddy's dead."

I have no memory of the next few minutes. I am told I went
stark white. My right hand clamped onto the chair in front of me.
Staring sightlessly out the window, I moaned over and over, "Oh,
my God. Oh, my God. Oh, my God." In my head I screamed the
words, "What have I done? What have I done?" If I had made
that one phone call to Edgar saying, "Come home," he would still
be alive. I had killed Edgar as surely as though I had pulled a
trigger.

I think the body takes over at crisis moments, knows what is best
for itself, ignores the mind where the hysteria runs riot. I shut
down, entered a strange sphere of detachment, floating above
reality. I heard myself talking to people, but that was not me
talking, that was my voice in an echo chamber.

The body also softens such a blow with disbelief. This had to
be a mistake, a waking nightmare that would go away. I was
waiting for somebody to call and say, "Wrong person. Terribly
sorry. Gee, what an error." I think that is what Melissa wanted
from her mother, who had always taken care of everything—
confirmation that nothing had happened, wanted me to say, "Oh,
it's all a mistake. Don't bother yourself."

She would find me—in the bedroom, the office, my dressing
room, the bathroom, the kitchen table late at night—and we

would shut the door and talk and talk and talk, going over the same ground again and again. Sometimes I put my arms around her or held her hands. On that Friday, as we sat together on the small step up to my bathtub, she told me, "I can never be truly happy again. I'll always be thinking, If only Daddy were here. He's never going to see my children. He's never going to meet the man I marry."

She was devastated that her own father had lied to her, had said he was coming home. She flayed herself for not telephoning him a second time on Thursday night; maybe the sound of her voice would have changed his mind. She looked for some rationale to ease her guilt. She said, "Nobody ever made a decision for my daddy, and we should allow him the dignity of making his own final decision." Then she reminded herself that in Philadelphia he was not the rational man she admired and said, "He was my father, but he wasn't my *father.*"

I tried to help her by interpreting Edgar, giving her reasons why he had been so terribly ill and frightened. We talked angrily about what the article in *People* magazine and Fox did to Daddy. I linked together for Melissa his disintegrating health, his Germanic background, his uprooted, displaced, isolated childhood, his belief that you always had to be what you were supposed to be and live up to that standard, his belief after Fox that the career was finished. I showed Melissa a little picture of Edgar on his first day of school in Germany, wearing a cap in the sun, the apple of his parents' eyes, standing there still healthy, carrying a cone container of candy for the teacher. Ahead lay Hitler and TB and the heart attack and being tossed and turned and frustrated— and then his fulfillment was taken away, and again he was not allowed to have his dream.

But I was helpless to heal my daughter. To me motherhood had always been teaching and protecting, giving Melissa as much knowledge as I had about any situation that came up in her life. Though children totally reject advice, you hope you are planting a seed. When Melissa was little, I would say, "Don't waste your tears. God only gives you a certain amount, so don't waste them on this." Later when something bad happened—when her first romance broke up—I said, "Trust me. The pain will pass." My counsel had always been, "Whatever is bothering you, write it down in a book. Close the book, and a year later you'll open it up and say, 'Big deal.'"

Now, those lessons were empty. This was what she had saved her tears for. This would forever be a well of pain. I had no comfort to give Melissa, no way to protect her. For the first time as a mother, I felt helpless. There was no one I could call to make it okay, nothing I could do. I was now a failure as a mother as well as a failure as a wife. Instead of protecting my daughter, I had been the catalyst in the death of her father.

In the afternoon of that Friday my numbness gave way to anger—anger at myself, anger at Edgar for doing this to both of us, especially to Melissa, the one person for whom he felt unconditional love. In direct proportion to Melissa's shift from shock into grief, my anger grew. I hated myself for giving in to it, for my weakness against it, for being so disloyal to this man who had loved me. I desperately wanted to dwell on my love, on our friendship, the way I felt I should.

I tried to tamp down the anger by seeking out people who had loved him. I tried to draw their mourning into myself to push away the rage, but then I would hate myself more because I felt I lacked the decency to grieve properly. I would see some sign of Edgar—his desk drawer slightly open and his pencil tossed on the top—and I would feel impaled by pain, and I would weep— then the sight of the pure despair on my daughter's face would refuel my anger.

Late Friday afternoon, after my talk with Melissa in the bathroom, I sat by myself on the bathroom floor. My eyes went to the glass door of Edgar's cabinet, the rows of pill bottles visible inside. Our life together had ended up in that cabinet. "You bastard!" I yelled out loud.

I wrenched open the door and swept every pill, shelf after shelf, into a big wastebasket, dropping them, spilling them, flinging them, clumsy with rage. Then came the terrible tears of guilt. What kind of person was I? What kind of woman would drive a man to suicide and then strike out at him?

But, strangely, in my rage I also felt bonded with Edgar, with the anger at me that must have consumed him. Like my own anger, his must have been a sickness that ran away with his reason. How many of those tranquilizers, how many swallows of brandy, had been aimed at me?

I think possibly my life was saved by two women—certainly my daughter, and Mariette Hartley. That evening Mariette, then the hostess of *The Morning Program,* telephoned me. Her father had killed himself when she was twenty-three, and now she was part of a network of suicide survivors who rush to help people like Melissa and me.

She wanted me to know that every single feeling I was having was valid and necessary. She said, "Grief is not graceful." She told me that my fury at Edgar was natural and even healthy, and that she had needed years to finally feel her anger and deal with it. When she told me, "There was nothing more you could have done," I still thought, I could have gone to Philadelphia.

Mariette put me in touch with Iris Bolton, whose twenty-year-old son had committed suicide and who now ran a support group for suicide survivors at her family counseling center, called The Link, in Atlanta, Georgia. Melissa and I talked with her on the phone for an hour and a half.

I was impressed that she knew so well what we were going through—the shock, the disbelief, the wondering. She said, "The 'why' *must* be asked and asked and asked until the question is worn out and you can let it go and just live with your hunches." She insisted that my anger was appropriate, telling me that suicide is the ultimate act of control and power. Edgar had had the last word and left me dangling, unable to resolve our conflict, unable even to say good-bye.

She warned Melissa and me that blaming was inevitable. Struggling to make sense of a senseless act, people find answers by blaming others, by blaming themselves. She said my guilt was really grandiosity—"We think we are so powerful, so important in their lives, that they killed themselves because of what we did or did not do." I told her I felt guilty about ignoring Edgar's signals, and she reminded me that his signals were mixed—and survivors have trouble believing that anybody would hurt that much—while the suicide misreads *your* signals and decides you do not care.

Iris and Mariette did not lift my anger, did not soften my guilt, but their clear voices, still tender with their own pain, reassured me that I was not crazy and not evil. I understood that Melissa and I were going through a double whammy, the regular grief process plus the special hell of a suicide. I was miserable, but in my misery I was normal. I was not alone. When they both said, "You will survive," I thought, Yeah, maybe, but I felt hope. If they had done it, so could I.

When I told Iris how worried I would be about Melissa, alone in the East in college, she said I was right to be concerned and urged us both to get counseling and offered to suggest a therapist for Melissa in Philadelphia. She also made us promise each other that we would not harm ourselves. That night Melissa slept with me—on Edgar's side of the bed.

But I could not sleep. Now in the solitude, in the silence, of the house, the way was open for grief. All night in a mindless haze of pain and tears, I wandered through the house, walked upstairs, walked downstairs, into the library, the dining room, the living room. In grief the bad memories are washed away, the good ones stay.

Walking, walking, I felt so sad for the house, knowing it was going to change, remembering the warmth and light that had been in those rooms, the good times, the formal dinner parties with the women dressed to the nines, the major jewelry out and sparkling. I thought about the small gatherings for really good friends—the good times when we sat with the fire going and talked and laughed and talked and laughed and Edgar was optimistic and feeling good.

The kitchen was the place where I did my crying, sitting at the table with Dorothy and Annie, who were still awake. And then I wanted to be alone again and wandered away into the library, a room steeped in memories—such as the wonderful trip to London when we bought the Chippendale chairs, our first big-time purchase, when we thought we were on easy street.

Every single thing in that house we had collected together.

The grandfather clock we bought in England played eight Scottish tunes. I remembered how worried we were that it would get broken and we would have to say to an American clock man, "Do you know 'The Bonnie March of the Ninth Brigade'? Because you've got to fix that."

Everywhere through the house were photographs—of Edgar, of his parents, of his ancestors, of Melissa at all ages. I picked up an unframed snapshot, the last picture taken of Edgar. In our suite at Atlantic City, one end of the room was full of friends and relatives, but Edgar stood apart, isolated at the other end, leaning on the back of a chair, head down.

As I wandered, I talked aloud to myself, telling the air, "He was my rock. I didn't mean anything I said." Unable to focus, I just moved slowly through the house, carrying one of the gardenias Edgar had sent me in the hospital, peering at everything like a tourist in a foreign country. Traces of Edgar were everywhere. "Look at his date book," I said to myself. "Look at his writing on that pad. There's his note on the freezer door. His briefcase is leaning against my bookcase; I don't ever want to open it."

The enormity of Edgar's death was beyond my comprehension. Unlike a death preceded by an illness, where life has already been altered, there was no evidence that the center of my universe for twenty-two years had been removed. Nobody took me upstairs and showed me a person on the floor. His death was an abstract concept. The house was exactly the same, waiting for him.

In the bedroom his books and pills and notepads were on his night table. When I wandered into the dressing room, his pajamas hung from the hook. In the bathroom, behind the glass door of Edgar's floor-to-ceiling cabinet—his sacrosanct preserve—I could see his meticulous arrangement of combs lined up, his gold manicure set, his can of shaving cream—with eight in reserve behind it—his lemon-lime cologne with spares behind it, his security in case of catastrophe.

I realized, heartsick, that I could now invade Edgar's sanctums that had always been off-limits to me—like a mother's bureau to a child. Now I could take over his side of the bathroom, could now go into his closet, could use his desk. Yes, he was gone. Yes, everything *was* different. Nothing would ever be the same. I stood there, utterly lost, thinking, What will I do without you?

I felt weak and sat on the edge of the tub. My last words with Edgar had been an argument. In my last talk with my mother, I had been angry. When my father was in the hospital with a heart attack, she refused to hire a live-in nurse for him when he came home, saying she wanted to do it herself, and I angrily insisted on it. The next day she was dead of heart failure.

Why do we fight with the people we love the most—and never with the people who do not care about us? Is this the human condition, hurting and being hurt by the ones you love—no way to make up, to be forgiven, blaming yourself for what you did or did not say, and should have done? May both Edgar and Beatrice rest in peace. May *I* rest in peace.

On Saturday, Michael Greenstein, a therapist suggested by my friend Wallis Annenberg, came to the house. I was open to the idea because I had done family counseling with Melissa to get us both through her period of teenage rebellion and individuation. Edgar came to the first session and sat there, silent, then refused to come again.

I knew the value of a nonjudgmental person you can tell the truth to who will help you, get it out so you can look at it and deal with it. A therapist will not solve your problem for you, but eventually *you* will solve it. Emotional troubles are like landfill. Get them outside, and the air disintegrates them.

I think when you are ill, you are torn between your rational mind and irrational emotions, and the guilts and fears have the upper hand. Getting well is gradually having the rational become your reality. I knew in my head that the suicide-support ladies were right, that Edgar's death was not my fault. He had been a very sick man—and without therapy he would have dragged me down into his morass. Michael immediately began reinforcing that truth, telling me the bottom line: "After Edgar's complete loss of control, his rage at himself and the world made life intolerable."

. . .

Edgar's body arrived in Los Angeles on Saturday. Melissa and I decided to have Edgar dressed in his best Savile Row blue suit with a pink shirt and a red-and-blue striped tie—dressed the way he would have wanted, with class and dignity, like an English gentleman. I invited the staff to send personal mementos to the funeral home to go into the coffin. Marcia Tysseling, our all-purpose assistant, sent a loving note and Edgar's morning vitamin packet and a business card from Frank's Deli. Melissa put in hair from the dogs who loved him. Both pairs of glasses went in—and a roll of Tums. Dorothy sent his phone list, and I added a can of the Diet Slice he loved and a bottle of 4711 cologne—and a note saying, "I love you. How can I go on without you?" It was all very Egyptian. I think death beats every primitive drum we have in our genes.

That afternoon I went to the funeral home by myself—Melissa decided to spare herself that memory of her father. I made no announcement of a "viewing" because I did not wish to be there receiving people, but I did not want him to be alone. In the midst of my anger I was still trying to nurture and protect him.

I was nervous about my reaction to seeing him. Bending over the casket, I saw that he had shaved off his beard. He had grown it after the heart attack because he could not lift his arms high enough to shave, and then, even though he knew I hated it, he left it on, perhaps because it was one thing he could control. Maybe shaving now was a peace gesture.

I saw a face that was young again, the inner Edgar, his sweetness, the untroubled man who had come courting with two dozen roses and thought we were going to live on Fifth Avenue forever and own the world. I was pulled back twenty years to the fun and the excitement of becoming a couple and having our baby, the adventure of growing and moving forward together. I thought, Oh God. What have we done to each other? I thought, What a blessing we cannot foresee the future.

Feeling the terrible waste of this man who could have had everything, feeling a crazy urge to goad him back to life, I said, "Why? Why? This is the dumbest thing you've ever pulled. Look what you've done to Melissa." I waited. Nothing.

I told him the gossip, who had arrived, who had called, who was flying out from back East—a friend talking on the telephone. I cried, the tears falling on his hands and face. I said things that would have made him laugh: "You'll be happy to know I've banned two of your cousins from the funeral."

Back home I told Melissa how important it had been for me to see him so serene and how pleased she would have been to see him looking happy again.

That night I went back a second time alone to make sure he was okay, to let him have a visitor. The third time was at 4:00 A.M. Sunday morning to see him once more before he was cremated. Strangely, as long as he was lying there, he was still not dead. I felt tremendous pity for this man who had spent all those years on the run—from the Nazis, from his TB, from his pain and bitterness and secrets—so continually on the run that he could not get help.

On Sunday Edgar's ashes were delivered to the house in a small square box. I left it on my dressing table with a rose and a good-luck stone on top.

The funeral service was held in the Wilshire Boulevard Temple, a very beautiful, very large synagogue. We traveled in a long file of stretch limos escorted by motorcycle police, all of us saying how much Edgar would have loved this parade. The family and close friends went in a side door—and were joined by an old friend of Edgar's, Roy Zurkowski. Ill at ease, he blurted out, "Edgar was a classy guy. Classy dresser."

That destroyed me. Nobody in California had understood that Edgar was a classy guy. I turned blindly down an empty hall, leaned my forehead against the wall, and wept. Melissa touched my hand and said, "It's all right to cry. It's all right." I answered, "It's not 'classy' to cry in public." Melissa, so sweet, reaching for our prescription for pain, made a joke, saying, "Princess Di cried in public when Charles's horse died." I laughed and said, "Then the princess has no class."

The temple was full. A thousand people came, including Mayor Bradley, Milton Berle, Bea Arthur, Jon Voight, Tony Franciosa, Jackie Collins, Michele Lee, Angie Dickinson, Nancy Walker, and Cher. Lovely eulogies were given by Roddy McDowall, Tommy Corcoran, and Vincent Price. Hundreds of people stood outside.

Left to myself, I would have had a very small, totally private ceremony with none of the display. And, believe me, *People* magazine would not have been in there. I decided to have these elaborate ceremonies for the sake of Edgar and Melissa, to show Edgar, "Yes, your life *was* important. Yes, you *were* somebody. Yes, a thousand people came when you died."

In these first days ceremony is soothing, satisfying. A funeral allows the grievers to feel this person was worthy of their grief. And when somebody dies, ritual brings a form to life, a forum where all grievers can speak, get out their feelings, vent, cry, be told they are right, their loss *is* major—and no matter who died, people will have to listen and be polite.

Melissa said to me afterward, "If only Daddy could have seen it—and he thought he was so despised. It was like, 'Daddy, people understood you.' " After a pause she added, "I'm sure he knew how much we loved him." I said, "Yes, he knew. He knew."

Following the service, there was a reception at the house, which looked wonderful, luxuriant with flowers, and was filled with people and talk and laughter. I grieved that Edgar was not there to enjoy the gaiety, enjoy his pride in this place we had built together, enjoy the white-gloved waiters serving from silver trays, enjoy the people who came.

But there were also the people who came through the receiving line and put their arms around me and said, "Are you all right?"—and I wanted to put a knife in their chests because these were the ones who had sneered at Edgar behind his back. But that was how I kept going, the anger pumping the adrenaline through me as I played the role of dignified widow.

I remember Jill Eikenberry, Michael Tucker, Dom DeLuise, Dolly Parton, Barbara Walters, Allan Carr, Mariette Hartley, Rona Barrett, Anne and Kirk Douglas, Sandy Gallin, Pamela Mason, Elton John, Florence Henderson. I was amazed that I never heard a syllable from Johnny Carson. Forgetting that Hollywood is purely a business town, I thought he would have, for a moment, remembered that he had known Edgar even before I did, and let bygones be bygones. But dozens of people did arrive from the past, from years ago in New York. They looked to me as though they had put lines in their face and grayed their hair—as though they were going from the *shivah*—the Jewish ritual of mourning—to rehearsals of *Our Town.*

Insane things happen when you are a celebrity. Virtual strangers arrived to console the star. When my mother died, a rabbi and his daughter came to all seven days of *shivah* before I discovered they were complete strangers. Now, the same rabbi called from the East and wanted to come out with his daughter to Edgar's *shivah.* The mother of one of Melissa's nursery-school friends, a woman I had met three times, flew out unasked and was angry that others were monopolizing me. A girl who had been a friend in my sophomore year at Connecticut College did the same thing. After the funeral, she hired a taxi and followed the cars to the house for the reception. Late in the afternoon she erupted to Dorothy Melvin, furious and feeling slighted because I was not taking advantage of her comforting shoulder.

During those evening ceremonies when the rabbi came and spoke—and I was playing the brave widow—I felt like an utter hypocrite. I am sure that this is part of the first months of mourning—every lousy thing you ever did comes flooding back. I would think, Don't you all know? He killed himself because of me. We're playing this game, and I wish you'd all go home. In my craziness I was half waiting for the police to come in and arrest me for murder, come up to me and say, "Mrs. Rosenberg, can we talk to you for a minute? We have this witness—you said to your husband, 'You can't come home.' "

The best therapy for me would have been to go right from the mortuary onto a stage, but my advisers agreed it would be unseemly. We decided I would reappear in public as a presenter on the Emmy Awards September 30 and return as a performer in mid-November. In any case, my agent said, since the Fox firing, booking me was extremely hard, and Caesars Palace was cutting me from fourteen to ten shows a week, which almost halved the money.

Additionally I was fearful that any audience, including television viewers, might not accept a new widow trying to be funny. If you are in deep mourning and *People* magazine has just given you a cover and you're on every CNN newscast in black, people don't want you coming out and saying, "My boobies are so low, I can nurse China from my bedroom." They will not understand that by saying it, you are keeping the door locked to sorrow. I could imagine people thinking, Look at her. She must be some piece of change. No wonder he killed himself.

Then there was the question, "What should the act be?" No longer could I come out as a married woman. Nobody wanted to hear about problems on my wedding night. I would have to find a new persona. What could I joke about? Finally having all that closet space?

I was terrified of crying the first time I walked onstage, but did not want a sympathy audience. I did not want a warm hand on my shoulder. I felt like Bea Lillie, who went back onstage in a London play the night after her son was killed in World War II. She had a sign posted backstage—DARLINGS, I KNOW WHAT YOU ARE THINKING. BUT PLEASE DO NOT TELL ME.

On Wednesday we received the envelopes Edgar had left behind. My manila envelope contained estate-planning papers, lists of the contents of the house, insurance-policy numbers, bank-account numbers—and all the keys in his key case. The police had had his farewell tapes transcribed to be sure his death was suicide. Melissa and I read our transcripts in the kitchen, and she bravely went upstairs to listen to her tape. Afterward, she told me, "It's very hard to hear his voice because he sounds so tired and so strained and so upset—he kept clicking the machine off and on."

I could not bring myself to play Edgar's farewell tape. I was still feeling too guilty. According to the transcript of the tape, he told me, "I cannot bear to be shunted aside and be a fifth wheel. I know this is not your fault. This is all my doing. I had the heart attack, and I'm a changed person. But believe me, when I fought, I always fought for you. The anger is something I have not been able to control since the heart attack, so forgive me for that. That people are angry at me . . . well, sometimes I'm proud of the enemies I made. If somebody had not been the bastard, you might have been cut up like a salami."

He told me to trust only Tom Pileggi. He told me the financial provisions he had made, told me to keep thrashing around and I would land on my feet because I am a survivor, told me not to reduce my life insurance. He told me, "I cannot in effect institutionalize myself for an indefinite period. I have spent too much of my life, more than you really know, the years and years and years, in TB sanatoriums in South Africa. I cannot see myself lying more weeks and months in hospitals. I'm tired. I ache mentally and physically. I've had it." Then he said, "It's very hard for me to show emotion because I was not brought up that way, but you made those twenty-two years a heaven for me. I miss you desperately, and I love you." The sadness of his words, of his defeat, of his capitulation, was just too much to bear.

On the last Friday of *shivah* I went to temple for the little ceremony to remove my mourning ribbon. On the way into the service our friend David Chasman stopped me and said Barry Diller had called, asking his advice about sending a condolence card. Too late. I cried through the service—that man had started the whole chain of events.

The *shivah* cushioned the first week of shock, and I was terrified of the day it would be over. I decided we all needed a little time of escape, a gap in reality, a time to postpone thinking and heal a little. I decided to take my support group on a two-week cruise among the Greek islands. My accountant said I could not afford it. I told him we were going anyway. I was crazy.

On that first Sunday after Edgar's death, I left with Melissa and Spike and Tommy Corcoran for an overnight in New York—traveling business class to save money. We checked into the Westbury Hotel, and I had a long dinner with Tom Pileggi. I felt a rush of affection for this man who had wandered into our lives as a business partner and stayed to become our friend and my salvation. Amid all the disaster and despair, my one good fortune was his presence, his brilliant financial mind when I was on the ropes, his absolute integrity when I could trust nobody else, his love for Edgar when I clung to those who shared my grief. More than anybody, Tom had forgiven Edgar his faults and treasured his virtues.

When I returned to my room in the Westbury Hotel Melissa was in bed asleep, and I lay next to her, lost and lonely and aching with guilt. I opened a book, always a sure solace and distraction, but at the end of the first page had no idea what the hell I had read.

How could I have missed the signs? . . . Edgar had married his murderess. . . . If I had been nicer to him, would he be alive now? . . . How smug and sure of myself I had been. . . . Would Melissa ever get over this?

The next morning I went across the street into the Madison Avenue Bookshop to get reading for the trip. I bought books Edgar would have chosen—Tip O'Neill's autobiography and one on Harold Macmillan. I had to educate myself, fill the gaps left by Edgar. The French history books I liked did not count. They were boudoir history.

Next I drove out to Larchmont and prayed at the graves of my parents and then Edgar's parents, because I thought he would want me to do that. Standing there, I prayed that he was with these people who really loved him.

The graves were unkempt, and I cleaned them, thinking, "This is what my life is all about now—loss, loss, loss." Weeping onto my hands as I pulled weeds and talked to my mother, I told her, "Some mess, this is. How am I going to get through it?"

How *was* I going to get through it?

2

ooooo

Looking back, I think Edgar and I were, from the beginning, headed for tragedy. We were two people obsessed with success, obsessed with my career. Show business is a tar baby. If you touch it, you cannot let go. Ask anybody—the group called the Singing Lawyers, who once sent me a tape to get on my show—Henry Kissinger, who once appeared as the TV weatherman on *CBS This Morning*—even Princess Di, who once danced in London with an English ballet company.

Show business is the ultimate wish fulfillment, the dream of being eternally beautiful, eternally talented, eternally loved and wealthy. It's the fairy princess gliding through the streets while everybody waves. It's Madonna in white satin. It's Julia Roberts getting her handsome prince.

Show business can be an addiction. That's what kept me going in the beginning of my career, what surely keeps Jay Leno on the road most of his life. An audience would laugh at me one night, and I would chase that high for another three months. One night in Philadelphia recently, the audience hated me, and I walked offstage swearing I'd get out of this business. The next night they loved me, and I fell back into their arms like a baby.

The ultimate high, the ultimate happiness, is when the audience is standing up at the end of the show and they won't let you go and you love them and they love you and you put your arms out to them and they love you more and you walk off and you've got to go back, and you say to them, "I love you," and they call out, "We love you, Joan!" Once you've had that, you spend the rest of your life trying to keep it coming.

Edgar was hooked into that high when I met him. He was producing five movies for the United Nations and was Mr. Big—called *Monsieur Le Patron* on the movie set in France, telephoned by the likes of Cary Grant, Ava Gardner, Sean Connery, and Joe Mankiewicz. Edgar was launched into production at the top, and he chased that feeling for the rest of his life. The bigger I became, the more power he, as my husband, wielded behind the scenes.

My career became us. Success in life equaled success in my career, and Edgar and I knew how to build my career. But we arrived at our heights in the grip of our pasts. Edgar was driven by his need to prove himself a major player. I was driven by my insecurity, my need to be loved, my easily hurt feelings, my obsession with loyalty, and my need to win. We were united by the anger that waited in both of us, the rage at accumulated, half-remembered injuries that set us side by side against the world. Ultimately we fell off our high wire, and took the wire with us.

A few months after Edgar's suicide, I cleaned out the garage and found the small black metal box he had brought out to impress me the first night I met him in June of 1965. It was a device that would let people join in TV quiz shows from their living rooms. He thought it would make him a fortune. Holding it, I felt again the excitement of that time—felt the glamour *he* had, the expectations *I* had.

Edgar was working then for Anna Rosenberg Associates. (No relation to Edgar.) She was the queen mother of public-relations consultants, advising tycoons and presidents on a personal level—sitting with President Roosevelt when he received a wire from Russian ambassador Averell Harriman saying that Stalin was breaking his Yalta commitments.

Edgar was Anna Rosenberg's public-relations emissary. His accounts were the Rockefeller brothers, Jack Heinz of H. J. Heinz Company, companies like the Encyclopædia Britannica and, particularly, American Machine & Foundry. Their automatic pinsetting machine had turned bowling into an American family sport, and Edgar had the idea of promoting it by using the endorsements of celebrities and society figures such as Lady Bird Johnson and Princess Grace of Monaco. Edgar sold AMF on the first simultaneous two-city stockholders' meeting, linking New York and Chicago with closed-circuit TV.

Hooked on show business, he convinced the *Today* show to do on-location broadcasts—in the Mediterranean with Cousteau diving with AMF scuba gear, in Puerto Rico with Sam Snead using a client's golf gear.

When anti–United Nations hysteria was sweeping the country, Edgar had the idea of a series of television movies dramatizing the UN's good works and received the enthusiastic support of Anna and her husband, Paul Hoffman—former CEO of American Motors, now managing director of the UN Special Fund—and U Thant, the UN secretary general, and the ABC network. He persuaded Xerox to sponsor the films to the tune of 4 million 1965 dollars.

Anna represented the Motion Picture Association of America, and had powerful personal connections in both Hollywood and the White House. Using these, Edgar enlisted names like Peter Sellers, Maria Schell, Edward G. Robinson, Alan Bates, Sam Spiegel, Eva Marie Saint, Yul Brynner, Rita Hayworth, Marcello Mastroianni—and they all worked for scale.

Under the umbrella of Anna Rosenberg Associates, he formed a production company called Telsun Foundation, Inc. Through Telsun, Edgar became friends with Peter Sellers, who asked him to help develop a movie about a traveling clown. The script needed a rewrite, and Edgar asked *The Tonight Show* to recommend a comedy writer. They suggested he watch my next appearance with Carson.

My first appearance on *The Tonight Show*—my miraculous, instantanous career turnaround—had been four months earlier on February 17, 1965, soon after Barbra Streisand hit in *Funny Girl* and Neil Simon went over the top with *The Odd Couple*. Soupy Sales was going strong on television, and Joey Bishop was still a major comedian. Allen Funt's *Candid Camera* was very big, and I had a job there as a writer. *The Tonight Show* was, of course, *the* show for a comic, and by then I had auditioned there seven times, once for a secretary who was eating a sandwich at her desk. Finally, my manager, Roy Silver, who represented Bill Cosby, used his clout and got me a guest appearance on Carson.

Virtually all of my jokes then were autobiographical, jokes I used to write down on scraps of paper and stuff into my handbag and see if they worked next time I managed to get in front of an audience. So my conversations on the air with Johnny Carson were really strings of jokes that told the story of my life: By six years of age I was a fatso who finished her midnight snack just in time for breakfast and ate so much she had stretch marks around her mouth. In high school my acne was so bad, blind people tried to read my face. In biology class a frog tried to dissect me. I sat out more dances than FDR. I was petting with a boy, and his hand went to sleep.

My father was a general practitioner—our family motto was, "A good epidemic means meat on the table." My mother could make anybody feel guilty—she used to get letters of apology from people she didn't even know. She was desperate to get me married. She used to say, "Sure he's a murderer. But he's a *single* murderer." I was dating a transvestite, and she said, "Marry him. You'll double your wardrobe." She was a very elegant woman. When a flying saucer landed on the lawn, she turned it over to see if it was Wedgwood.

One area of my life was too painful for jokes—the relationship between my mother and father. They had emigrated as teenagers from Odessa, Russia—Meyer born into poverty, Beatrice into wealth.

Meyer's mother came to New York, where the family chipped in to send Meyer to medical school. Beatrice's mother hated her much older husband and ran away to New York, where her jewels were soon sold and she ended up as a midwife taking in boarders. Beatrice worked in a shirtwaist factory and slept on two chairs. Her brother became a dentist and installed his mother and sister in fake luxury on the Upper West Side, where Meyer met Beatrice and married her.

I grew up in a home where my overworked GP father could never bring home enough money, and my mother, married to a man she didn't love, was ashamed of poverty and consumed with upward mobility. Without money, we moved from Brooklyn to the snooty New York suburb of Larchmont, always with household help, always with my sister and me going to the best schools, always with screaming fights about money at home.

Though neither Beatrice nor Meyer knew how to express affection, I knew I was deeply loved. Meyer did not have the time to build a relationship with his children, and I resented him for working so hard for so little in return.

My mother, Beatrice, a formal, queenly woman, was my rock of security, always there for me, solid, always taking my side, defending me, totally loyal. Her children, by God, were the best. If she saw any faults in me and Barbara, nobody heard about them. I adored her. But her love could not come out as tenderness. There were no loving arms encircling us. I remember reaching over and touching my mother's hand in the theater. I do not remember her ever touching mine. Her love was expressed as worry, making sure Barbara and I had everything we should—education, good manners, know-how in society, the right clothes.

I was a disappointment to her. She could not understand why I wanted to be an actress. In her head I should be like my sister, Barbara, who, at that time, was one of only two women at Columbia Law School. My mother did not realize my need for the love and approval that can well up from an audience.

I first discovered that euphoria way back in nursery school, playing a kitty cat in a class play. Knowing that people thought I was terrific, I had a feeling of safety—fat or thin, rich or poor.

From that day on I had tunnel vision. I still have it. I was going to be an actress in big-time Broadway "theatuh" and the classics—Shakespeare, Shaw. I saw myself arriving nightly at the stage door, stepping out of a limo wearing a major fur coat with an orchid corsage and my hair in a pageboy—it was the forties, remember—and hurrying past a throng of adoring fans to give my all to my art. My parents made me feel wrong in what I wanted. They thought I had no talent. My father, who thought "actress" was a euphemism for "prostitute," was terrified for me. My mother thought the stage was low class.

I had a joke in my act: "When I told my mother, 'I want to be a Broadway actress,' she said, 'I'm not going to tell you no just now . . . first go to college and get your diploma. Then I'll tell you no.'" Obediently I spent two years at Connecticut College and two at Barnard, majoring in English and graduating with high honors.

After I graduated from college, I tried it my parents' way. I went to work at Lord & Taylor, rising very fast there and then moving to Bond's, where I met the son of the vice president. He was what I thought they wanted—WASPy, Columbia graduate, a businessman, and cute, cute, cute. So we got married and moved to East End Avenue, and it was all terrific and it lasted eight months.

I became an office temp and kept auditioning for acting jobs. At the same time I was hanging out with all the other hopeful nobodies in Greenwich Village. My parents were wild. I was twenty-five years old, my friends were getting married. Everybody *good* was taken! I was inviting home people like Woody Allen, George Carlin, Richard Pryor, and Bob Dylan. Did you ever see a picture of Bob Dylan before he became Bob Dylan?!

I was taking the 9:25 P.M. train into New York, going downtown, and taking the last train home. They didn't know where I was going, whom I was with. And they expected the world. They knew I wasn't that attractive. How could I make money from being a performer? I had always been funny, using humor as a way to be accepted and wanted. Laughing got me through the hurts, made life palatable. When I was eight or nine, my mother used to dress me at the fat kids' shop in Macy's, and I called it the Henry the VIII Shop. Nothing has changed. Jokes still get me a place at the table.

I discovered that stand-up comics could make six dollars in an evening, so I tried that to keep me going until I was tapped for

Ophelia. I humbled myself before sleazy agents, the kind of people who shed their skins every year. One stiffed me for six dollars. Another promised the actress Rosalind Russell to a Catholic church bazaar—and pushed me, instead, onstage into a wave of boos and hisses. My stage name came from an agent, a full-blooded American Indian named Tony Rivers, who told me that my name, Joan Molinsky, did not make it as a stage name. Without blinking, I said, "Okay, how about Joan Rivers?"

I was a loser working with losers—with a ventriloquist who moved his lips even when he wasn't talking, with a trainer and his three tap-dancing chickens. I was "Pepper January, Comedy with Spice" in a strip joint where men with their hats on their laps yelled at me, "You stink! Fuck off!" In another club the manager fired me right onstage over the loudspeaker—"Get her off!" I worked at a nightclub where you passed the hat and the hat didn't come back, at a club where the cigarette girls sold bullets, and, truly, at a Catskill resort where a man stood beside me translating each line into Yiddish—so the jokes bombed twice. I spent those seven years in my twenties fantasizing that I was Audrey Hepburn acting in a movie about all this. There was no way I could be myself and live through so much rejection.

But then came *The Tonight Show.* At the end of that first, life-altering segment with Johnny Carson, he said, still laughing, "You're going to be a star." Years of failure and frustration fell away. In that instant, I put my dreams of legitimate acting on the shelf and became the hot girl in town.

Edgar telephoned me about rewriting the Peter Sellers script and, to discuss the project, took me and my manager, Roy Silver, to Chambord, which was the most elegant French restaurant in New York. At that time I was living in a tiny apartment over the Stage Delicatessen and existing almost entirely on doughnuts and macaroni salad. During dinner Roy and Edgar talked. I was very shy.

Edgar was short, relatively thin, with black hair, a round face, and big, thick glasses on his nose. I could see that this forty-year-old winner producer in a Dunhill blue suit and Lanvin shirt had class—a classy way of talking, a classy way of dressing. He read classy books, had a classy mind. He did not wear a pinkie ring.

He mentioned his crème-de-la-crème English education at Rugby and Cambridge, and dropped lots of names: Marcello Mastroianni, Alan Bates, Ben Gazzara. He insisted we come back to his place for a drink, and on the way told the limo driver, "Charles, don't forget to pick up Miss Cardinale tomorrow." I knew he meant Claudia Cardinale. He was too good to be true.

Roy and I went home in the limo, and we were blown away. "Son of a bitch," Roy was screaming, "if he can make all that money, so can we!" Just five months earlier I had been performing in Greenwich Village dumps. Here, treating me as a professional screenwriter, was a man with four movies going in Europe, friendly with Peter Sellers and hobnobbing with the Sam Spiegel set—the highest echelon of show business.

I had a vision of doors opening to me—door upon door upon door to the horizon. Hugged in my arms was a real script bound in leatherette, the first I'd ever seen. Inside was a note from Peter Sellers saying, *Edgar, let's see what we can do about this.* Everything was very, very heady.

Edgar set up another meeting to discuss the script. I was running out of black dresses. He arrived in a limo in front of the Stage Delicatessen and climbed the stairs to my tiny apartment, which featured a Castro Convertible bed and Aunt Alice's desk. It had been Carol Burnett's apartment before she hit. He came in the door carrying two dozen long-stemmed roses in an ugly green vase—which I kept for years. Then we went to the Four Seasons with a Telsun associate producer, and there was more charm and name-dropping and show-business talk—but nothing about the Sellers script.

The restaurant served huge strawberries glazed with sugar and dipped in chocolate, but I didn't dare eat one, worrying, Do you use a knife and fork or your fingers? These strawberries were too big to put whole into my mouth, and I was scared that if I took even a little dinky bite, the juice would squirt all over, and everyone would get red.

Roy closed the deal with Edgar. In a week I was to go down to Jamaica, where he would work with me in the mornings and with a writer named Eugene Burdick, author of *The Ugly Ameri-*

can, who was doing a Telsun script, in the afternoons. Peter Sellers would join us in a few days. I was thrilled.

On the plane I did not sit with Edgar. Coming along as guests were Joe Mankiewicz's son Chris and Chris's wife, and I sat with her. I was a little surprised. I thought the trip was pure business. We landed at Montego Bay, and Edgar drove us to Round Hill, an incredibly posh enclave of cottages. No Jews allowed. No Christians, either. Talk about *exclusive!*

Jamaica seemed to be on a different planet from the United States, where civil-rights protests in Mississippi were making national headlines and troops were being readied for combat in Vietnam. Driving to Round Hill, I saw tourist women in flowing caftans, diaphanous cotton skirts, bare brown legs, and sandals and lots of toes. In a tropical paradise where you stuck a flower in your hair, my suitcase was full of nice little sweaters, pleated skirts, panty girdles, stockings, matching leather pumps and bags. I felt humiliated. Not knowing what to bring put me into a different class—I felt like Stella Dallas.

Waiting at Round Hill were two telegrams, one saying that the married Mr. Burdick was in California having an extramarital tryst, and the other that Peter Sellers was held up shooting a movie. So it was to be a foursome—with me still saying "Mr. Rosenberg." The Mankiewiczes were in one cottage. I shared the other with Edgar. What's going on? I wondered. If he brought me down there for romance, that was a turnoff. I have tremendous pride. I would not stand for an attitude of "Oh, she's there if I want her." I marched over to lock the door between the bedrooms, but before I could turn the key, I heard the lock on his side go *click. Click?* How dare he!

At breakfast time the servants knocked and came in with knowing faces and two trays. "No, no, no," I heard myself saying frantically, "Mr. Rosenberg is in the other room." I was even more uncomfortable when Edgar showed no sign of wanting to work on the script. What had I got myself into? I did not want to be a date. I wanted to be a professional screenwriter.

I felt so embarrassed and self-conscious that I slipped away by myself and hid all day, wandering around this fabulous, absolutely empty rich man's compound. On a hill, along a winding road bordered by huge bougainvillea bushes—orange, purple, red, pink—were big white one-story villas bought by people like William Paley and Adele Astaire. They used them in the prime months and rented them out in other months to equally wealthy people. Paul McCartney goes there. This was the off-season, when nobody was there. Our villa had been opened especially for Edgar, who had filmed a promotional documentary for Round Hill. I swam in a deserted pool.

That night the four of us sat on couches and played word games. I was good at them, but felt so wrong in my clothes, I clutched pillows in front of me as a camouflage. Edgar knew *all* the words. He knew history, politics, current events, music, theater. He had seen everything, heard everything, read everything, and worse, retained everything. We played Facts of Five, and while I was good at movie stars over thirty signed by MGM, he could do rivers that flowed into the Mediterranean.

I found myself liking him. He got my jokes, which is essential for me. And he had a great sense of humor himself, very dry. Edgar never laughed at his own jokes, which were ironic and sophisticated, very black, and tuned in to the ugliness of life. We had so much in common. He was looser then, more accessible, not yet so self-protective. He was simply charming.

I felt he respected me, but there was no outward sign of affection. As our relationship grew, I came to see he was not the type to express feelings directly. "Joan works very hard" or "Joan is the highest-paid opening act in the business" was all he was apt to say, even after many years of our being together. His emotional reticence never bothered me, though, because our relationship was not about passion, it was about friendship, support, protection—and business. At the best times in our marriage, we were loving partners.

There in Jamaica the British public-school accent and reserve came off as courtliness, an elegance that was extremely appealing because it reminded me of my mother and was what she wished she had married. People called him "sir," and he knew how to treat servants with a perfect blend of graciousness and distance. He knew how to eat those glazed strawberries and knew it was all right to eat the brie with the crust.

He also understood right away what my life was all about, knew that the mouthy girl onstage was not the real me, knew the real me wanted to live well and have beautiful things. I realize now that he understood because he had the same dream, the same consuming obsession with show business and success—and the same insecurity and hunger for respect. He had spotted a soul mate.

The second day in Jamaica the Mankiewiczes had a huge fight. While Edgar was off consoling Chris, I sat on the beach with his wife, an Italian model he had met during the filming of *Cleopatra*, fabulous in her bikini with her tan and dark hair and flashing eyes. While she talked and talked and talked, telling me that Chris had become a different man when they got back to the States, telling me the pain she was in—she kept poking at crabs with a stick, flipping them over, tormenting them. I was on *his* side.

They left that afternoon, and suddenly I was alone with Edgar in this lush, incredibly beautiful romantic resort with nobody else around. Our pool was just above the aqua Caribbean. Two white-jacketed servants were assigned to us alone. Everywhere were fresh flowers.

I panicked. What did this man have in mind? We still had done no work. I needed protection. I called my writer friend Treva Silverman in New York and told her, "Get down here fast."

I wanted career, not romance. Eight years earlier I had had the grand passion of my life, an all-enveloping love affair. In the end—at a time when he was saying he could not sleep or eat or exist without me—he got one of his old girlfriends pregnant. I could not endure such pain and grief again.

That night at Round Hill I felt a little nauseated. When I complained, Edgar brought a brown leather Dunhill case from his room. Inside was every pill for every ailment known to man. I was frightened of this traveling drugstore, and took nothing—and thought, How strange. He's prepared for anything.

On the third day at Round Hill, with Edgar still postponing any work, I went off again alone and swam at another empty villa.

Afterward, I came back to my room, and there was Edgar, standing in the doorway. Suddenly, when I saw him, I had a deep sense
of well-being, of coming home, a certainty that he was what I had
been looking for, that this was absolutely right! Yes, so quickly.
It was as if . . . in a split second, with one step forward, we went
from absolutely nothing to everything. We made love, and then,
as though it were the natural order of events, he proposed and
I accepted.

Everything fit. Here was a man I could trust who was going to
take care of me. We were a good match—he gave me class, I gave
him warmth. We filled each other's gaps—he was the intelligent
one with the English accent, and I was the performer, full of the
fun he did not know how to have.

After Edgar proposed, we took out our date books to find the
earliest day we could get married in New York. "Okay, I can do
it on Wednesday." "Wednesday's not good for me." "How about
the afternoon of Thursday?" "You got it." Then he asked me, "Do
you want a ring or pearls?" I said, "Pearls." No ring. Can you
imagine? Me?

So when my duenna, Treva Silverman, arrived in Jamaica, she
was too late. The three of us spent two days in the swimming
pool, finally working on the script. On the flight back to New
York this elegant gentleman leaned over and took my hand and
held it and stroked it. In public.

The Peter Sellers script was never finished. In New York I moved
immediately into Edgar's apartment, and when I told my
mother, the dowager queen of Larchmont, she was in shock. "No,
no, no." I said, "We were married in Jamaica. We're just going
to get *remarried.*" I know its hard to believe: out of college eight
years and still lying to my mother!

I took Edgar to Larchmont to meet my parents. We pulled up
to the house in a limo, and the driver got out and came around
to open our door. Just then my mother rushed out of the house,
saw this nice-looking young man in a dark suit, called "Congratu-
lations," threw her arms around him, and planted a big kiss on
the driver. "No, no, Bea, *this* is Edgar."

They got along immediately. Despite the scene at the limo,

they were both formal and set great store by dignity. They were loners who had almost no friends and trusted very few people. They wanted the finer things. As Edgar used to say, "We're both snobs."

I was about to marry my mother.

On July 15, 1965, three days after we returned from Jamaica, Edgar and I were married by a judge in the Bronx courthouse. The couple ahead of us were Filipinos escorted by the whole Philippine Navy—the first and last time that Edgar and I were the tallest people anywhere. I had on a twenty-six-dollar dress, black with cream lace, from Bloomingdale's. Like Edgar, I do not show affection in public; I play the game of "Oh, it's nothing. It's nothing" when it's everything. So the ceremony was brisk and businesslike. Treva Silverman stood up for me, and the elusive Eugene Burdick for Edgar, almost the last act of his life. The next day Burdick flew to California and died shortly thereafter of a heart attack on a tennis court.

Before I left for Jamaica, I was performing at the Bitter End in Greenwich Village. When I came back, I asked the owner, Freddie Weintraub, if I could have my wedding night off. He said, "Sure! Hey, you're getting married. Just get me somebody comparable." We said, "Fine." He said, "Get me Woody Allen or Bill Cosby."

So I did two shows that night. My agent, Irvin Arthur, came down. Six months earlier he had told me to quit the business because I'd never make it—but I stayed with him out of loyalty. Now, everybody thought he was my husband and congratulated him. Edgar had refused to come. "I'm not going to be a backstage husband," he said. Famous last words.

3

ooooo

During that first year of marriage to Edgar, his smart friends were having trouble matching in their heads this elegant intellectual with what, to them, was a lowly, uneducated stand-up comic. I was sure Anna Rosenberg thought he could have done much better. I acted like a mouse around her. Barbara Walters, who was then the hostess on the *Today* show and friendly with Edgar, said the first time she met me, "We never thought he'd marry somebody like you."

In fact, nobody had thought Edgar would even get married. He had been coddled for forty years by his mother, Frieda, and her housekeeper, Heddy, who cleaned for us daily and disapproved of Edgar even having a wife. She continued to do his laundry, but left mine in a heap on the floor.

The main woman Edgar had ever had in his life—except for a six-year relationship with an actress—was his mother, who lived just down the hall in an old-lady apartment with sparse, heavy blond thirties furniture—memory furniture, bits and pieces from a grander time of life—some beautiful handmade lace, and lots of pictures of dead relatives. Everything was meticulously neat, as though ready for her to die in the next five minutes.

Frieda was a short, heavy woman. Edgar had her stocky build and the same piercing dark eyes, heavy nose, and round face. She had just one close friend, a nurse she had met in the hospital. Frieda was so proud of this friendship, proud to say, "I'm going to the movies tonight with Marjorie" and "Marjorie and I were shopping yesterday." It was sad.

Going from bachelor son to married man was a major adjustment for Edgar. For the first time there was another person interfering with his privacy. One night I discovered him taking a Valium. I said, "What is this?" He said, "I do it every night. I need my sleep." I was shocked, I am vehemently opposed to taking any kind of drug. I hardly touch an aspirin. I said, "No, no, no, you cannot do that. You must stop." I still don't know if he ever did.

We had another big fight when I wanted to lighten up his apartment, which was decorated in blacks and tans and brown leather. I suggested off-white, pale celadon, and pale, pale apricot. He said, "Never! This is the way I like it, and this is the way it's going to be." He told me all this macho stuff—"I am the man, and I will not help you with housework, and I will not help you cook and clean. None of it." "Absolutely," I told him. "You're not expected to do anything." Oh, shit, I thought, here we go. But I kept quiet.

But Edgar wanted me to be happy. Within weeks, Heddy was working only for his mother, and he was scraping dishes and taking out the garbage. Edgar had to assert his CEO front because, like all men of his generation, he was insecure and needed to know he had an old-fashioned marriage in which he was the head of the family. Once I had said, "Okay, you're the boss" and checked decisions and got permissions—he could relax—even though I actually ran the household. But I enjoyed hiring the help, worrying about the dry cleaning and laundry, planning the parties, arranging the flowers, being the woman of the house.

Edgar was comfortable with those dynamics. His father was a mensch, and the powerhouse Frieda was actually in charge. Later, as executive producer of my Fox show, all Edgar really wanted was to hear Barry Diller say, "You're the boss of the show"—and then everybody could go about their business. But

I could not have kept those two men from their collision even if I had realized from the first the enormity of Edgar's pride, how great his need for recognition. And I *never* would have blocked him from being the show's producer. By then, our business partnership was an unspoken bargain at the core of our marriage.

I look at pictures of myself in those days—my 1960s hairdo and pink nails—and feel absolutely no relationship to that girl. She still believed in happy endings. She was naïve about the treachery, about the pitfalls, the backbiting, the meanness, the stupidity in big-time show business. The success that was happening for her seemed absolutely right and logical. She had worked hard and, by God, was a rising star with a wonderful, successful husband. Well, the movie should have ended there.

The day I was married, I escaped my old struggling life—living in a dinky struggle apartment over a deli, wearing struggle clothes. As I crossed Fifth Avenue, all my hand-painted struggle furniture turned back into pumpkins. The second half of the sixties was a sweet, happy time.

Overnight I made the tremendous psychological jump of saying, "I'm grown up now and no longer a kid in Greenwich Village." I could release the side of me suppressed under those black dresses and hairpieces and boa, the me that wanted to bring out the Georgian silver and be my mother's daughter.

Edgar was making a very good salary with Anna Rosenberg, and we pooled our incomes. At that time in our marriage he had that WASP caution over building and preserving capital. But I began relishing the money I had never had. Immediately I bought new clothes. No, not Oscar or Geoffrey Beene or Galanos. Those designers were still far in the future. And my husband was conservative—anything other than a black dress and pearls to him was like wearing a scarlet letter. I had my parents' house painted, put on a new roof, bought my father a Cadillac and my mother a fur coat. I had a great time.

There was a playfulness to everything then. Our lives were young and adventurous and unpredictable, our expectations unlimited. Edgar had never had fun friends, was always the bachelor invited to dinner, and now I brought serendipity into his life—running out together to six different coffeehouses to see six different comics, going to three movies one after another, popping out to the Hamptons on Long Island to see friends.

When I performed in the Catskill Mountains, Edgar drove me up, left hand on the wheel, his right hand reaching out to mine, or conducting the Broadway show tunes we played on a tape recorder. Sometimes friends came, six of us in the car, everybody silly, all laughing, driving back the same night and stopping at the Red Apple Inn for sandwiches. We'd get home to New York at 4:00 A.M. and go to the Stage Delicatessen where the other performers were just back from their Catskill dates—Rodney Dangerfield, George Carlin, Dick Cavett, Dom DeLuise, Stiller and Meara—and the generation ahead of us—Alan King, Steve Lawrence and Eydie Gorme.

I joined Edgar's career as the producer's wife. I was there by his side when he went to Nice for the filming of the Telsun movie *The Poppy Is Also a Flower,* starring Yul Brynner, Trevor Howard, and Rita Hayworth.

Everybody stayed at the Negresco Hotel. In the middle of the night Rita woke up and did not know where she was and panicked and began smashing furniture. I was in the lobby when she was led through at 3:00 A.M. in a Chanel suit, surrounded by the doctors and orderlies that Edgar had called, all trying to calm her—"Rita, Rita, Rita"—and she was pushing and fighting and yelling, her hair disheveled and wonderful. We thought it was alcohol, but maybe the Alzheimer's had begun.

In show business everything is credentials, and in France Edgar was the one with the credentials, the producer from America, a man to be cultivated. Sam Spiegel's yacht was in Monaco, and he invited Edgar and the little wife aboard. It was huge, part of a herd of white trillion-dollar whales docked side by side. Onassis's yacht was there too. On the blue water the yachts were like scudding white birds. As dusk flowed across the hills of Monaco, topped by the Palace, the green slopes were laced with lights.

Spiegel's upper-deck salon was packed with the international crowd—people telling amusing stories about the Windsors, Onassis, everybody witty in several languages. David Niven and his wife were aboard—and Nureyev, who had just defected and was on the cover of *Time* magazine.

Edgar could deal with Niven by talking about history. He remembered what Nureyev had danced. It was natural that he went off and talked business with Spiegel. This was one reason I had married him. But I was left alone with those tall, thin, wonderfully coiffed and made-up women who to this day make me feel dumpy and intimidated. As I have done ever since I was a fat child, I played the Shadow and pretended I was invisible and just watched.

Nureyev was beautiful, his white shirt open, golden-brown skin, perfectly muscled, wearing white ducks and loafers with no socks—as though a Greek god had come aboard, charming and laughing, just returned from visiting Bacchus for a while. Suddenly the hostess plopped him next to me. He said something in French. I tried out, *"Le livre est sur la table."* He got up and left.

David Niven was the grand, elegant movie star with mustache and ascot. The missus was a society woman, exquisitely groomed, perfectly dressed in silk slacks and silk shirt, thin as a rail with that smooth Riviera tan that comes from months of being outside for just twelve minutes a day. She was in a group next to me talking about vacations, about New Year's Eve at the Plaza Athénée in Paris, Easter with Grace and Rainier. Suddenly Mrs. Niven turned to me with a gracious smile and said, "If we're not in Marrakech, it just isn't Christmas."

I did not know what to say, except "Me, too." The smile never left her face, but her gaze passed over my left shoulder and never returned. There was no way I could cry out, "Would somebody please ask me about Henry James—or Ed McMahon? And I can tell funny stories about my father and his patients."

From below deck came two golden-brown girls with long blond hair and beautiful lithe bodies, no bras, and little boobies poking against see-through shirts. Sam Spiegel never introduced these languid water girls. I was agog, sitting there so proper, in my head feeling as though I were wearing a hat and gloves and holding a handbag.

As we drove back to the hotel, Edgar said, "I feel sorry for Sam, he's such a lonely man."

I said, "If he wants to be happy, that crowd is never going to do it. If he wants happy, I've got my aunt Lucy who's living in New York. She's sixty-four and a really well-to-do widow. And she's got a pair of deck shoes."

Edgar told me I didn't understand. Sam was a man who couldn't let anybody get close. I now realize he was identifying strongly with Spiegel. I said, "You don't understand. There's a fool back there on that boat with those stupid girls and those senseless people." We had a major fight—really because I was furious that I could not handle that crowd, and Edgar was furious that I had not clicked with them. We always pretended we did not care if we fit in—but we both desperately wanted to be accepted.

I could only stay with Edgar in Monaco for a week; I had performance dates in the United States and was glad to leave. On my flight back alone from Nice, I changed planes in Paris and, while I waited, through the lounge swept a fabulous woman in a beige turban, a beige cape, long beige gloves, a radiant rush of glamour. I did not know who she was.

I boarded the plane and was sitting in first class when in came two lesbians, butch beyond anything, rough trade in leather and short-cropped hair. They stowed luggage in the overhead, and behind them came that woman, who I now realized was Marlene Dietrich. One of the leather ladies kissed her on the lips, and then Dietrich sat down next to me.

I was hysterical. I was sitting next to *Marlene Dietrich.* She was all the glamour of the movies—a m-o-o-v-ie star. I had seen her when my mother took me to the movies. Now, I had reached the height in life of sitting next to Marlene Dietrich on a plane from Paris to New York. Incredible!

I wondered if she had seen me on TV and knew that I was not just a civilian. I prayed that she would speak to me in that voice, even say, "Excuse me," and get up. I decided not to talk to her unless she talked to me.

Marlene Dietrich did not say one word. All she did for ten

hours was eat—eat as though she were going to her death. This beautiful woman became a German hausfrau, constantly calling for food. There was pastry wrapped in paper, and she scraped the icing off the paper with a fork. The sad thing was, when this epitome of glamour fell asleep, everything sagged, the skin on her face, her hands, everything. She crumpled into an old lady. Doria Gray.

Very early Edgar became my unofficial manager—because we both saw him as the one person in my life who was 150 percent in my corner, the man who would protect me from all those people in show business who try to use and exploit you. My official manager was Roy Silver. He was hip, funny, brash and full of energy. After John F. Kennedy's assassination, when the security was at its highest, Roy put on a dinner jacket and crashed a reception for Lyndon Johnson. He even managed to have his picture taken with Johnson. That was Roy.

Roy, God bless him, had promoted me onto that original *Tonight Show* in 1965, and then moved me right ahead during that year—into headlining at the Bitter End in Greenwich Village, onto *The Mike Douglas Show*, into Mr. Kelly's in Chicago as headliner, back onto Carson, into the hungry i in San Francisco, back on Mike Douglas. He signed me up for my first comedy record. Roy managed me brilliantly. With him I became the country's hot young comedienne.

But not long after my marriage, Roy began living my success—which often happens. Booking agents and especially managers work intimately with the artist, shaping their acts, steering the careers, listening to the problems—becoming the mother superiors and father confessors. Many times managers and other members of your inner circle come to believe that the performer cannot work without them, that they are the power, and the limos and suites and press conferences are as much for them as for you.

I had a hairdresser for years named Jason Dyl, who traveled with me everywhere, always first class. One time we stayed over at a motel on Cape Cod, everybody settling into duplicate rooms.

Suddenly I got a call from the front desk. Jason was standing there screaming that his room was "unacceptable."

The fact is, nobody in the entourage is essential. Sinatra does not need the lights. Or the conductor. Everything is augmentation. The performer needs only one thing: Talent.

When Roy Silver booked me into Mr. Kelly's, he escorted me to Chicago, where he settled into a suite in the best hotel, the Ambassador East, at my expense. "You will need a suitable place to meet the press," he explained. I said nothing and moved into the kitchenette rooming house where I'd lived when I was with the improvisation group Second City. I still had my old grateful struggle mentality and thought I was not yet entitled to a suite.

Roy, who got 15 percent of my fees, began rushing me onto the big-money fast track long before I was ready. I had been developing my fragile little act in front of audiences of two hundred adoring people, who allowed me to be different from the average slick comic. Suddenly I found myself opening for Jack Jones in a huge place in Pittsburgh, and during my act they gave out bowling awards in the back of the hall—"And now for the woman with the most strikes . . ."

Roy sold me to the vast Basin Street East for two thousand dollars a week, big money then. I was terrified. Edgar was leaving for Europe on business and had a huge La-Z-Boy lounger delivered to my matchbox of a dressing room so I could rest—and it *filled* the room. I had to sit in it during makeup.

The audiences at Basin Street were hip sharpies, guys with big cuff links, the Copacabana crowd, not there for comedy but for Duke Ellington and Mel Tormé—who were warring with each other over who got top billing. I was the rest period between their performances, and they refused to use each other's band setups, so during my act, right behind me on the stage, no curtain, Tormé's band moved its equipment off, and Ellington's musicians set up.

While the drums and music stands crashed and banged, I was up there telling the crowd how I was such an ugly baby when I was born, I had to slap myself; that I went to a wig farm and bought the runt of the litter and taught it tricks—"Curl! Set!" When I looked out over the audience, all eyes were riveted on

Louis Bellson setting up his drums. When I paused for emphasis in a joke, I could hear the buzz of audience talk. I felt invisible.

One night after coming offstage, I stood crying on the sidewalk with Roy, telling him I was not ready for this. He said, "Don't worry, baby, it's all in your head. You can do it. You've got to. This is the big time."

When Edgar arrived home from Europe, he found his bride miserable and stuttering and bombing, losing all the assurance I had built in the six months since hitting on Carson. When you lose confidence, you lose yourself, your persona, your timing, your humor. When people are not laughing at what you think is funny, you begin doubting that you are funny, you begin to wither.

Onstage you must communicate total assurance, which tells the audience that you are funny, gives them permission to laugh whenever they want. They do not have to make a judgment call. The same line out of the mouth of Joe Blow will get a totally different reaction when spoken by Robin Williams.

Edgar understood everything immediately. In the corridor outside the dressing rooms, he bawled out my booking agent, a man named Bendett. They began pushing each other, then went into the alley behind the club, and Edgar began punching the guy out—while I held on to his jacket, screaming, "Edgar, stop it." It was wonderful. My knight was wearing my colors into battle.

My contract was up with Roy Silver, and Edgar hired one of the top managers in the field, Jack Rollins, who handled Woody Allen. This was a definitive moment. Not realizing how it would take over our relationship, I had put myself permanently in Edgar's hands and thought this a great perk of my marriage. With Edgar behind me, I could become that carefree, crazy madcap I had imagined myself.

Edgar was a tiger for details, and I was not. Throughout our life together he ran the business side—balanced my checkbook, filled out the checks for me to sign, picked my photographs, answered the mail, met with the accountants, invested the money that was starting to come in, handled the bank transfers. So I would not be upset and distracted, he solved problems he never told me about. He protected me by reading all the contracts, and amazed the lawyers by spotting the weaknesses, by knowing nuances, the legal difference between "and" and "or." The lawyers, the best he could find, chafed under the second-guessing, but had to admit, "Yeah, you're right."

He trusted no one. He always said, "Have three lawyers." He got independent opinions on everything. The lawyers did not like that, but too bad. Edgar cared only that the deal was solid. He taught me to always go to the top, go to the person who can give the answer, get the action. If you go too low, everybody up the ladder makes the decision over and over, one by one. I would worry about alienating the underlings. Not Edgar.

Edgar's judgment on building my success was continually sound. A career is a succession of choices, and he worried about them all—is the publicity right, is it better to be inside *People* magazine or on the cover of *Us*? He had a rule: Never perform in a city more than once every three years, so you don't wear out your welcome.

He brought me along slowly, so I would not burn out. He believed I should never go after the most money: I should only do what was right for the career. Because we did not feel I was ready for the pressure of Las Vegas, which really *was* the big time, I turned down an eighty-thousand-dollar offer and continued in New York developing my material. Without Edgar, I would not have had the strength to say no.

When Jack Rollins took me on, he insisted I go back to my roots to develop my act, and he put me into a little hothouse club called the Downstairs at the Upstairs, where Mabel Mercer had been appearing. Throughout the rest of the sixties and early seventies, except for prearranged blocks of time when I toured, it was my base of operations where I worked five nights a week.

The Downstairs at the Upstairs was an exotic little jewel box of a cabaret in the old Wanamaker mansion on East Fifty-sixth Street, all oranges and pinks and art deco. On weekends limos delivered lacquered women in mink coats who climbed the grand curving staircase to the tiny upstairs showroom where five interchangeable, superpersonable preppies in evening clothes sang bitchy, sneering, snotty, trendy songs. Sort of a *Spy* magazine with music. Downstairs in an even smaller room, I reigned under a tiny stained-glass canopy over the little stage.

In the Downstairs my act was still evolving, but getting stronger. It seems I was voicing more and more what people were thinking but were too embarrassed to say. When the wedding pictures of Jackie and Ari appeared in the *Post,* she was so much taller than he was, I came onstage that night and said, "Did you see the picture? All I kept thinking was, Please God, let them be standing on a hill." That got a huge laugh. Pretty soon I was saying, "Jackie O. spent twenty-eight million dollars her first year with Ari. Can you imagine the trading stamps she has? She can get a Naugahyde suitcase with those." America hated her for the marriage to Onassis. We wanted her to be the Queen Victoria of our generation.

Jackie once came into the Downstairs at the Upstairs with Mike Nichols. She parked a major sable in the coatroom—so before the show I went right in there and tried it on. I had never seen her more than ten inches tall in a magazine; for all I knew, she could have been that height—and here I was in living Technicolor wearing her perfect sable that came down below my fingers and dragged on the floor. Her gloves were in the pocket, a wonderful perfume was in the air. I was astonished. She was always underplaying, wearing those elegant little cloth jobbies. She could have come to temple with me in that coat.

The maître d', Archie Walker, seated her smack in the middle of row one. Having her there in front of me was surreal. The whole audience pretended they didn't notice her, but when she laughed, they laughed, when she did not laugh, nobody laughed. For a long time I refused to look at her. Then, when I did, her eyes dropped. Jackie did not want to be the woman whom I asked, "Where are you from? Married or single? Let me see your ring. Boy, didn't *you* do well."

Talking with women in the front row was increasingly important in my act. You can tell who is married by the amount of attention you're getting. If a couple is married, you have their undivided attention. The unmarried couples have a hand on each other; there is something happening between them. I avoid the woman who is really pulled together; she'll be too uptight to talk.

I go for the woman with a corsage, because if she thinks it's hot stuff to wear one, she's already open. Sometimes a woman in the audience will call out to me—and I know *she's* a friend. And when I have true rapport with one person, she becomes everybody in the audience.

Women in the audience tell me their intimate secrets, sometimes something devastating. One time I asked a married woman about her husband, "Do you think he cheats?" She said, "Yes." And he's sitting right there! Another woman said, "He beats me up." I said, "Call the police. Get out of the house." Her husband beside her had paid for the privilege of having a thousand people know he's a wife-beater.

These women have jumped the fence between remembering it's an act and being onstage. For them there is no performance and no stage and we're just talking about things, girlfriend talk. Everybody wants to come in from the cold.

The Downstairs was the place where career began to be Edgar's and my whole life. It was our league—small-time show business on a level we could understand and enjoy. We were not dealing then with millions of dollars and high-octane lawyers and their egos and chicanery. The whole career did not seem to ride on our decisions. My every move was not amplified in the press.

We felt as though the Downstairs was *our* club, and in it Edgar was *Edgar.* People said, "Let me check that with Edgar." He was the paterfamilias, a role he loved and tried to achieve on the Fox show, one of the roots of our troubles.

Since neither Edgar nor I had a lot of friends, we also came to the Downstairs to socialize. A duck finds other ducks. I was at home with the comedians and actors, the writers and musicians and makeup people and agents, the bookers and managers—with that whole backstage world. With them I knew who I was. They gave me a place. They welcomed me in. I did not have to prove myself.

Everybody loved the club and was proud to be there, felt tremendous camaraderie. Of course I operated best in this atmosphere of total love. Almost every night, after the last show when the doors were locked and the waiters were changing into their civvies, a little group would gather at the bar—Edgar; Archie Walker, the maître d'; Rod Warren, my friend from my struggle days who wrote the revues for the Upstairs. Others would join us—Lily Tomlin when she was performing revues at the Upstairs, Madeline Kahn.

My opening act was Barry Manilow. Barry played as I went onstage and offstage at the end. He was a gawky-looking, bright, very ambitious kid who had an attaché case filled with songs and jingles he was working on—always writing and arranging, always coming and going to TV networks and advertising agencies, always hustling. We liked him a lot.

This inner circle was part of my addiction to show business. We all had youth, playfulness, daring, all felt we were on the way up, but living dangerously at the caprice of the public and therefore full of humor—because survivors laugh more. In show business we are all children. Nobody says, "Your skirt's too short for your age."

We laughed a lot about the owner, Irving Haber, whom we tormented and adored. He was a man in his late fifties, short, paunchy, loud, crude, blustering, always yelling at the help. "Don't throw away the swizzle sticks. You can use them again. Bunch of fucking assheads. You know what swizzle sticks cost? Ten dollars a thousand."

We laughed about the nights when hundreds of people were in line outside to get in and people inside were virtually standing on each other's shoulders and every door was locked—and the fire marshal would come in and accept an envelope from Irving and say, "It looks fine to me." We laughed about the illegal aliens in the kitchen and the steaks that were green with mold in the refrigerator, about the people who ordered steak and the chef refused to cook it, and Irving said, "Wait, wait, we can scrape them off."

Irving was an immigrant boy who grew up with the attitude that you can be generous, but in business you count your pennies and get ahead of the other guy before he takes advantage of you. He had worked his way up, gone to night school to be a CPA, was very smart, and opened a lucrative chain of sleaze-bag restaurants called the Gypsy Tea Kettles, each with a big kettle over the door and a blowsy woman inside who read your tea leaves. He did not need the Upstairs; it was a labor of love.

My six years there were a giant game, like checkers, Irving against Edgar and me, each trying to outfox the other. It was fun to say, "We beat Irving." But sometimes he won, and he knew it was a game and enjoyed it too. Basically, if I filled the Downstairs at the Upstairs, I won. If I did not, then we had to do what *he* said. All the rest was silly, so we could play about it.

I was being paid by the head, and Archie would give us an honest count of customers in the room. If there were 110, then Irving would tell us there were 94. "Irving," Edgar would say. "There are a hundred and ten."

"A hundred and ten?" he'd answer, astonished. "I swear to God, ninety-four."

"Irving, come and count."

"Jesus Christ, where did they come from?"

The bar was set off from the showroom behind a glass wall where those customers could not hear the show. Since I was paid by the head in the showroom, I did not collect for anybody in the bar. But Irving would go through the bar collecting an extra two bucks and snap on the loudspeaker. I would stop the act and yell, "Irving, I'm not saying another word because I can see people laughing out there."

Irving would say, "Jesus Christ! Who turned the sound on? We've got to put a tape over the switch." We had such good times.

The other side of Irving was jolly and generous. He cared a lot about the kids who did the revues in the Upstairs. If he walked into a neighborhood restaurant and saw one of them eating, he would pick up the check. When their parents came to a show, he told them what wonderful kids they were raising. He had a house in Mahopac, New York, and each summer invited everybody up there for a day of softball and a cookout.

But this same man could not bear to pay these kids decent wages, though they were making him big bucks doing two and three shows a night. When he found out they were making sandwiches for themselves in the kitchen after the second show, he went crazy, screaming, "No sandwiches! If youse want to eat, go down the street to the coffee shop." But they found a way to win. Lily Tomlin walked into the kitchen and said to the chef, "I am sleeping with Mr. Haber, and he said my friends can have all the sandwiches they want."

For a long time Irving's brother had a good thing going, making sandwiches in the kitchen and selling them at lunchtime on the sidewalk to workmen. When Irving found out, he kept the club locked until 6:00 P.M., and he fired the Puerto Rican day man who took the phone reservations and installed an answering machine.

Edgar and I liked the day man, so we had friends telephone and leave a message perfectly timed so the tape ran out in the middle of the last sentence. Here is what Irving heard when he played back the machine: "Downstairs at the Upstairs? This is Harry Schwartz. Next Tuesday night I'd like to bring a party of twenty to dinner and the show. Money is no object. It's a birthday party. Please call me back at 478-09 . . ." Click. Within two weeks the day man was back.

In our games with Irving, Edgar always held the trump card. The club was small enough to be a little kingdom, and as long as I gave Irving the kingdom by pulling in the crowds, Edgar had a lot of power. He could say, "Joan won't go on." Twenty years later at Fox, when he went up against Barry Diller, Edgar still thought he had that power, could still play that ace. Irving Haber knew it was a game—Ha, ha, now you outsmarted me—Ha, ha, now I outsmarted you. With Barry Diller, it was, Now I kill you.

Just the fact that all of us pretend to be adults is silly. We are role-playing. Everyone is an actor. Irving Haber was playing Benevolent Dictator to the Kids and Mr. Pinchpenny out of Dickens. My role was Innocent Performer Who Knew Exactly What She Was Doing. Edgar was Show-Biz Dabbler and Adviser to the Semigreats. During my Fox show, Barry Diller played Head of Studio, so he had to be very strong and very firm and certainly no-nonsense.

Life is a game to see how far you can get on the board before the opponent catches you. That is the fun—matching wits but really liking each other. I basically left *The Tonight Show* because the game turned into an endurance contest. Fox was so devastating because there was no humor about business in Barry. To him business was a struggle to the death.

4

ooooo

Thanks to the titanic power of television, I rose rapidly in show business. I was a guest on *The Tonight Show* about once a month, and each time I was seen by millions of Americans. To get on the show, all I had to do was call up and say I was ready. Life in those early days was simple: write my jokes in the daytime, and try them out at night.

Unfortunately I cannot take a pencil and write jokes. I am entirely verbal. I need to sit with somebody and bounce ideas back and forth. To do this, I hired Rodney Dangerfield, who was just beginning to be known. By that time Edgar and I had moved to an apartment on Fifth Avenue, and Rodney would arrive looking like such a *zhlub*, the doormen would stop him in the lobby. Finally Rodney told them he was there to deliver seltzer. Then they let him in.

We sat in the den, Rodney at the typewriter, I on the couch, and we would start bantering on some topic—any topic. Maybe something as banal as tape recorders. Rodney might say, "He was telling me he loved me . . ." And I would say, "Yeah, how about, the marriage was . . ." And Rodney might finish it with ". . . on Fast Forward." I might think of Heidi Abromowitz—"Her tape recorder has only one speed on it. Fast Forward." Then Rodney could say, "Yeah, she's such a tramp, her tape recorder has only one button—Fast Forward." I might rearrange it, "Yeah, she's such a tramp, the only button on her tape recorder is Fast Forward." Not a great joke, but that's how it works. You just let the mind go. It's a mysterious, wonderful process.

At that time jokes were more difficult than usual. My act is mainly complaining about my life, and in those New York years I was content. There was no humor in being happy and having a terrific husband. Can you imagine Roseanne Barr with nothing to complain about? I was no longer a single girl, so my jokes described marriage. I told audiences that I knew nothing about marriage when I went into it. On my wedding night, I had a nightgown with feet. I said that Edgar brought his ex-girlfriend over. She said, "I've heard all about you"—and presented me with *The Joy of Sex.* I went on, "I know nothing about sex. All my mother told me was that the man gets on top, the woman gets on the bottom. I bought bunk beds."

People were shocked. I was breaking new comedy ground with talk about women's intimate experiences and feelings, with jokes like, "I have no boobs. I went to nurse my daughter. She sucked on my shoulder. I moved her to the breast, and she lost four pounds." But compared to the standards of today, my act then was extremely mild.

When I listen to Andrew "Dice" Clay, I marvel that I ever thought Dick was a proper name and blow was what you did to balloons. Sam Kinison insults everybody—including AIDS sufferers and Kurds who were killed by parachuted food supplies. He says all old people should be put to death after eighty-five, and brought a crippled dwarf onstage to call Jerry Lewis a son of a bitch. He insults Christians. Kinison pounds on the floor and shouts Christ's last words: "Ouch! Ouch!" He's outrageous but brilliant.

But Kinison and Clay are not being *new.* The public is just more tolerant, more accepting. And every generation rediscovers the past. Comedy does not change. We just dress it up differently. Men and women, our bodies, does money matter or doesn't it—I'm so ugly that . . . these themes are still universal themes. On my show I recently had a hot young performance artist talking about how it felt to be pregnant. Robin Williams talks about his wife being pregnant. *I* talk about being pregnant. In the forties, the joke might have been "My wife's so fat that when she sits around the house, she sits *around* the house!" In the nineties it might be, "My wife's so fat that you don't walk with her, you walk among her!" Comedy addresses the daily problems we all face. So thirty years ago we laughed about the dishwasher. Today we laugh about the fax machine.

In the sixties my breakthrough joke came just after Melissa was born. I said on Carson, "When I had my baby, I screamed and screamed. And that was just during conception." That joke was quoted all across America. People were calling Edgar to ask, "*What* did she say?" That's how repressed we all were in those days.

But those jokes also shocked because they came from a winning young girl in a nice little dress and pretty little pearls, her hair in a cute flip. I was everybody's married daughter saying things no lady would *ever* talk about in public.

In those days funny women were expected to look weird and ugly and therefore nonthreatening to the ladies out front. At that time the two top female comediennes were Phyllis Diller and Totie Fields. A major part of Phyllis's act was her wild drag-queen outfits, the gloves, the long cigarette holder and crazy hair, and that mad, cackling laugh.

When she came to see me at the Downstairs, I had no sense that she might have been envious of me. She laughed the loudest and afterward was gracious and charming. That night she looked as if she could have been the head of the Mellon family, so chic and pulled together and understated. Little did I know that twenty-five years later, people would be saying "She's so different in person" about *me*.

Totie was a throwback to the tough, vulgar Catskill comics—a chunky woman with pudgy hands and silver nails and Sammy Davis Vegas rings. She was probably sorry she did not have twelve pinkies so she could have a ring on every one. She was a brilliant comic, singing a couple of songs, talking, doing routines about panty hose, about her husband, George, about being fat.

She came out of the lowest levels of show business, from toilets, a fat girl doing strip joints. And she was a total professional who knew how to work an audience, how to sell a joke.

Totie was a gutter fighter who must have been contemptuous of this earnest college graduate with a circle pin and a small delivery, this comedy parvenue who she thought had never paid any real dues in comedy, never done three shows a night in Sheboygan—and was coming into her territory. I could not understand why certain major clubs around the country refused to book me, and I learned later that Totie Fields was spreading the word that I was dirty and vicious, not funny.

Much later, in the mid-seventies, she lost her leg to diabetes and sent me a sweet letter from the hospital telling me she had watched me on Carson and liked my routine. A few months after that, when I was performing at the MGM Grand in Las Vegas, there was a knock on the dressing-room door and it was Totie, alone, a hundred pounds lighter, limping badly, going blind, and brave, brave, brave. She had climbed two flights of steep metal stairs with her wooden leg to tell me she was in the audience and loved the show.

We talked for an hour—muted and soft. The room was garish with gangster furniture and flower arrangements. Sitting on the red velvet couch was this skinny lady with her cane. We talked about jokes—what works and what doesn't work—about club owners we knew, funny things that had happened, and where comedy was going. This night was a rite of passage for me and, I hope, for her, too.

I adored Totie in that hour. We were just two women alone together; we both knew that she was dying and I would never see her again.

While choosing my material for the Carson show, I was extremely tense. In this business if you aren't worried, that means you're not working hard enough—which means you will not be around very long. The preparation was like studying for a test: Am I up-to-date? I would ask myself. Can I make this better? Are people bored with these subjects? The first time a joke comes to me, I'm tremendously amused, but after that I coldly rate them: good, medium, lightweight—fillers or killers.

Everybody's appearances on *The Tonight Show* are loosely scripted—like a rigged Ping-Pong match. I would arrive early at NBC and go over my routine line by line with a talent coordinator, working out the questions I wanted Carson to ask and my answers: "Have Johnny ask me, 'Are you entertaining a lot?' and I'll say, 'Well, Edgar had his ex-girlfriend, Fatima, over and . . .'"

The coordinator decided what would make Carson laugh, and when the lines were set, I memorized everything so I could act them out—and then put my notes in my purse to study onstage during the commercial breaks. When the show was over, I marked the material not used—preparing already for the next time. I was the woman who keeps the crusts and makes bread pudding.

Waiting to go on, I would sit in the dressing room gazing at the monitor, studying with horrible fascination the guests who were not doing well, watching Johnny stop laughing and the guest speed up or slow down and twitch and stumble and sweat. In those early days I would be terrified, wondering, My God, is it the audience? Or the guest? Or Johnny?

I would hear reports on Carson—"Johnny's in a good mood," or "Watch out for Johnny; he's upset." You did not really have to be told. If his mood was bad, the halls backstage were quiet, the makeup room empty while he was there. Nobody wanted to be picked on, get that displaced anger, his cutting, sarcastic remarks. On the air he might not play with you during your spot, might just turn off and leave you marooned in silence. He would even sometimes behave this way with people he liked.

The stage manager would bring me from the dressing room to wait behind the curtain. As soon as I could hear what was happening onstage, the adrenaline would begin to pump. But maybe Carson would go off on a tangent, and I'd have to wait a few beats longer to make my entrance, and the adrenaline would fall away. Then suddenly I would hear Johnny say, "Now let's bring her out"—and the energy would flash through me again. It's a miracle I didn't have a heart attack. . . .

The lights always blinded me at first as I would go to the guest chair and fumble with my dress. At that moment I never looked at the audience. The whole relationship was just the two of us. I would start by saying, "Johnny, Johnny, if you only knew . . ." as though a camera had been snuck into an intimate lunch with my brother, the confidant I told everything to because he wouldn't tell a soul. That was the game I played in my mind. And Johnny went along, listening and commiserating with me.

Carson played me like a harp. He knew where I was going, knew when to come in and when to lean back. We were George Burns and Gracie Allen, Mike Nichols and Elaine May. I do not think Johnny Carson is in tune with many people, but I believe that somewhere inside him I was a kindred spirit, absolutely in tune comedically.

As a stand-up comedian, Johnny had an easy, WASPy charm. He came up as a boyish MC, and he never seemed to want to develop any great routines. You never thought, Jesus Christ, that was *funny*—like Woody Allen's moose routine, George Carlin doing the Seven Words You Can't Say, or Bill Cosby doing Noah. But Carson is still one of the great straight men of the century. He is a brilliant reactor who becomes the audience, asking its questions, having its reactions. This is extremely difficult. He has to know when to cut in with a question, when to stay out, when to make the face, when to be sincere, when to lean toward his guests and be *entre nous,* when to look at the audience and give the joke an extra twist. He has to know when a joke is big enough to sit back in his chair and laugh out loud.

His timing must be masterful. If he comes in with "How fat is she?" one beat off, the joke won't work, because comedy is half music. So much has to do with rhythms and timing—when a beat comes, when a rest comes. If somebody sets you up wrong, it's like a conductor tapping his baton; you have to stop, reset yourself, and start again.

Johnny never left me alone in the lifeboat. If a joke wasn't working, he didn't turn to the audience and give them a look that said, "She's a kook," while he rowed away and left me sitting there.

I felt so grateful to Carson, so loyal, I refused for nearly two years to go on Merv Griffin's show when it started in 1965. I would not appear on any network but NBC. I thought I was back in college—NBC, rah, rah, rah. I bought an NBC T-shirt. They were my family, and a family is sacred—your own through thick and thin.

Johnny Carson worked because he's an old friend. America wants to be with someone comfortable at night. You have to laugh and cry over and over again with someone before you feel comfortable. Look at Phil. Look at Oprah. Look at the years it took to establish their shows. Look at Jay Leno. He's wonderful, he has great humor, he's ebullient. We know him. I think and hope he'll do well.

I adored Johnny Carson. His leaving late-night television signifies the end of an era, an end to his audience's youth. Many performers of an older generation—whom you won't see on Letterman or Arsenio—have lost their final theater. And Johnny's absence, of course, will leave a big gap in America's viewing habits.

He was kind and considerate to me. Many people thought he was aloof, but he is a loner who has nothing to say to a lot of people, and I understand that; I am the same way. Johnny was proud that he had found me. He found a lot of people—Woody Allen and Bill Cosby—and they moved on and became his equals. But I constantly thanked him for turning around my life, for saying, "She's right," and bringing me the career, the husband, the major break of doing Ed Sullivan.

I started on *The Ed Sullivan Show* right after I became pregnant. Edgar had shown no interest in having a child during the first two years of our marriage. I was caught up in my career and had never been the one who went "kitchy-koo" to that baby in the park, never said to the neighbor, "Oh, let me baby-sit little Tiffany." I did not reinvite people who brought their kids over.

But one day while I was performing in Detroit, I stopped at a soda fountain for coffee and an English muffin, and a dark-haired woman came in with a baby. It was so cute, bundled up to twice its size in a snowsuit. They were having a great time together, blowing on a straw, the kid laughing. The relationship was so tender and dear, so total, I said to myself, "I want one of those."

I was shocked at this revelation. Shocked! But suddenly it was the right next step. For the first time, my life was stable and structured. I did not want to be telling jokes in nightclubs all my life, and part of growing out of that would be having a family. I had never been able to lavish love on anybody without thinking they might say, "Oh, stop it," and make me self-conscious. My mother was wonderful, but basically cold. My father was preoccupied. Edgar was not a sponge for love. I was a touchy-feely person surrounded by repression.

Buried in me was a need to have somebody really, really, really my own, a baby I could kiss all over, up and down those little toesies. God knows I need love, but *loving* is what is truly wonderful. Having somebody to go home to, somebody to care for and worry about, is what takes you out of yourself. Being loved does not fill you up in the same complete way.

From that moment in Detroit I could not wait to conceive. I threw away my birth-control pills and telephoned the Roman Catholic archdiocese to find out about the rhythm method of birth control—how to take your temperature every day and avoid the days you are most fertile. The information was invaluable. Backward.

I was pregnant within two months. Edgar was just as thrilled as I was. He loved seeing me so happy, and I think, too, he was proud of this proof of manhood. He was no longer the outsider, the bachelor friend on the fringes of adult society. He was a family man with a rightful niche. By that time, after Frieda's death, we had moved to Park Avenue, and now the proud father-to-be went out and rented a larger apartment on Fifth Avenue.

I put on maternity clothes after six weeks. I talked constantly to everybody about my pregnancy, figuring if I talked enough, God would not allow any problems. My baby was my friend from the day that rabbit died. I had read that if you talk directly to a baby growing inside you, its brains come alert faster. "Okay, sweetie puss, here we go," I would be saying as I drove alone in the car. "The sun is shining. When you see the sun, you're going to love it. Your father wants to name you Carl or Carla. Trust me, that will never happen."

Pregnancy went right into my act. I told audiences I was such a fabulous mother, I was breast-feeding my unborn child—and I was carrying so low, the kid's feet were sticking out. Then I'd lean toward the audience and say, "Want to see?"

I complained that I was carrying so big, I looked like a mother kangaroo with everybody home, and felt like such a big fat tub, I was looking for a college kid to carry the baby for me. Then I could be down in Jamaica and she would just call me up and say, "Guess what? The kid's here." "Great!" I would say. "What did I have?"

By then I was performing regularly on *The Ed Sullivan Show,* and when I tried to use those jokes—television was so strait-laced in those days—Ed said he would not even allow the word "pregnant" on the air. We finally compromised on "Soon I'm going to be hearing the pitter-patter of tiny feet." Now movie stars are posing pregnant—and naked—on the covers of national magazines. Some change.

I first did Sullivan in 1967 because of a mistake. Ed had agreed to book Johnny Rivers, the folksinger. But by then in his career, Ed was getting more and more confused from what I think now was early Alzheimer's. "Next week we'll be having Joanie Rivers," he announced on the air. So they *had* to let me in the door.

But before the final okay, Ed Sullivan wanted to see my act. So Edgar and I reported to his apartment in the Delmonico Hotel on Park Avenue. In bright sunlight he sat behind a lacquered French desk in his living room on a pretty Louis XVI chair. I stood in front of the desk like a child before a teacher and said, "My hairdresser, Mr. Phyllis? We're very, very close. As a matter of fact, he was one of my bridesmaids."

The most powerful man in TV entertainment sat stone-faced. He never smiled. Not once. Feeling that I was drowning in the pool of silence, I pushed on with, "Somebody broke into Mr. Phyllis's apartment, and they took his roommate. They thought he was a piece of pop art." I was so afraid of seeing Sullivan frown that I did the whole act to a French Impressionist painting right above his head. "Hey, the stewardess was such a tramp . . ." I told the gold frame while Ed's wife, Sylvia, sweetly tiptoed through the room.

I was right back to the first time I stepped on a stage and bombed. When you are a success, audiences take you on faith; they no longer judge you. But here in Ed Sullivan's living room, I knew the jury was still out. I felt sweaty, felt myself shrinking into my skin, felt my shoulders hunch, my feet go pigeon-toed. At times like this you cannot as an adult run screaming from the room, so you force yourself to finish and leave whole. But in the midst of that kind of panic, I talk too fast, get too loud, and don't wait for the punch line. I swallow the key words of a joke: "I was so desperate I wrote my (mumble) on men's room walls. All I got back was (mumble) towels." Nobody knows *what's* going on!

But Ed must have had an inner chortle that day, because he let me on the show. He somehow decided, though, that Edgar was a doctor, and so for the rest of our relationship he would say, "Hi, Doctor, nice to see you, Doctor. The little lady is doing just fine."

Sullivan had the pulse of America. He had hunters who looked for acts, but he was the one who made the final decision. He personally saw the crowds for the Beatles at Heathrow Airport in England and decided to bring them to America. He was the first to put Elvis on TV. Every performer in America fawned over him. I was in Sullivan's dressing room when he was angry at Shecky Greene for a particular joke. Shecky, then one of the top American comics, was saying, "Ed, I didn't mean it that way, Ed. Ed, that's not what the joke is. Ed, I'm telling you, please, Ed, Ed, Ed." Nobody now has the power of Ed Sullivan. Today there are too many channels, network clout is diluted. I think that's a big reason why Johnny Carson is quitting while he's still somewhat ahead—before his ratings are dragged down by all the cable channels and new late-night choices.

I was once on *The Ed Sullivan Show* at the same time as the Rolling Stones. They were white-hot. The limo bringing Edgar and me to the theater could not get through the police cordon holding back the mob of teenagers. We had to get out and walk. In the midst of all this hysteria, Ed Sullivan walked into their rehearsal, took one look, and said, "They're not going on my show unless they wash their hair." Fifteen minutes later I went into the makeup room, and there were these four scruffy guys with their heads leaning back in the washbasins.

Their dressing room was big enough for a Steinway piano, and their idea of a joke was to destroy it. My dressing room was next door, and, given what I was about to do, my idea of a joke was not much better. Our windows looked out on Fifty-second Street, and a throng of screaming, hysterical, lovesick teenagers. Ed had sent me a dozen red roses, and foolishly, for laughs, I took one and threw it out the window. Thinking it came from Mick, the girls rioted, hundreds of them breaking through the police line, turning over the sawhorse barriers, trampling each other to get the Jagger rose. I was terrified.

The police came up looking for the person who started the riot. "Do you know who threw the rose, Miss Rivers? Somebody could have been seriously hurt."

"Disgusting!" I said. "Who would do such a thing!" Meanwhile, staring them in the face was a vase with eleven roses in full bloom.

The show was live—rehearsed and performed in one day: Ed Sullivan Sunday—in a theater so old, to get to the front of the theater from backstage, you had to go through the men's room. When I was called forward to check my cue cards, I would knock on the men's room door and yell, "Here I come! Shut your eyes! Shut your eyes!"

During the last years before Ed had to give up the show, he became increasingly dotty. Once Jane Morgan was singing "Bolero," and he walked on the stage and said, "Everybody clap along." To a bolero beat? Sometimes on the air he would ask questions that made no sense. He called Woody Allen over after Woody's act and asked him for no discernible reason, "How's your father? Is he better?" Woody, improvising, said, "He recognizes me now and he's able to blink."

Talk about potentially embarrassing moments, Kate Smith, everybody's substitute Statue of Liberty, was, close to the end of her life, also getting a bit dotty. In fact, one of the most horrifying symptoms of this was . . . well, she had a reputation for flashing. One year, during the Academy Awards, Bob Hope wheeled poor Kate out onstage to sing "God Bless America," so afraid she would flash that people backstage fastened the hem of her dress to the wheelchair! The whole time she was singing she was plucking at her dress. I swear.

Now, back to Ed.

After months of jokes and talk about the patter of tiny feet, Ed called me over—I was nine months pregnant—to ask on the air, "Are you married?"

"Yes, Mr. Sullivan."

"That's right. That's right. The doctor. The doctor."

As he declined, Sylvia became so protective of him. She was wonderful. I admired her, admired their marriage. She was Ed's best friend in the world, the one he could turn his back on and not worry. They did everything together, made all decisions together. Very much a team. This I understood.

Regardless of how successful I was becoming, I continued to see comedy as a stepping-stone to a legitimate acting career and the respect I believed only came with acting. Stand-ups are considered funny, but not artists, not sensitive—there's no talent to it, anybody can do it: "Hey, you want to hear funny? You come down and talk to my secretary. She'll kill you. Ask her about her mother-in-law."

From girlhood I saw myself as Katharine Cornell, treading the boards, the toast of Broadway. I tasted that respectability in Barnard College, where I was the leading actress, performing in every play I could—starring in *Lady Windermere's Fan* and *Juno and the Paycock*.

In 1967 I wangled permission to sit in on Lee Strasberg's classes at the Actors Studio, a tiny, beat-up theater in the West Forties. The women wore corduroy slacks, crew necks, no makeup, hair plain—because an *actress* isn't bothered with worldly thoughts. Everybody knew each other—very cliquey. If you were accepted, you were royalty, a *Method* actor, which meant that if you were not yet famous, you soon would be, because you are talented and part of the elite.

Marlon Brando always took classes when he was in town, as did the Wallachs—Eli and Anne Jackson—and Paul Newman. Major actors, struggling to advance their craft, did works in progress by major writers. Strasberg, who sat in the center of the front row, criticized everybody equally, and the response from these talents? "That's right, Lee. Thank you. It's true. I was working for heat and didn't get it." Just being in the room was the most exciting thing in my life.

I talked about this at brunch one afternoon at Steve Lawrence and Eydie Gorme's apartment, and Eydie asked if she could come with me. When I picked her up, she was dressed as if she were going to a Hadassah luncheon—a fur stole, suit, hat, gloves. At the Studio, I turned toward the back row where I always hid. Eydie, being Eydie, led me right down to the front. Right at our shoe tips Joan Copeland did a scene from a Tennessee Williams work in progress.

It was one of those fabulous acting moments that leaves a stunned silence, that stillness that is an appreciation far greater than any applause. In that silence Eydie Gorme—with her Eydie Gorme voice—said, "Listen, we can do better than that. Let's show 'em. We'll get costumes and makeup and do a scene from *Arsenic and Old Lace.*" Every head turned.

Eydie sat there impervious. I was mortified. I never could make myself go back. My stage acting mattered to me so desperately, I did not have the courage, the confidence, to push myself into that charmed circle. I could not bear the possibility that they would say no, that I might find I did not have talent.

I longed for the Eydie Gorme brass, envied her strength and confidence. Barbra Streisand, recording a song, does fifty takes; Eydie sings a couple of times, and it is done. We did a *Carol Burnett Show* together—the three of us were playing the Supremes in a comedy skit, and Eydie took me aside and said, "Let me show you how to read this line to get a laugh." And she was right. I got my laugh.

I have never been able to step out front and say, "I'm Joan Rivers and I *know!*" I have always worked to get what I want through subterfuge, through winning hearts to get people's minds, through men—through Edgar. I have feared that people are going to smell my fear, my ingrained terror that in fact I am a fraud. That has been my Achilles' heel. I am too fearful to just go in and push and make the sacrifice. I so admire Cher, who just stopped her income and said, "I'm going to act." I've heard she went so broke she had to sell back a diamond bracelet to David Geffen, the man who gave it to her in the first place. I never had the courage to say, "I'm giving up everything, the house, the cars, Melissa's private school. I'm going to take a year off and act."

The only feature film I was ever offered came early that same year, 1967. Edgar and I were invited to dinner by Frank and Eleanor Perry, who had done *David and Lisa*. Edgar had become a friend through Telsun, and they were my first taste of Park Avenue liberalism. After dinner the women discussed a march on the UN—but I never found out what they were protesting. The big issue was what to wear.

"Shall we wear our mink coats? Is it too upper class?" "Well, I'm wearing the Dior coat with the matching dress—and I'll carry a Hermès bag. I am not embarrassed by who I am." "Should it be the Hermès or the alligator one?" "Well, maybe you're right. I'll do the mink after all. They should know that people like us care." I was asked if I was going to march. I said, "I don't have the outfit." Nobody laughed.

Frank was directing *The Swimmer* with Burt Lancaster and wrote in a part for me. The film was an adaptation of a John Cheever story about an aging Lothario who decides one afternoon to swim home cross-country, pool by pool. At each pool are people and incidents that peel open his entire life. By the end you realize he is a fraud and failure.

I made a joke and called my role "Chaplinesque." That is, I played a tramp. Burt Lancaster reaches the pool of a former mistress, played by Janice Rule. To get back at her, he picks up a slutty girl with a heart of gold named Joan. That's me. I am excited because I think he'll come away with me; then Janice tells him off, and I get dumped. Typecasting.

On Monday we went to Burt's trailer and read the lines through, and Frank explained what he wanted. As we left, Lancaster said, "Honey, wait a second." I went back in, and he said,

"Forget everything he just told you. This is how we're going to do it."

He redirected every line so that there would be no sympathy for me. Frank wanted a happy girl who then got hurt. Lancaster was going to be Mr. Wonderful who came up against a mean bitch, and was right not to go off with her. Trying to please both men, I was going back and forth between line readings, and nothing made sense.

I was also experiencing what acting in the old Hollywood movies must have been like with those big stars fighting for their screen time, using every trick. In my scenes with Lancaster, he would step backward, forcing me to turn my face toward him and away from the camera. While I was speaking my lines, he was constantly in motion, shaking his drink, wiping his mouth, moving his hands. Since eyes go to motion, the attention would be on him.

No actor was allowed to touch him. If I laid a hand on him, then the camera would have to show whose hand that was. That is the old movie rule for bit players—"Always touch the money." Then they cannot cut you out of the scene.

I had been a Burt Lancaster fan, but here he was refusing a little bit player her moment in the sun. This was the first time I came up against a star who was not generous, somebody totally self-centered, somebody out to kill. However, Frank Perry was smart. He just kept saying, "Cut. Do it again." My scenes were supposed to take two days to shoot. Finally, after seven days of reshooting my two little minutes on the screen, Frank said, "I know what the son of a bitch has been doing all week. Now do it the way you and I want." That was the wrap.

The picture was semipanned, but I got singled out with some positive mentions. When Vincent Canby of *The New York Times* said I was "especially interesting," I was thrilled.

No movie offers came as a result of *The Swimmer.* I thought doors would open, thought somebody would read the reviews and say, Let's take a look at *her.* I was so young and optimistic I even thought a Broadway musical might fall in my lap, and just in case, I should be ready.

I had never been able to sing. The first time I tried to carry a tune, my voice got a hernia. But if there was a song in my throat, I was going to find it. I began studying voice twice a week with the man who coached Lauren Bacall in the hour just ahead of me. To me, Bacall was a major star. Twice a week I would arrive, and the teacher would say, "Miss Bacall, do you know Joan Rivers?" And Bacall would say to this little piece of garbage that was following her, "No, how do you do." I'd say brightly, "Yes, we met last week."

That little scene was repeated month after month as I grew bigger and bigger and bigger with my baby. Each time I thought, Sooner or later, she's got to remember me. A blind woman would say, "How are you feeling?" I mean, I could no longer button my coat. Finally I decided not to remember her, either. When she said, "No. How do you do?" I would answer, "No. How do you do?" At that time, standing up to Lauren Bacall, I felt great.

Though I intended to have anesthesia when I had my baby, I decided to go to natural childbirth class, and know everything, have every tool there was for the birth. Edgar dropped me off and picked me up, but refused to come inside, so I looked like a widow or a divorcée, and the teacher had to be my partner. But I told myself, "That's Edgar." So stubborn. To hell with it. Maybe Lamaze fell into the same category as therapy, which he had always scorned.

The baby turned sideways in the ninth month—which meant a breech birth. "You have no right to do this to us," I kept telling my stomach, "you must turn back. This is ridiculous." The day before she was born, she turned back. Typical Melissa. Had to do things her way, when *she* was ready.

On January 19, 1968, when I was onstage at the Downstairs at the Upstairs, the first contractions began. Between shows I did an interview with a writer from *The Milwaukee Journal.* I finished the last show at 2:00 A.M. and went home. At noon the next day Edgar took me to the hospital, and two hours later I had Melissa. Talk about timing!

I saw her the minute she came out, bright red, her nose flattened all over her face. I was so excited—but also upset. I had made such a connection with her, my feelings were hurt when she did not sit up and say, "Mommy! Wow! So that's what you look like!"

For a permanent nanny, I put an ad in the paper with the come-on "Show business couple, meet and greet the stars." We got calls: "Are you Barbra Streisand? Are you Goldie Hawn?"—followed by sighs of disappointment. One applicant was Scottish, spoke with a burr, arrived elegant in the white uniform and the blue cap, very proper. She had worked for Vanderbilts and Firestones and literally interviewed *us*. Finally she said, "I will take the position, but only on one condition. I insist that the parents, no matter how busy they are, spend a half hour a day with their children."

I told her she didn't have to worry. In fact, poor Lily Anderson did not know what hit her. She was thrilled to meet the show-biz people who came through the apartment. She even became a little show biz herself. Once I heard her saying to another nanny in the park, "When Miss Ann-Margret came to our house, Melissa wore her white didee." Then there was the time when Lily, in her uniform, went on a TV quiz program, where the panel guessed what the employer does—and nobody could imagine she worked for a stand-up comic. She won a mink stole.

Over the years a series of nannies became part of our lives, but *I* raised Melissa. I put her on my schedule. When I arrived home around 2:00 A.M. after performing at the Upstairs at the Downstairs, I walked a lot through her room, and the minute she stirred, I got her up and we took a bath together. The next morning I would get up and have breakfast with Edgar while she slept. When Melissa woke, we'd play in bed for a while. In the late morning I would go see my manager, check in, find out what offers had come in, and maybe have a business lunch.

I was usually home in the afternoon, and there was never any "Here, Nanny, she's wet." That little bottom was wiped by me, and shake, shake with the wonderful talcum and "We smell so good now" and the kiss on the stomach before the diaper. And then I would put her on my bed and tell her *everything*.

Unless she could come with me, I usually stayed home all afternoon. If I had a dress fitting, I took her into fitting rooms.

Once, when I went looking at jewelry, Tiffany opened its side delivery door for the carriage. If I was driving somewhere, Melissa came in the limo and we played together. I have a picture of me at a woman's luncheon with Melissa on my lap. I am sure nobody wanted Melissa as a lunch date.

Of course, having a baby continued to be a big section of my act. I told the audiences that while I was in labor, the nurse had tried on my dress and said, "If you die, can I have this?" The intern was so young, he expected the stork to come through the window. I said that Edgar didn't understand much about the whole thing. After Melissa was born, he stood and waited for her luggage to come out.

Edgar used to wonder, "Doesn't she bore you?" I would say, "No, we have the best time. We just went to the park and bought a balloon." Probably because of his own solitary childhood, Edgar did not know how to do children things and was made uncomfortable by them. I knew he loved Melissa and wanted to be the best father he could manage, but he was so fearful of emotion, of opening up and being vulnerable, he seemed in pain trying to express love. Sometimes he tried to unbend with her, doing Halloweens and Easter egg hunts. But he did not spend time and connect with Melissa until she was truly verbal and they could exchange ideas.

That was okay with me. I was happy that she was all mine, the little person who could absorb all the love pent up inside me. The first time I *really* knew she loved me back, Melissa was nine months old. During her nap time she somehow climbed out of her crib and crawled all the way to my room to see me. I said, "Oh, look. I have a visitor," and my heart melted, and I got down on the floor with her.

She was my pal. When she was older, we watched late movies together. The day after *Zulu,* I took her to Temple Emanu-El nursery school to be interviewed. She ripped off the sticker that said, HELLO, I'M MELISSA. She would not play with the other kids. The teachers said, "Your child is very antisocial." I said, "That's because there was a wonderful late, late movie with Michael Caine, and we stayed up together." They just stared at me. As we were leaving, Melissa threw clay at another little girl. I told her, "We blew it, honey," and we went to Schrafft's and had breakfast.

From the minute I had Melissa, I would rather spend time with children than with adults. Their innocence is so unscathed. Their trust, their unquestioning belief, makes *you* a better person. The layers of social deceit have not yet formed, and they call things as they are. You hear a child say, "I don't want to play with you because I don't like you." Good! Now we know where we stand, and we can go from there.

At the same time, children have not learned to ration their love, and they accept your love totally. Their joy is complete— and they get rid of unhappiness so easily. A child is crying, and in three minutes you can have her smiling and laughing again. I love that.

Having Melissa to come home to, looking forward to spending time with my daughter, was all-important. My career had not yet become the glue that held my life and marriage together. The rock at the center of my tiny universe was still the baby and the home and the marriage.

5

ooooo

Just because I talk about plastic surgery on television, people think I'm a plastic-surgery addict, that I have plastic surgery every day. I think every woman should have plastic surgery if she wants. My mother always told me, "There's nothing good about old age, so accept it with dignity." To me plastic surgery is like a touch-up, a tune-up that makes me feel good about myself. You take your car to be Simonized. You get your dresses cleaned. Why not a little job under the chin?

After shooting my movie *Rabbit Test* in 1977, I was down and depressed. I figured, get the whole face done and nobody will see me while I'm editing the film. So I told the best plastic surgeon in Los Angeles to do everything, and he did, and I was sitting in the editing room thinking, Gee, my eyes are great—you can't even see the stitches. Then I went for my first checkup, and the doctor was taking the stitches out behind the ears, and I told him, Boy, my eyes look terrific. Suddenly he turned bright red. He'd *forgotten* to do the eyes! So I got an IOU for one eye job by Los Angeles's number-one plastic surgeon. I wanted to give it as a raffle for a charity, but no one would take it. *Now,* they'd grab it!

Right before the Fox show I finally had my eyes done and along with it I did a very light acid wash. It was nothing, like a sunburn. It takes away the top skin, and with it, all the little lines. For me, it was no pain, no burn. Three days later I was performing at Lake Tahoe.

I once wanted to make my nose thinner, not a whole big job. Unfortunately I was on the cover of *People* magazine that month, and the doctor looked at me and said, "What can I *do*? Everyone has seen this picture." "Just thin it," I said, "no one will notice." They didn't.

When I had to have a hysterectomy, I asked if a plastic surgeon could sew me up. There were four other ladies in the hospital crying, "Boo-hoo, I'm no longer a woman." Me? I was thrilled. My tummy was as flat as a washboard. Nothing like a tummy tuck at the end of a hysterectomy.

In 1968, long before *I* did, my career got a major face-lift. Because of my comedy success, the William Morris Agency offered to package a TV talk show for me, using the syndicator, Trans Lux, to sell it to independent stations around the country. I was ready. I felt I had done stand-up comedy, had proved I could succeed, and longed to move on to less confining, more diverse ways to communicate.

Edgar wanted to be the show's producer—which meant quitting Anna Rosenberg. I kept saying to him, "Are you sure? Are you *sure*? What's going to happen if the show doesn't work?" To me he was already a movie producer, and this little half-hour morning show seemed like a comedown.

I worried that he was giving up his power base. What would happen if this man, who was used to going to work every day and wielding power, was now home all day? Would that put a tremendous strain on the marriage?

I remember I was sitting on the bed with my legs up, and he was taking off his shirt and tie and he said, "I've always wanted to go back and produce for television. If the show only lasts thirteen weeks, I'll produce other things." I did not realize at the time that Telsun was winding down and he had no other film possibilities. Anna Rosenberg Associates was a public-relations firm, a far distance from show business, Edgar's addiction, where he had tasted its glamour and power at the top level. In New York Edgar enjoyed the perks of an important producer, had offices on Fifth Avenue near Rockefeller Center, and his secretary, Ruth Feyer, had been General George Marshall's secretary. Romancing clients is no longer stimulating when for years you've been flying from New York to France to Yugoslavia to walk onto movie sets and solve everybody's problems.

Edgar earned the right to tremendous pride in what he had done. And Edgar's pride as a man—along with his intellect and experience as a producer—was a big asset for me because I was so vulnerable, so constantly in need of support and reassurance. I did not realize that the roots of that pride extended dangerously deep into his psyche, that it was rooted in lifelong emotional needs that would handicap him for the next logical step into the film business.

Through Telsun he had access to major movie people like David Lean, Tony Richardson, Peter Sellers, and Sean Connery. All sorts of doors were open. With a partner named Sidney Kaufman, he looked for production projects, but they always seemed to be holding out for the perfect deal. If Edgar did all the development work on a film idea that interested Sam Spiegel, Edgar thought he deserved half the money. It was not in him to give away 80 percent to get Spiegel's backing, though that would make the project happen. To Edgar the unfairness was a breach of honor and principle, an insult that diminished him. For better or worse, he was not a compromiser, and you had to respect that.

Also, Edgar did not have a gambler's soul. Closing a deal is shooting crap, putting your reputation and self-esteem on the line. He could oversee my career, but was terrified by risking his own personal failure. Once a package had been put together, he could run it brilliantly—but somebody else had to throw the dice.

The William Morris TV-show package was irresistible because it put Edgar at the top with complete control. Where my show-business addiction is drinking in love on a stage, his drug was to be the boss, answering to no one. At the time I believed he was simply a strong, take-charge person, but ultimately events turned that need into a flaw that brought us both down. I think Edgar craved control because he had such a hard time handling uncertainty. And I believe the reason lay in his past. Whenever a goal had been in his grasp, it had always been yanked away.

Born in 1925, Edgar grew up in Bremerhaven, Germany, doted on by his dominating mother and three aunts. His father, Berthold, owned a prosperous butcher shop. In that family they believed that if you did well financially, you were smart. If you did poorly, you were dumb.

The family, threatened by the Nazis, fled first to the larger city of Hamburg, and then, when Edgar was eight, to Copenhagen, Denmark. Edgar told me that they crossed the German border with only what they could carry, and he had chosen his pet canary and toy soldiers. At the crossing a Prussian guard took these most prized possessions away from him.

Perhaps this one terrifying moment of helplessness accounts for his continuing need to own things. Edgar did not have one shirt, he had fifty. I do not know how many watches he owned. After two years, as anti-Semitism grew in Denmark, the Rosenbergs decided to move to South Africa, a haven for many European Jews. They settled in Cape Town. By now, after all the uprooting and losses, Edgar was a loner—shy, introverted, awkward at making friends, indulged by his mother. But he was a star student who read a half-dozen books a week. I suspect his whole persona—what inner security he had—was built around being that voracious reader and superior intellect.

Six months before he died, he told me his darkest secret. As a boy in Cape Town, he developed tuberculosis. "Don't tell Melissa," he kept saying, his voice aching with shame. In those days in South Africa—and much of Europe, too—tuberculosis carried a social stigma. Virulently contagious, Edgar was instantly ripped out of school and sent three hundred miles north to the Neelspoort Hospital in a desolate, arid region called the Karroo. "It was horrible, *horrible*," he told me. "Don't tell Melissa."

When he came out of the sanatorium, he was more than ever an outsider, kept at home, nursed by black servants, educated by a tutor. And then a relapse sent him back to Neelspoort.

His escape during his adolescence and young manhood was reading theater biographies and playing over and over the songs of Noël Coward and Cole Porter. So he was thrilled when, to be close to relatives in the New York area, the family moved in 1948 to America, the very seat of show business.

Starting as a night clerk in a bookstore, Edgar moved on to an advertising agency, and then made it into show business. He was hired at NBC as a production supervisor and coordinator, planning and arranging the labor, materials, and equipment. As the expediter and budget controller, he was involved in every move in a production, and eventually became a troubleshooter for the semilegendary producer Manie Sachs. During those early days of television, Edgar wrote the network's first handbook for production supervisors.

That was the perfect job for Edgar—details, details, details, checking, checking, checking. He must have been brilliant. My secretary found an NBC memo thanking Edgar for his job on a Martin and Lewis telethon—"a rare combination of long range planning, continued rechecking, and talent that had appeal, sincerity and dignity."

In 1954 he joined an NBC subsidiary as a full-fledged producer, doing closed-circuit TV shows for demonstrations and sales meetings at major corporations like Pan American, Ford Motor Company, Humble Oil. During that time he had become good friends with Tom Rosenberg, the son of Anna Rosenberg, who sold his mother on hiring Edgar to add television expertise to the office, and considered him "one of the most creative guys I've ever seen, prolific with ideas, many of them first-rate."

The decision to do the show began the fusion of my career with Edgar's. That was not our plan. It just happened. I was frightened by the responsibility of carrying a show on my shoulders, and Edgar and I obsessively hashed out every decision. I had a joke based on the truth—"My marriage is wonderful because when I wake up in the morning, I'm thinking of me and so is he." Still in bed, Edgar would say, "I figured out during the night that the contract should read . . ."

Telling me, "You deserve better," he handled the agents. He was the one who said, "No, she won't go into Mr. Kelly's for less than a thousand dollars a week; that's what George Carlin got. She's headlining and she's hot and she's on the Carson show. She doesn't have to prove herself." I was in the background saying, "Oh, we're going to lose the job." And he was saying to the agent, "...and we want a car to pick her up at the airport." But by God, we got what he asked.

And he was the one saying to the William Morris Agency, "You're making more for packaging the show than we are for doing it. You've got to take less." And they did.

Increasingly the romance in my life was my career. My lover was my career. My career gave me the flowers and the candy. And that is the way—twenty-four hours a day of wondering and worrying—you have to be if you are going to stay in the mainstream.

I did not worry about any flaws in the marriage. As my mother used to tell me, nothing is perfect, and this marriage was working. A lot of people, I think, go into marriage expecting it to be all honeymoon and huggy-kissy the rest of their lives—but the passion goes, and the lucky ones end up with the best friend, the trusted confidant who shares everything and gets the jokes. In my career Edgar and I had a common interest like nothing in the world, one that consumed us—and the child we loved.

Particularly in show business, marriage is a long-term commitment to somebody you dare turn your back on. Edgar knew my history and knew the fears, knew the enemies and was there to protect me, whether or not I was in the room.

I was so lucky. My husband may have second-guessed everybody and annoyed everybody—but he did something right. I look at, for example, the *Laugh-In* kids, wonderful talents who were coming up at the same time—Jo Anne Worley, Ruth Buzzi, Arte Johnson. In the long run, they needed an Edgar.

We named our show *That Show,* and designed it to be one of two transition shows between the 1968 *Today Show* and the morning game programs. In five major cities we were on NBC. For the pilot, which sold the show to the independent stations, we asked Johnny Carson to be a guest. At the time he was in delicate contract negotiations with NBC, but he ignored his lawyers' advice and did us this tremendous favor.

I wanted to thank him with a present—but you can't go to

Tiffany and buy him a cigarette box. He already had six. We asked ourselves what we could give Johnny that he didn't have. The answer was Melissa.

She was still an infant at the time, so we dressed her up beautifully. The nurse in full uniform and cape took her over to NBC and actually got right through to Johnny, who was in a meeting with his whole staff. "Mr. Carson," she announced, "this is for you." The joke around the show was, Johnny went white because he thought maybe the baby was his.

He read the note pinned to Melissa, which said, *Dear Mr. Carson, my parents don't know how to thank you for what you did for my mother, so they wanted to give you something they really love, and that's me. My name is Melissa Rosenberg. I weigh 12 pounds. I eat very little. Please bring me up Jewish.* The color came back into Johnny's face, and he laughed and cradled her; she fell asleep gripping his little finger. He finished the meeting with Melissa in his arms.

That Show ran from 9:30 to 10:00 A.M. Barbara Walters had a show then too, and we ran back-to-back and shared a hairdresser. Ours was a tiny, inexpensive little effort; what we saved out of the production fee was our profit. We hired writers so young, the writers' room smelled of Clearasil.

Edgar did everything. He assembled the contracts and the budget and the lawyers and got the meetings going and worried whether they spent twelve dollars for the typewriter rental. He made himself the senior member of the show's units, and he probably drove people crazy micromanaging each detail. But the machinery ran like clockwork. His decisions were right, he found the guests we needed.

When he was working for NBC, people would sit around the casting table and say, "This is a part for So-and-so, but he'll never do it." At which time Edgar's boss, Mannie Sachs, would say— "Did you call Sinatra?" He meant, always try for the best first. Never assume you'll be turned down. In our meetings, if somebody would say, "Of course, Robert Wagner'll never come on," Edgar said, "Did you call Sinatra?"

We taped three shows one day and two the next—which gave me time for club dates, and in January of 1969 I became a regular guest host on *The Tonight Show.* All I had to do for my own show was read the books, learn my notes, show up, and put on the clothes they gave me. It was a proud, happy time for everybody.

Doing the show, I was one of the first hosts to go out into the audience for my opening monologue. In one of the first shows I said, "Today our guests are Don Rickles, star of his own network series, and Mr. Vidal Sassoon, hairstylist extraordinaire and author of the book *Sorry I Kept You Waiting, Madam.*

"Do I look different today? I just spent the entire day at the beauty shop. They really dolled me up. They worked on my hair, not the color because I happen to be a natural blond. True, the roots are black, but that's just because my hair grows faster than my color. When they finished with me, I looked great. They gave me fake fingernails, false eyelashes, a wig, and a padded bra. For once I felt like the real me. When I got home, Edgar took me in his arms and kissed me and made love to me like never before. Then he drew me close and whispered, 'You better get out of here before Joan comes home.' "

After the commercial I sat down in a little French set with three chairs and two armoires. Don Rickles came out, and we talked about his show—he was brilliantly funny, insulting everybody. Then Vidal Sassoon came on and talked about hair. The ladies got some laughs, some celebrity, and some practical hints—which was very important because they didn't feel guilty about wasting part of their morning.

We had an expert on marital fights along with James Earl Jones, and he and I improvised a fight—"Where, Jimmy, did we lose the magic?" When we had on the old-movie actress Joan Bennett, I was thrilled. One of my earliest memories was licking Joan Bennett's face. As a child, I had bought ice cream in Dixie cups with a star's picture on the inside of the top. Amy Vanderbilt was booked to talk about etiquette—but the day before our show, she got a better offer and canceled. I talked about that on my show, on Carson, everywhere I went, saying, "Let's talk about manners, shall we, Amy?"

Getting Ed Sullivan as a guest was a major coup, and frightening because he was more than a little dotty by then. So we put all the questions up on a board where he could see them. On the show he got what we called "perky"—"Watch out, Ed's had a nap. He's perky"—and when I asked the first question, he decided it was funny to give the answer to the second question. Catching up to him was impossible. I went to the third question, and he went to the fourth answer. Soon he was totally confused, the audience was totally bewildered, and I was panicked. "There goes *The Ed Sullivan Show.*" But Ed was having a great time, and nobody said a thing.

Jerry Lewis, when he was a movie star, came on our dumb little show like the big king, demanding everything. He arrived late, full of being Jerry Lewis. He wanted a bigger dressing room. He wanted champagne. He wanted flowers. Two thirds of the way through the show, he looked at his watch and said, "I've got to go," and walked out.

His was the arrogance of the big star: When I get there, the show starts, and it ends when I leave. I followed Jerry Lewis at a club in Detroit, and the hotel put me in the room he had used. Lewis had made them redecorate it just for his stay. Yul Brynner used to make places repaint his rooms for him in brown. The Sands in Las Vegas rebuilt a dressing room overnight to keep Sinatra happy.

Arthur Godfrey came to talk about air pollution, and was so rude and demanding to the talent booker who handled him, she ended up in tears. Edgar asked me to go cheer Godfrey up. When I reached his dressing-room door, the voice I had grown up with was calling somebody four-letter words, and I had to go in and say how thrilled we were to have him, and how I was such a fan of his.

But whatever it takes to get the show on you do. You accept that you're a slave to the show. I wanted to get Whitney Houston as a guest for my present show, and was told her father was the best route to her. When I got him on the phone, he made me feel like a piece of dirt, dismissing me with, "No way. No way." But you shake that off, and an hour later you're trying somebody else—and the pleading and prostrating keeps you healthily humble.

In the middle of the first season, *That Show* was getting good ratings when it was in its proper morning time slot. But in syndication you have no control over when a show is aired. The stations that bought the show were little kingdoms making their own decisions, willing to do anything to get higher ratings. If one of their slots had terrible numbers, they would put me into that time and hope for the best—"She's doing great in the morning, maybe she can win against the soaps in the afternoon." We found ourselves, a little morning show, put on in the afternoon and even in prime time against shows like *The Hollywood Palace* and *The Carol Burnett Show.* There would be Carol on CBS, an hour of stars, music, and skits, and over here Joan Rivers was asking, "How do you make a Danish sandwich?" When, sure enough, that didn't work, I was dropped entirely because there was now another show in my old morning slot.

After our first season we lost a lot of stations. Edgar was extremely upset, and I was very tired. NBC, which had kept me in my morning slot on its own stations, was happy with us, and we were part of a big *New York Times* ad the network ran for its fall schedule. But I wanted to retire. I was very young, very cavalier, and thought this was just a way station to bigger things. I was still performing at night at the Downstairs at the Upstairs, three shows on weekends, and I was bored doing a half hour on how to pack a suitcase. So we pulled the show off the air ourselves.

Though I had stayed at the Downstairs at the Upstairs, I was not "happening" on the comedy circuit around the country. Our booking agent, William Morris, was completely discouraging, telling me, "You're too New York. You're too Jewish." Edgar said, "Find us the hardest place in America for a Jewish comedienne to work." The agent said, "Milwaukee," which was a center for German-Americans.

They booked me into the Pfister Hotel, and I opened in a tiny little showroom next to the swimming pool on the roof. The crowds were so big, they overflowed into the pool area. I played to women with falling hairdos and men with limp collars. Within days, they moved me to the main ballroom—and William Morris believed.

For the next year and a half we were in and out of New York, performing in showrooms throughout the country. I began appearing as an opening act in Las Vegas, and had guest shots with Carol Burnett, Jim Nabors, and Flip Wilson. But I was still frustrated by the lack of acting offers, even though I had done well in *The Swimmer* and had toured successfully one summer in the play *Luv* with Dom DeLuise and Mickey Rooney.

Well, I believe you can do anything if you are willing to try hard enough, so, in a moment of chutzpah, with only one unproduced movie script under my belt, I decided in early 1970 to write my own stage comedy, starring me. I had read all the backstage sagas about putting on a play, but nothing could prepare me for surviving what turned out to be a definitive turning point in my life and particularly Edgar's.

The enterprise started out happily. My collaborators were a funny former agent named Lester Colodny, who had written jokes for me, and Edgar, who was excellent at plotting, but with his precision mind, he would say about a joke, "That is grammatically incorrect." And we would say, "But, Edgar, that's *why* the joke is funny."

During a year and a half, much of it touring, the play evolved into a comedy about women's liberation and the difficulty of urban living. My heroine, Jill, wanted New York to secede from the Union and become a country. Because she was so busy going to rallies and being the liberated woman, she was breaking up with her boyfriend of seven years—while enduring the barrage of troubles that can happen to any poor schlepp who lives in a New York City apartment house.

Our agent sent the script to Alexander Cohen, a top Broadway name, very experienced. One day in 1971 he arrived in his chauffeur-driven Mercedes at our summer rental in Bedford, New York, and sat on our terrace and told us he wanted to produce the play.

We went into rehearsal in Washington, D.C. We had very little interest in anything else. The Vietnam pullout negotiations, Nixon directing NASA to build the space shuttle, were insignificant. Edgar and I were living the romance of those books we had read—rewriting the play late into the night, sleeping four hours, memorizing and rehearsing new lines, running on all cylinders, making huge decisions like, Should my liberated-woman character go braless on stage.

Edgar was in his element, standing in the back of the theater each night making notes, telling us afterward that this line is not working but that one is. Then reality hit us. The day before our opening in the National Theatre in Washington, a stagehand grabbed me and said, "A play just like yours was here last month. *The Prisoner of Second Avenue.*" We were competing with the same theme as Neil Simon, the undisputed master of Broadway comedy.

To keep myself functioning, I started my mind games, saying to myself over and over like an incantation, "There's room for both of us. The audiences are laughing. There's room for both of us." Then the second hammer blow hit. The Washington reviews were bad. I started a new mantra, "We'll *make* the New York reviews good. We'll *make* the New York reviews good."

Then the *real* crusher came. Alex Cohen announced that he was closing the play out of town. Still, I refused to give up. After the evening's performance I left on my makeup, kept my hairdo, and over my sweater and slacks put on a gorgeous, dramatic purple Yves Saint Laurent velvet cape. Then in Alex's suite I played a scene so melodramatic, so worthy of a grade-B movie, that I cannot believe that Alex never laughed.

Full of theater, I stood in the middle of the room, stumpily regal at five feet two inches, and said, "You *cannot* close the play. You've *got* to let this open. You *must* bring it into New York. Just listen to the audiences laughing. The play is funny."

Alex, right in the mood, said, "Only Vivien Leigh could move me this way." He had an investor come down from New York the next day, and I did the same performance, this time adding tears, and he gave us the money to open on Broadway.

After a month in Washington we moved to the Morosco Theatre in New York and into the company of such plays as *One Flew Over the Cuckoo's Nest, Butterflies Are Free* with Gloria Swanson, *Applause, Jesus Christ Superstar.* I remember standing in front of the theater and looking at the cast pictures they had posted. I was so happy. My name was up on the marquee. Just bliss. I was on Broadway at last. Next would be the movie of *Fun City.* At last I was on my way. And so was Edgar. In the city that never sleeps. For the first time in my life, I put aside my expectations of disaster and allowed myself to truly believe.

We opened on a Sunday night, January 3, 1972. The TV reviews were good. But the next day's newspaper reviews were poor. So we put all our hope on Walter Kerr, the premier New York critic, who would appear in the Sunday *Times.* He had come to dress rehearsal and Edgar and Alex had watched him laugh. Even the stagehands had peeked through the curtain to see his reaction. We were elated that he would save the show.

I was up late Thursday night waiting for the preview edition of the Arts and Leisure section. Alex called us. "You're not going to believe this," he said. "Kerr panned it. He loved Joan. Hated the play." I said, "That's impossible. You saw him laughing, Alex." I told Edgar, "Walter Kerr hated it." He got on the phone, too, and was devastated. Afterward, he did what became his pattern. He took a sleeping pill and checked out. I tried to talk to him, and he said, "Joan, I took a pill. I'm going to sleep."

This was our first failure as a team, the first major stress on our marriage, and we did not band together. We did not go to each other for comfort. We drew apart. That is what sometimes happens when you are husband and wife *and* business partners. When the business goes sour, you somewhere down deep blame each other—"It sure wasn't *me.*"

That night, I could not sleep. I did anything to distract myself from my helplessness—checked Melissa, made coffee, went through the mail, tried to read—but could not concentrate. I felt utterly defeated. Nobody can buck the *Times.* Its power to take away your dream is absolute.

I wanted to be in theater so badly. Melissa was crayoning at the Morosco in Ralph Richardson's old dressing room. I wanted to be part of that room's history. I wanted the stage doorman to say, "Good night," and I'd say, "Pops, here's the key." I wanted to walk down Forty-fifth Street—the street where I had gone as a child with my mother, my head full of dreams—and see my name in lights.

So I decided to buck the *Times* anyway. As long as there is any possibility, you cannot give up. I did what I always do. I worked twice as hard. Alex had said, "If we can run six weeks, we'll run forever. If you can get the money, we'll keep it open." We put twenty thousand dollars of our own money into *Fun City,* and I went on every television show, every radio show, saying, "I'm looking for somebody very rich. It's a funny play . . . somebody very rich."

You try anything. I called a warlock; I figured it couldn't hurt. The warlock had been a guest on *That Show,* and his great-great-great-grandfather had been hanged in Salem. I told him, "You've got to help me." He said, "My whole coven is meeting Friday night."

Sure enough, a southern gentleman flew into town in his private plane and loved the play. He offered us sixty thousand dollars, which would have kept us open another two weeks. But by then we knew Alex had no faith. He had not even printed posters. Our agent warned us that Alex would not mount an advertising campaign. He would just use the money and close anyway. At dinner at Sardi's we gave the gentleman back the check.

We closed on January 8, 1972, after eight performances. I have a tape of the last performance, and the audience was screaming with laughter. After that we went to Sardi's—the only time in my life I got drunk. I drank a full bottle of wine by myself. At home I lay on the bathroom floor in my dress, vomiting into the toilet and passing out and waking and vomiting again. Melissa came in and said, "Daddy, why is Mommy sleeping in the bathroom?" Edgar said, "Mommy's unhappy."

For three days, in an agony of confusion and fear, I wandered and paced. The foundations of my life had been shaken. Whether *Fun City* was a good or bad play was not the point. The issue was one that would return again and again—with *The Tonight Show,* with Fox Broadcasting—each time altering my life. What I thought was funny had been rejected. This attacks a comic's very being. In stand-up, at least the audience decides whether you are funny and whether you remain onstage. But I had tackled Broadway, the cruelest arena, and for the first time I was facing one of the brutalities of show business, the fact that a few individuals, this time the critics, can carry your fate in their hands.

My sense of helplessness was a kind of grief. For the first time I had put all my energies behind something—everything I had— and been unable to move it with sheer force of conviction. At my very core—then and still today—is the belief that willpower can do anything. Will plus hard work equals success. But now—as it would be again with my Fox show—my faith was shattered. But only temporarily. I have another article of faith: If one door doesn't open, you can find another. That faith has kept me going all my life.

A few nights later Melissa fell asleep listening to a *Sesame Street* record. I came into her room and turned off the machine. I flicked off the light and suddenly from the shadows of this enchanting child's room I could see, spread out seventeen floors below, Central Park white with snow, backed by dark towers twinkling with lights. I said out loud, very dramatic, "You don't want me, New York, I don't want you. We're out of here!"

So Edgar and I moved to Hollywood, seeing ourselves as two talents moving to a land of larger show-business opportunities. Every friend who had gone there was doing well. We had no idea that as the plane flew over the Mississippi toward Los Angeles, Edgar's doom was sealed. After so much struggle in his life, after finally experiencing his dream in New York, he was on his way to the one place in the world where he could never be appreciated for himself, on his way to becoming a star's husband.

6

ooooo

When I moved to Hollywood, I thought I was the golden girl. I was arriving as a hot new comedy name, a guest host on *The Tonight Show,* which was now in California, a television veteran.

Together Edgar and I were the team who had created and produced a TV show that ran for a year. And how many people write a play that actually reaches Broadway? Our friends who preceded us were doing very well. My bridesmaid, Treva Silverman, was writing scripts for the Monkees and Mary Tyler Moore. Kenny Solms and Gail Parent were a team writing sketches for Carol Burnett. Rod Warren was musical director for *The Pearl Bailey Show.* Edgar and I looked down on Hollywood from the altitude of our New York sophistication, symbolized by a moving van full of something never seen out there before—namely, boxes of books. We thought this town was going to be duck soup.

Edgar planned to be an independent producer, and he immediately rented himself an office and hired a secretary, Tracy Hotchner, the daughter of the writer A. E. Hotchner. Though he would still keep a paternal eye on my affairs, Edgar had every intention of making it on his own. He put me in the hands of one

of the top management firms, Katz, Gallin, which also handled
Mac Davis, Dolly Parton, and Cher.

We wanted to conquer Hollywood and, indeed, doors did seem
to open immediately. Jim Nabors, that lovely man, gave a huge
party for me. The party was extremely California—catered by a
major French restaurant, twelve men waiting to park your car.
Jim Nabors's public-relations people had done the invitations, so
he, too, was being introduced to some of the guests—in his own
home. "Joan and Jim, this is Tony Orlando and Dawn." "Oh, very
nice to meet you." Can you believe it? That was my first lesson
that in Hollywood what really matters is names, and whether in
the business you are hot or cold.

Edgar and I, so sophisticated, laughed when a string quartet
played a little recital and some of the guests applauded in the
pause after each movement, thinking the piece had ended. I
felt superior about my dress. The other women wore the California look—whatever was the latest trend to make them seem
fourteen years old. I had on a spectacular New York dress designed by Halston at his height, the sort I could wear only because I was extremely thin then. It was made of a lightweight
silk crepe, very slinky, all one piece, no seams, cut low in the
back with a halter in front that tied around my neck. All I
could wear under it was panty hose. In that dress you did not
slouch.

My second Hollywood lesson came when a producer's wife
walked up to me and said, "How nice to meet you. Next time I
would like to meet you dressed." That was my introduction to the
not-so-subtle competition in Hollywood.

I also was unprepared for the opulence in California. Size
meant success. Everything—sofas, lamps, tables—was oversized.
Jim Nabors had the biggest marble bathroom I had ever seen—an
all-glass shower with room for four, a double-sized tub, a TV
recessed into the marble work, fabulous plants everywhere. I was
so stupid, I thought he must have a real green thumb.

So Edgar and I right away felt like fish out of water—or in very
shallow water. But we handled our new environment in diamet-
rically opposite ways. I was willing to play the Hollywood game.
I had never been a Greta Garbo—"I am here. I am a star. Come

to me." My persona had always included self-deprecation—"You think you've got troubles? My body is so bad, a Peeping Tom looked in the window and pulled down the shade."

Through my years of struggle my reflex had always been to play up to anybody with power—"Help me. I'm a little piece of nothing. Help me"—and then "Thank you, thank you." That was my role professionally with Johnny Carson. I once kissed Ed Sullivan's hand on camera. I had no trouble going to Hollywood parties and saying to Shirley MacLaine, "You're the best actress in the whole world"—which is what you do in a town where Barbara Eden in *I Dream of Jeannie* was a power. You had to be able to say, "You're absolutely right. The Hunchback of Notre Dame *should* be played by a woman."

But such sucking up is not the basis for friendships. I think Edgar believed he was married to a show-business insider who could bring him in—only to find that I was an outsider, too. Like him, I never fit with the right people, never had that knack, have always been a white-and-black penguin when all the others were black-and-white.

Edgar, for better or worse, had too much pride to try to fit into that California world—and I respected him for his integrity.

In Hollywood power is the ability to get a film made. A few stars have it. Kevin Costner has it, Eddie Murphy has it, Julia Roberts has it. But the *real* power is in the hands of a very few kings, the potentates who can grant your destiny, bestow your dream, your fantasy. Phone calls by these men are returned within an hour. They can get important people out of meetings. Nobody disagrees with them. They have reached the top after a series of right decisions, a run of hit movies, and seem to know the secret that nobody else knows. They watch out for each other and can also make sure you never work in Hollywood again. When Michael Eisner, CEO of Disney, opens his mouth, all other conversation stops. If Mike Ovitz of CAA sneezes, six people say, "God bless you"—and mean it.

These executives that Edgar needed to like and help him were not impressed by Rugby and Cambridge. Edgar's British accent was a turnoff. He was not a candidate for that Thursday night poker game or the football betting pools. He did not care about the Los Angeles Lakers. He was not into whoring around or picking up boys in West Hollywood. He would never drive a Jeep or use his car to bring cocaine out to the gang in Malibu for the weekend.

To these kind of men Edgar's producing credentials at Telsun were small potatoes. Nobody cared about the United Nations' testimonial dinner for Edgar, nobody was interested in the silver cigarette box on our coffee table inscribed by the secretary general, U Thant, *In grateful appreciation. . . .* Nobody cared that Edgar had been important at NBC. He was just a star's husband.

Ignored by the power elite, Edgar became even more intimidating, more superior, made more certain they heard about his English education. And he hugged to his bosom each and every slight, remembering them like a father whose child has been hurt. His attitude became, "I'll show those bastards."

When he went to his office down in Beverly Hills, he sat frustrated and unhappy. He had not learned to work on several projects at once, and getting properties onto a screen is a long, slow dance, a tantalizing exercise in waiting.

The only way I could deal with Edgar was to expect something would happen for him and also to include him in all my deals. From the day of our arrival my comedy career was percolating. In addition to *The Tonight Show,* I often appeared on the original *Hollywood Squares,* a big hit show then, and I traveled increasingly to Las Vegas to work as an opening act. In Beverly Hills I found a version of the Downstairs at the Upstairs, a small place called Ye Little Club where I could "write" new material—"I like California because it's insane. My gardener is a Nazi Quaker. He declares war, and then he refuses to go."

I also set aside three hours almost every afternoon to push the scriptwriting I had begun in New York. I desperately wanted to make the next step up, to follow Woody Allen, Lily Tomlin, Bette Midler, who were living my expectations.

I loved the intensity, the tunnel vision of the writing process, building something from nothing, giving the characters their own lives until they take over in every situation, reacting the way they must. They become your friends, and you see them in your head. Through them you are bringing shape and meaning to your own chaotic life, to the disconnected impressions, memories, insights that are the raw material.

Writing is a fabulous escape from the realities of life. In the last fifteen years I have constantly had a project under way. With George Furth, who wrote *Company* on Broadway, we did the first draft for *The Rose*, starring Bette Midler. Hired by the producers, I sat with a writer named Tom Perew and wrote the lines Bruce Willis spoke for the baby in *Look Who's Talking*.

In those first months in California I was so inexperienced that I was not surprised when ABC bought my script for a *Movie of the Week*. It was called *The Girl Most Likely to . . .*, and the idea started with a blind date I had when I was a freshman at Connecticut College.

The boy was from Yale, and he was standing at the foot of the stairs in my dorm as I descended—132 pounds of chubby pulchritude dressed in a gray-flannel dress and little gray-flannel shoes to match. He turned to the girl who had fixed him up and said, disgusted, "Why didn't you tell me?" All evening he ignored me. It was a weekend, so he had to come by the next day. He arrived for breakfast at 1:45 P.M., just in time to say, "Well, let's have a cup of coffee; gee, I gotta catch my train to New Haven." I had been waiting since 9:00 A.M.

I transferred after my sophomore year to Barnard College in New York, and this boy married a girl I knew there and became a doctor. Years later in California that girl called me, and I invited her to a large supper party I was giving by the pool. This same boy walks in with her, fat now and bald, fortysomething. He had no idea I had been 132-pound Joan Molinsky.

He was all over me; everywhere I went, there he was, obviously a cheater, following me into the kitchen to get me alone— "Can we meet for lunch? Isn't that a pretty dress [looking down my cleavage]. You're much younger and prettier than on the TV." There was a lot of "Let me help you"—and his arm would touch my arm.

As his car pulled out of the driveway, I told everybody the story. "I should have said, 'Does the name Joan Molinsky mean anything to you?'—and whipped out a gun and killed the son of a bitch." My friend Kenny Solms said, "That's a movie."

The Girl Most Likely to . . . went right into production starring Stockard Channing and Ed Asner. Its first showing was seen by 50 million people, a rating record then for a movie written for TV. I wrote the first draft by myself in eight weeks, and ABC had a writer rework it, and then I reworked what he reworked. It became the story of a fat ugly girl who gets thin and beautiful and kills every boy who ever slighted her.

That script came right from the heart.

After six months Edgar's office had become an unnecessary expense, and he gave it up. At home, my office was in the tiny guest house, and Archie Walker, the maître d' from the Downstairs, had come west with us to be my secretary. There was room for only one desk, which Archie used, so Edgar created a setup to make his phone calls from an antique bench jammed in a corner.

Lost in California, Edgar was getting up in the morning, getting washed and dressed, only to wonder, "Now what?" I told him, "Go to a network and get a job, go work at Katz, Gallin." But Edgar had done those jobs. He said he would feel humiliated as somebody's assistant.

We decided that perhaps I was the missing piece in his projects, and we should get together as writer and producer team. I thought *The Girl Most Likely to . . .* showed I had solved the secret of Hollywood scriptwriting, and I would have the clout to demand Edgar as producer. He would prove himself in the industry, and I would be guaranteed a producer who put my interests first.

Should I have known better by then? Of course I should.

Edgar and I were hired by Freddie Silverman at CBS to do a pilot for Florence Henderson about a strait-laced girl who inherits a rock band that takes off. After many meetings, many rewrites— everything positive, no serious doubts expressed—the script was accepted. Everybody loved it, and CBS set a January shooting date. Florence was canceling engagements. We were ecstatic.

Suddenly CBS changed its mind and canceled the pilot. And the powers that be chose 6:00 P.M. L.A. time on Christmas Eve to make the call, which meant somebody in New York had nothing better to do at 9:00 P.M. on Christmas Eve than telephone California and deliver crushing news. Edgar said on the phone, "Would it have hurt you to wait till the day after Christmas?"

I couldn't believe it. I had been living with my characters for months and months and months. Now they and I had been rejected. I felt as though close friends had died, and I was starting again at zero.

Yet now I know better.

The decision to cancel our pilot at CBS could not have come out of the blue at the last minute. Those people who had been saying "Great, great, great"—lifting our expectations to the skies—were not playing honestly.

I learned never to put all of my heart and cards on the table— which is hard for me because I am so emotional. I dared not allow feelings to intrude for fear I would be manipulated. I became more and more closed, believing few people at face value. When somebody said he liked me, I wondered, "What does he want in return?"

But if you want something, the way I wanted to establish myself as a writer, you go forward, you work and work for it. In our second year in California, 1973, I went to work alone on a script about a guy who kidnapped the Radio City Music Hall chorus line by mistake. I called it *Roxy Haul.* I sent it to one of the Hollywood kings, David Begelman at Columbia.

I would still be waiting for Begelman's return phone call today had I not camped in his outer office, telling the secretary, "I'll just sit here. Don't worry about me. I've got my needlepoint. I'll catch Mr. Begelman on his way to the men's room." I sat there for three days.

Because he "loved my spirit," Begelman saw me. Edgar, as the producer, had done the figures and computed that we could bring the movie in for exactly a million dollars. George Segal and Michael Caine were interested in playing the leads. Begelman told me to send him the budget, and if it checked out at a million or below, he would give us a go-ahead.

One would think that by now we would be more cautious, but something about show business made us behave like children, and each time Edgar and I had something accepted, we became hysterical with joy. Now, two days later, we *did* get a call—from our lawyer. Edgar had not included the 10 percent studio overhead in the budget. The cost of the movie was more than a million. Begelman had canceled.

I was enraged at Edgar. I had humbled myself in Begelman's office for three damn days only to find out that, wait a second, *my* team made a goof! . . .

That was my first hint that maybe Edgar and I were *both* amateurs in the big time.

I could not endure the possibility of a house husband. I did not want to come home and have him tell me what was for dinner. That was not my idea of a marriage. So I persevered with our writer/producer package.

But for all my willingness to play the game in Hollywood, I might just as well have kept my pride. I was no more successful in the movie business than Edgar. I was more and more in demand in Las Vegas—but that increasingly pigeonholed me as a Vegas comic. No acting jobs were being offered. My new scripts were being turned down.

Edgar handled his frustration by withdrawing into himself. He broke my heart. He pretended he was not suffering, but I knew he was. He was constantly reading books for properties, had ideas, tried to form partnerships with people—he worked on four projects with Larry Kasha, who later produced *Knots Landing*—but he was miserable. And I was miserable. With our wounds from *Fun City* still raw, we could not comfort each other. Our marriage was shaky.

He resented me for being busy, and I felt guilty for being busy. I would go into the bathroom at night and sit on the floor, leaning against the tub, which is how I prepare my comedy routines, organizing the flow of jokes. Edgar would be on the bed, impatient, watching *Masterpiece Theatre* and calling, "Hurry up and come in." I would have to say, "I can't. I've got to get ready for my Carson shot." I would be resentful. Then I would feel guilty about being angry—which made me even angrier.

My irritation broke out in the wrong places—"Since I'm sitting here writing, why don't you pick up Melissa at school?" Then he would do it and come back and tell me he was the only father picking up a child. I wanted to die. But much as I loved being a mother and wanted to be his companion, there was less and less time. I was making the money.

Edgar was not the man I married. I wanted the Edgar in New York when we were happy, the husband who was the breadwinner and held a long gold chain with me at the end of it, romping like a little puppy, the Edgar who handled the heavy business stuff while I was Marla Maples, worrying about what gown to wear.

I did not know the Edgar who more and more was the one who talked to the gardener and checked up on the pool man. To see my husband go to the market—the idea of him pushing a cart— was a nightmare. He would report that Jack Lemmon was there, too—but I knew Jack was between films. I became Edgar's topic of conversation. Somebody would ask, "How are you, Edgar?" And he would say, "Joan is just doing so well." That used to kill me.

We were beginning to lose honesty with each other. Walls were being put up. I buried myself in the present, worked even harder, and kept on hoping. I never suggested getting help. The word "therapy" then was not in my vocabulary.

If I realized then how much our role reversals could affect the future of my marriage, perhaps I wouldn't have been blind to the possibilities of therapy. But I was running too fast to see clearly the trouble we were in. So I would just rant and rave, saying, "We're miserable. We're unhappy. We've got to figure out something different." But Edgar would put on that stiff British upper lip and say, "There's nothing wrong. Everything's fine."

This state of affairs continued into the fall of 1973. Although my comedy career was booming, my husband was lost and I, a woman who depends on roots in a place that is basically rootless, was, too, in a way. Almost everybody in California is from somewhere else, which means people have no history there. Roots to me mean family, the loyalty one only gets from a family. Home really is the place where they have to take you in, and I didn't have a place I could call home since I left New York.

Returning from an engagement at Harrah's in Tahoe, I suddenly could not make myself go back into that house and rejoin that atmosphere of pain. Aching with sorrow and guilt, I went directly from the airport to the Beverly Hills Hotel and settled into a cottage there with Melissa and her governess.

The first night my friend Tommy Corcoran, who cared about both Edgar and me, took me out to every sleazy bar in Los Angeles, showed me in one night the underbelly life of a single woman—"See So-and-so? He'll never marry her. He's got a wife. See So-and-so? She's with a paid escort. See those six women together there? They've left their husbands."

This move of mine was, of course, a tremendous shock to Edgar, a reality shock because he had blinded himself to my unhappiness—and now he was adrift alone in a foreign land. He chose, however, to treat the whole event as a joke, a game—"Oh, that silly Joan. She's such a child"—as though I would presently come to my senses. Which, in fact, I did.

The ties between us ran so deep, this separation never became more than a breather. Once the pressure lifted, the friendship resurfaced. We did not have other trusted friends, and the bond between us was very strong. Every day Edgar was in and out of the cottage, going over the mail, discussing business things, dropping Melissa off from school. We continued our life, but in separate spaces.

After a week of this I heard a prying noise at the back door of the cottage late one night. I was terrified. Somebody was trying to break in. My reflex, without another thought, was to telephone Edgar. He was there in ten minutes. The next day he took us home.

I felt tremendous guilt over the emotional upset I had caused—but also relieved. I had brought our problems to a head, and now maybe we could find a resolution. And making the decision to return had forced me back in touch with the foundation of our marriage. The trust, the mutual honesty, the certainty.

But I also had to acknowledge a dangerous syndrome: When Edgar passed a certain anxiety threshold, he would check out with denial and a sleeping pill. I, in turn, would lose myself in my daughter and a whirl of feverish activity. I did not want Melissa to have a broken home. I thought then that I could live with this pattern. I did not see it as a fatal failing.

I don't believe two people can build a life on wild, romantic feelings. That is a big reason marriages break up. These feelings are so ephemeral. Peter Passionate will not necessarily be there in the morning or nine months later when you are throwing up and need somebody to take you to the hospital—or when you are away working eighteen hours a day. I did a needlepoint pillow that says, LOVERS COME, LOVERS GO. FRIENDS REMAIN. It sits in a prominent place on the sofa in my library.

I wanted to be married—especially in predatory Hollywood. I didn't want to sleep around, didn't want to be a star all dressed up and going home for a TV dinner by herself. I admired long, nurturing relationships that must have had their rocky times— marriages like Paul Newman and Joanne Woodward's, Hume Cronyn and Jessica Tandy's. I still believe that in the long run, what wins out is the closeness, the relaxation that comes with marriage, the intimacy without fear of humiliation.

In the last analysis, Edgar needed me and I needed him—and Melissa needed both of us.

I do not know how Edgar came to terms with his failure to function on his own in Hollywood. This may sound odd, but for our separate reasons—mine was guilt—we both buried our agonies and never discussed the issues forming in our relationship. This unspoken accommodation worked very well for a long time—until, of course, it didn't. When Edgar described his role, he often said, "We run a factory, and Joan is the product." His pride was temporarily satisfied by exercising power from behind the throne. He adopted a persona, the brilliant intellectual who had created a star. He came to like being "Edgar," a character in my act, but a shadow man unrecognized by the public. That gave him a mystique, a feeling of celebrity.

Finally we both came to emotionally accept Edgar's role as the star's husband. It was built into our life. We could not escape it—any more than other couples like Ann-Margret and Roger Smith, Lynn Redgrave and John Clark, or Jackie Collins and Oscar Lerman. Stars' husbands really protect their wives. They know the side that nobody else sees, the vulnerable you, so frightened, insecure, the terrors of childhood repeating in adulthood. The husbands fight in a way no agent or manager ever will—like a mother protecting a child. Today, when I see a star's husband backstage doing battle with the stage manager or the orchestra conductor, I may roll my eyes, but I understand completely.

Once when Suzanne Somers opened for me at Caesars Palace, there was a major argument when Alan Hamil insisted on a huge set that required I work in front of the curtain on three feet of stage. He was crazed like a bulldog—you can be sure that while he was playing the son of a bitch, Suzanne was standing in the dressing room saying, "I've got to have the set." We gave in. When I saw her act, I realized she was right. She needed the set.

Being right does not prevent a lot of garbage from being piled on the husband. People were saying, "Joan's wonderful, Edgar's terrible." There was one producer, a woman, who said, "I will work only with Joan; I will never work with Edgar." I thought, Is she that stupid? What does she think? That I just go home and write jokes and go to sleep? That we don't go to bed together, that we don't know what the other is doing?

The husband is on duty twenty-four hours a day, so the emergencies fall to him. My contract stipulated that there be nobody under sixteen in the front row. This is because I cannot say, for instance, to a woman, "Are you good in bed?" with her child sitting there wearing Mickey Mouse ears. I would come offstage at 1:00 A.M. screaming, "There was a kid in the front row!" and Edgar would be the one on the phone to the headwaiter saying, "It's in the contract. Any children up front and she doesn't go on!" Who was the real S.O.B.?

I was being unfair, letting Edgar be the lightning rod for the hostility that floats around town. I, who preach honesty, was being dishonest. But that is built into the star/husband equation. That is the point, really. I was able keep the image of the easygoing sweetheart, smiling and joking—who later told Edgar what I really thought. Even my managers—who always want to come on to people as the good guys—would say to the maître d', "He's the trouble. If it was up to me, a kid or two . . ."

In my business the only place I can be honest is onstage. If you are honest in real life, you make so many enemies, you will never get back on that stage again. And we performers all want to be adored. I longed to be loved like Carol Burnett and bask in people saying, "My gosh, she's the warmest . . ." So I let my husband take the heat.

7

ooooo

One week as a single girl made me realize how much I needed structure in my life, a framework for my feelings, an environment that defined my identity. That is particularly true, I think, for anybody who is successful in show business.

The more I was in demand in Las Vegas and the more money I commanded, the deeper was the chasm that yawned behind me. Only a dozen stars manage to stay at the top, and I had been around long enough to watch Trini Lopez, Frank Gorshin, Bobby Vinton, and Lola Falana begin to slip. Helen Reddy was a major headliner when I was her opening act. Today she is happy to sing in Michael's Pub in New York. You can have the money and the accoutrements, the house and the cars, the clothes, the servants—but you have it all at somebody else's whim.

For our sanity, we performers must have stability in our private life, some form of law and order. I think that structure comes in big ways—for me it was my marriage—and in little but important ways—like my perfectly organized drawers and closets. The separation impressed on me just how much my home and possessions had become the reassuring definition of myself—and how much living in that rented house with somebody else's furniture and decoration, somebody else's organization, made me feel at sea. I needed my things around me, needed a permanent place that said, "This is where I will be and who I am." If I was going to survive in show business, I would have to sink roots to stabilize my soul. I wanted to buy a house.

Edgar had come to the same decision independently. He began looking not at what I thought we could afford but at Hollywood estates like Jack Warner's former home. The financial caution of New York was gone: Southern California does that to you. Anthony Quinn's house was for sale at $600,000, which would be millions now. The real estate agent, who had checked us out, refused even to show it to Edgar. "Clearly you cannot afford it," she said.

He shot back, "Well, obviously, if it's for sale, neither can Tony Quinn."

I did not like anything I saw. All the Hollywood houses looked the same—new, impersonal, as though they were furnished in one day. Cher sold her house complete—everything in it untouched—to Eddie Murphy. Nobody in that world seems to have a beloved house to pass on to their children. When people do well, they get a bigger house. When they do even better, they get an even bigger one. Hollywood is constantly transitional, of the moment. Nobody has anything that the past has touched, no wonderful treasures from a grandmother. When Joan Crawford's house was sold, the new owner ripped out an unbelievable thirties movie-star bathroom—all marble and columns—and put in all glass.

After we'd been looking for about three months, in January of 1974 Sandy Gallin called up and said, "I found your house"—a twelve-room bastard colonial home on Ambazac Way in Bel Air, a micro-Tara designed by Paul Williams, a major black architect in California. He designed a wing of the Beverly Hills Hotel, and later, when he wanted to stay there, they would not let him in.

We went to see it with Gail Parent, who is now the co–executive producer of *The Golden Girls.* The real estate agent was showing it to another woman, and took us along as a favor. The minute I walked into the two-story entrance hall with its balustrade curving up to the mezzanine, my heart leaped. Here was a set for an MGM movie. Off the foyer was a double powder room, and off the dining room was a small glassed-in atrium luxuriant with greenery. The library was paneled in English oak. The master bedroom had its own little sitting room at its far end with a fireplace—and it connected to what would be Melissa's room so I could get to her fast if she needed me. Sometimes it happens that you walk into a house and you know you belong there. I felt that way about the house on Ambazac Way.

The other client had first call on the house, and I was hysterical that she might buy it. We followed her and her husband from room to room. "Oooh, this is terrible," I said to Gail. "Look at the window in the bathroom. You'd have to do so muuuch." Gail, in her nasal voice, said, "Who would want a round breakfast room? Ooooh, it's so aaawful." We ripped that house to shreds. Finally the woman said to her husband, "This is not for us," and they left. I turned to the agent and said, "I'll take it."

We bought it in a day for $325,000, which then was like $5 million. I was terrified we could not afford it, but Edgar insisted, and he was right. However, we were in over our heads. I was constantly worrying about money. We needed a washer and dryer, and in exchange for the machines I appeared on *Truth or Consequences*. Pushing balloons across the floor with a toothpick, I said to myself, "Ten minutes on my knees, ten years of clean clothes." When people promised, "I'm going to send you flowers," I would say, "No, send me a rosebush." Pretty soon I had the most beautiful classic English rose garden in California. From May to December I never had to buy flowers for the house.

The house, which we referred to as Ambazac, was *tremendously* important to me. I let the house be my romantic fantasy. My bathroom overlooked the rose garden, which was lit at night, and when I bathed in the dark, I felt I was bathing among the roses—while over me washed the scent of the night-blooming jasmine.

Truthfully, if I had all the money in the world and one day to spend it, I would rent Versailles, live there as if I've always lived there, and bring my friends as my guests. No question about it, I would take over Versailles.

The furnishings in the main rooms were French, not country French, city French. I called Ambazac "my Versailles with contact paper"—the way Marie Antoinette would have lived if she had made it to America. A very formal house. Once a woman came into the living room and looked at the damask-skirted tables, the antique screen, the Chinese porcelains, and asked, "Who died here?" Edgar said I should have answered, "Louis the Sixteenth."

Edgar's office was in a large alcove at the top of the front stairs. I did not have an office and kept my things on a windowsill outside the living room. Later we converted a downstairs guest room into an office for Edgar—with a pretty love seat for me by the telephone.

But Ambazac dramatized what happens in the entertainment world when your standard of living shoots up along with your career. We now had a huge mortgage, major taxes, a bill of twenty-six thousand 1974 dollars for renovations, plus a new roof. A house like that requires a pool man, a gardener, and two in help in the house. As my career accelerated, in addition to the governess, I eventually needed two secretaries, a full-time accountant, and a public-relations man.

Safety also became a worry and expense. I had begun to receive threatening crank letters, and every public person knows these cannot be ignored. It takes only one nut to put a bullet through your head. Edgar and I bought pistols and learned to use them on a range in Las Vegas, and to this day when I go out, my gun is with me. At Ambazac we put up electric gates, outside beams, and indoor beams.

Within three months of moving into the house, our expenses were eight thousand dollars a week—and growing. My only regular income was *Hollywood Squares* at $750 a week and an occasional guest-hosting on Carson at $1,000 a week, neither of which brought in substantial money. So I went on the road for eighteen weeks a year; half my life was spent in hotel rooms, drilling my daughter in spelling over the phone. I had no choice if I wanted that house. Donna Karan does not have to go personally to Cleveland to sell her dresses. But *I* was the product. I had to go to

Cleveland myself. One year I missed the entire blooming of the rose garden, and Edgar cheered me up by bringing newspaper horns full of huge roses to my hotel room in Las Vegas.

Edgar and I began a happy, productive period in our lives. We had found our California mode. Knowing we were lucky—my career was only getting bigger, Melissa more extraordinary (every mother thinks that, I know—but she was!)—making sure the luck was not capricious, we worked like two little squirrels hectically gathering nuts. Edgar's line was, "We live an Italian opera." Each night we went together to where I performed, developing material. During the day the phone rang constantly—six lines lighting up—managers, agents, lawyers, publicists phoning. Edgar fielded the calls, when necessary turning to me with questions.

"Carol Burnett wants you for the March fourteenth show. Do you want to do it? It would mean giving up two weeks of Reno." "I don't know. What does Sandy Gallin say?" "I'll get him on the other line. . . . Sandy thinks we can switch Reno. He'll get back in twenty minutes."

"Okay, the Sands will switch, but you'll be opening for the Carpenters, and I don't think you'd be as good with the Carpenters; their audience wouldn't understand you. Maybe we can move the Carol Burnett date." Twenty minutes later: "Yeah, the Burnett people want you a lot, so they'll switch."

"Can you find out if the Burnett people will pay for Warren? He's doing my hair very well." Ten minutes later: "They won't pay for Warren. They already have a hairdresser." "Maybe they'll pay half." Ten minutes later: "Yeah, okay, they'll go for half. They want you to do fifteen minutes." "I can't. I don't have enough new material." "They want fifteen minutes." "I can't. See if they'll take seven." Twenty minutes later: "They'll take ten. And they want to know if you can sing."

Soon my publicity man would be on the phone. "*TV Guide* just called me. They're doing a thing on ladies in television and how they exercise. What does Joan do for exercising?" "I don't exercise." "Don't say that. You can get into *TV Guide*. Figure out something you can do." "How about that I go up and down on my toes while I'm brushing my teeth?"

Somebody in our staff was always having a crisis. Our secretary was single and dating, so we were part of her adventures. She went out with a doctor, drank too much and threw up in the toilet of his apartment and chipped her tooth on the rim. She thought he should pay for it because it happened in his house. "He won't pay," she told us. "What do you mean the son of a bitch won't pay," and I got on the phone with the doctor and said, "You should pay because it was your toilet and you bought her the drinks." Finally Edgar and I hired her a lawyer and she got the money.

I told her she should meet *my* lawyer—and they liked each other and began courting. "My wardrobe is your wardrobe," I told her. The day they got engaged, she brought me back twelve dresses.

At the end of each day everybody gathered in the office; Melissa would arrive on the bus from school, and we would talk over the day. Life was warm and busy and very exciting. Even the guard dogs were happy, eager to love us and kill everybody else.

The one selfless section of our life was Melissa. She was Edgar's sole object of unreserved sentiment. Her confirmation in Sunday school was the first time I ever saw him close to tears.

For me, Melissa was the one to whom I could give total affection and feel it being absorbed and returned. I relished being a mother, watching my child form and grow into a young lady. We wanted Ambazac to be a place kids liked to play. There were silly races in the back garden—giant steps, umbrella steps, backward steps. Kids into the pool, out of the pool. "Mrs. Rosenberg, Harry's got a nosebleed." Pizza trucks arrived, and Cokes were handed out. Churning life. Damp footprints leading upstairs. Terrific. Six kids on the floor of her room in sleeping bags, the sounds of girls' voices and giggling filtering into our bedroom.

When she was only eight, Melissa got into horseback riding in a big way. We sat outdoors cleaning tack at night, laid out her riding clothes on a chair and two ribbons for her hair, then up at six to go to the horse show. On Thanksgiving weekend it rained four days and was the best time we ever had. The WASP mothers looked like Paddington Bear working in the muck and the mire in their rubber boots and slickers and rain hats. Always cold, I wore an old, old mink coat. Melissa was absolutely mortified.

For years she would come into our bedroom in the middle of the night and go to sleep between Edgar and me, and then suddenly she was too big, but I would wake up and she was there on the rug in her Charlie Brown sleeping bag, the last present she got from my mother. Then came that first symbol of maturity— her own phone—but a Snoopy phone. I loved walking into her room to hear Melissa saying to a girlfriend, "Can't talk now about him, *she's* here." My big sophisticate was talking into Snoopy's arm.

But I fear that Melissa has suffered the burden of having a celebrity mother. When we went out together, I tried to make it *her* occasion, but there would be that commotion when I arrived, the paparazzi swarming in. She grew up always a star's daughter never sure of her own identity, never certain whether the teacher liked her for herself or wanted to come to dinner to meet Mom.

I worried that she would slip into that lazy Beverly Hills star-child syndrome. A lot of rich kids slide through school, knowing Mommy and Daddy will take care of them. Melissa, from age fourteen, always had a summer job; she got into the best schools and studied her way through. We had our fights, but she never ruled us. In the seventies and eighties with drugs in her school, and lots of abortions, she remained a real kid, making her own Christmas presents even though there were three Mercedes in the driveway. She never became jaded.

No doubt part of the parental equation was guilt. I am sure that my career seemed to Melissa an unbeatable rival, the fascinating, exciting sibling she could never equal. When I was home, I still locked myself away in the library in the afternoons to work on screenplays. In truth, there were some successes—a CBS series called *Husbands and Wives* that ran for nine weeks, for instance—but my real interests lay in a collaboration effort on a script with Jay Redack, the producer on the original *Hollywood Squares* and a brilliant comic writer. The idea for the movie was Jay's—what if a man became pregnant? Sounds ridiculous, right? But at the time it stole my creative heart. We called it *Rabbit Test,* and one of Melissa's childhood memories is hearing Jay and me at night laughing our heads off.

Rabbit Test was intended to be a movie of sight gags and foolishness. For example, we had a scene where a warm, wonderful housewife was so protective of her family that she sprayed their food with Lysol, a scene where Queen Elizabeth dropped her pocketbook in the Palace and out fell a picture of Nat King Cole, half a sandwich, a tampon, and a motel-room key.

Again, you see these sight gags on paper and they don't read "funny"—but think about *Blazing Saddles, Airplane!,* and *Hot Shots!,* lightweight movies that make you laugh out loud at nonsense.

The script was turned down by every studio. I had so hoped we could achieve even a modest hit so we would be accepted as a husband-and-wife partnership and do more projects, growing better and better.

Just at that time I had a cancer scare. A mole that had been removed from my side came back, and I thought, That's it. Everything is all over. I told Edgar, "If anybody who rejected our script comes to my funeral, you throw him out." I made him promise.

Then Danny Melnick of MGM, the youngest and hippest of the studio heads, called us on a Friday afternoon and said, "We're going to do this. I love it, and we can make it for a dollar thirty-five." Edgar and I were hysterical with excitement. The following Tuesday, Melnick left MGM.

For a year Edgar and I worked to raise the money to make the movie ourselves. We spent four and a half months courting one woman who wanted to be around show people and whose husband owned a lot of RCA stock. Finally she promised us twenty-five thousand dollars. Then at a large party that must have cost close to forty thousand dollars at one of the most expensive restaurants in Los Angeles, she said, "Well, twenty-five thousand dollars is a lot of money. I think I'll send the script to my daddy."

Courting a rich couple in Chicago, we flew there and talked and talked, and they brought us to their apartment for a party and showed me off. They had me autograph their living-room wall. We realized that none of these people had any intention of investing.

We courted a man who owned supermarkets in Indianapolis. We flew a Pennsylvania orthodontist out to Los Angeles and took him with us to a party at Johnny Carson's house. He finally gave us twenty thousand dollars—and then at the end called for an audit. Another investor, Sam Goldwyn, Jr., kept changing his mind—yes, no, yes, no—until he finally did send us a check. But he didn't sign the contract.

Then Embassy Pictures offered $500,000 if we could match it. I was performing at the MGM Grand, and in all my Las Vegas newspaper interviews I kept repeating, "Anybody wants to invest in a very funny movie, let me know." One night in my dressing room I received a letter handwritten in pencil. It read, *Dear Miss Rivers, I am very interested in investing in your movie. Please excuse the pencil. I don't have a pen with me.* It was signed, *Thomas Pileggi.*

I told my secretary to call Mr. Pileggi and find out if he was for real. She came back and said, "He truly wants to invest." I got on the phone and liked what he said. I learned later that he was in Las Vegas for a builders' convention and had seen me on TV and thought I was funny. "It takes a powerful person to make me laugh," he told me. "I'm a very serious person." And he liked to see people fighting the system, doing something on their own.

A week later Tom flew out to California at his own expense. I came into the library, and there was this cute, boyish man— medium height, brown hair, a round, deceptively innocent face—and he was holding two gift-wrapped boxes, which we immediately opened. They contained little gold Italian horns on ropes that men were wearing instead of neckties, and Edgar, who did not wear any jewelry, took his right out of the box and hung it around his neck.

We told him the terms—15 percent—and he said, "Fine," and wrote out a check for $150,000 and gave it to us. He did not want a contract. He told Edgar, "You're an honest man. I can tell by your face." Edgar said, "You may never see the money again. Nobody has ever trusted me like that." Tom answered, "You can only hurt me one time." It was friendship at first sight. Tom told me later, "I read him, and he read me."

With money from Tom Pileggi, Sam Goldwyn, Jr., Embassy Pictures, and some small investors, we had our $500,000, and we began signing up actors. Suddenly two investors dropped out and we were $100,000 short. I told Edgar, "We are going ahead. I'm not waiting. I'm going to mortgage the house." Edgar said, "Absolutely not." I told him, "Then I'm going alone. I'll get a divorce and use the settlement."

There was no stopping me. I was insane. Possessed. My brother-in-law had just died of cancer at age thirty-seven, and that reminded me, whatever it is you want, do it now. And the movie had become me. I had to prove that the script was funny, that I was funny.

Edgar knew I meant what I said. He got in the car and drove away. I have no idea what went through his mind, but he returned two hours later and said we should also mortgage the Larchmont house, which I could do without my father's knowledge. This was a moment when I truly needed my husband beside me—and he was there.

We began shooting, and Edgar invited Tom Pileggi out to California to watch. They became as close as brothers.

Tom saved our lives a second time. Sam Goldwyn, Jr., who had not signed the contract, suddenly threatened to pull out unless he got a much higher percentage on his money. We were already shooting—this could have been a financial disaster.

Tom quietly said, "Whatever you need, you got from me." He gave us another $150,000—and we let Edgar have the pleasure of calling Goldwyn and saying, "So long." Goldwyn was astounded. It was one of the great days of Edgar's life.

People were seeing our dailies, and the word went out that we had a very funny movie. Ray Katz negotiated a three-picture deal with Columbia Pictures—my own offices and a secretary. This was what I dreamed of having, but I turned it down. Perhaps I had been on the outside so long, I had an outsider's mentality, a fear of the establishment, a belief that all executives were the enemy who would find me out.

I thought my passion was to do my own movie, free of enormous studio overhead, free of executives with the power to tell me what to do and what was funny and whom to cast. When I chose Billy Crystal for the lead, Columbia would have thrown me out of the office because at that time Billy was nowhere.

I knew Billy from the comedy circuit, and my instincts were right—he turned out to be a good actor. He got everything immediately, was funny, needed little directing, and didn't overact.

Though I set out to make a slick, far-out comedy in the tradition of *Animal House* or *The Naked Gun,* I see now that it became, by necessity, more like a very funny home movie, full of awkwardness, but also full of freshness, energy, and spontaneity. We had no money; so when we needed a little girl, there was Melissa. If we needed a nurse to run through a hospital ward, I was the nurse. When we wanted a cashier to beat up an old lady, who better than my collaborator, Jay Redack? When we had a dinner scene, we used our own place mats.

To reassure investors, we promised in the contract to hire from a list of top-ten cinematographers. Only Lucien Ballard was interested—very macho, very Hollywood, an eyepiece on a string. I thought he would be my mentor.

Instead I worked six weeks with a man who hated me and hated himself for working on the film for only the money—three thousand dollars a week, the biggest item in the budget. At lunchtime he took a nap. He left on the dot of 5:00 P.M. He never stayed to see the dailies—unheard-of for a cinematographer.

Each day I would start the setup for a scene and ask, "Where do we put the camera, Lucien?" "Put it where you want." "Where do you want me to put it?" "Well, maybe over here. Set it up over here, Ernie." Variations of that exchange happened again and again. We had a scene with a mother and a fat daughter, and instead of keeping a height chart, the mother marked the girl's width on the wall and wrote down the date. Lucien refused to shoot it. "It's not funny."

I looked him in the eye and said to him, "I'll take that chance."

He shrugged his shoulders. At that moment I was defying a man who could shut us down, and I would lose my house and my father's house. Everything. I was terrified. But I was also furious. Furious. Yet I had to smile and pretend, digging my nails into my palms. To this day I can feel that anger.

But for the first time in my life, I was defying a male in authority, face to face without using Edgar. This was a real critical juncture for me. I had always kowtowed to male authorities, and let Edgar go into the final-crunch meetings of a contract negotiation, face those male lawyers. If I had to deal with men, I tried to wheedle them around with feminine wiles—pleading, cajoling, teasing, laughing—which is the way I sometimes still find myself handling them. Old habits die hard. The Joan Molinsky of 1973 would never have applauded at the end of *Thelma & Louise* the way I did in 1991.

During the filming I had stopped all performing, a tremendous financial loss that put us even deeper in debt—so when the editing phase began, I was grabbing any club date within reach of Los Angeles. The MGM Grand in Las Vegas turned an adjoining dressing room into an editing room. Every spare minute, even between shows, I was there. Show girls would come in half-naked and stand behind us and watch the editing machine and laugh.

But assembling the movie, the film editor would ask, "Where's the close-up, the medium shot?" They were not there. Sometimes we had to blow up parts of the frames to get from a medium shot to a close-up. Thanks to Lucien Ballard, we had ended up with little alternate camera coverage, and thanks to our tiny budget, we rarely had the luxury of retakes. Usually you have five hundred cans of film with lots of angles and distances. We had twenty cans.

The film was released in February 1978. The headlines on the reviews read, RABBIT TEST FLOPS AS FARCE; RIVERS' RABBIT FLUNKS THE TEST; RABBIT TEST NAUSEATING, BUT . . ."

The film bombed.

Today, I still resent the cruelty, the spitefulness of those reviews. Though, frankly, when I saw a videotape of *Rabbit Test* recently, the movie does look amateurish—bad photography, bad sound, bad lighting—everything unfocused and ugly—but there are fifteen hysterical minutes I am extremely proud of.

I believe that hell is not pain and fire, but boredom. I think you must take risks, must see how far you can push. If you really believe in something, you must try it, must do it. If you always take your shot, your life is going to be interesting. Failure is devastating, but here I am fifteen years later feeling that *Rabbit Test* was one of the most successful experiences I have ever had. It is part of my education, part of my consciousness.

It still managed to make enough money to pay off all its investors, and some say *Rabbit Test* has become a bit of a cult film. I had my movie set—they built my dollhouse—and people spoke my lines and I worked with a camera. I had the experience of sitting in my library and laughing for five minutes at the idea of our hero, Billy Crystal, sitting in a coffee shop going on and on about how money doesn't bring happiness while in the background a little old lady who can't pay her check is physically beaten up, and thrown out by the cashier. And then that idea became images on celluloid that were shown to thousands of people, who laughed the same way I had laughed a year and a half earlier. Hell, *Rabbit Test* may be on the shelf, but I can pull it out and know that I made it happen.

8

ooooo

In the showrooms of Las Vegas in the 1970s, doing twenty-eight weeks a year, I found my mass audience—the hardworking women of America. Vegas turned out to be *The Ed Sullivan Show* with red velvet.

During that time I worked all the hotels along the strip, opening for everybody—Paul Anka, Lola Falana, Lou Rawls, Robert Goulet, Mac Davis, John Davidson, Shirley MacLaine, Tony Bennett, Trini Lopez, Frank Gorshin, Neil Sedaka, Tony Orlando, Bobby Vinton, Ben Vereen, Andy Williams, Petula Clark. I called myself the Strip Slut.

Though in my head I know comedians are considered the lowest rung on the ladder, in my heart there are moments when I burst with pride—those times when I make fifteen hundred people in a showroom laugh all at once, a sudden crack of laughter, explosive. This is why comedy is so difficult an art form. We all share what is sad—a child dying in her mother's arms—but we wildly disagree about what is funny. Every joke must hit each of those fifteen hundred, each one feeling spoken to, one on one. When a woman twenty tables back says right out loud, "Yeah, my husband does that," she feels I am talking to *her*—and that is a big thrill for me.

I never look at the men in the audience, never deal with them. For at least a third of my act, I feel they don't know what the hell I'm talking about. The rest of the time they laugh for the wrong reasons—the shock of hearing a woman joke about forbidden subjects, the pleasure of seeing the wife laughing. They get caught up in the sheer energy I am throwing at them, running and screaming around the stage—bang, pow, sock!

Everything I say is woman-to-woman. I work hard to reach the college-educated, professional women, but I am thrilled that the heart of my audience is the ladies who are making this country continue, the ones raising the children, taking the part-time jobs, staying home and getting through life the best they can. They were pretty in high school and wanted to twirl batons, and instead of college they got married and had kids. These are women with a quiet determination, the survivors.

These women get my humor because it is earthy and basic and tells the truth, and these women know the truth. They live on paychecks, and buy lunch meat, watch the electric bill, turn down the thermostat. They have to make the rent, and just when they think they are ahead, along comes the dental bill. They would love life to be a little easy, would love to have some nice things. When I make jokes about marrying for money, they think, Yeah, because maybe they should not have married that unsuccessful boyfriend they thought they loved.

I like to think I am giving these ladies a moment of freedom, talking to them as though they are one giant girlfriend in the dark, so we can share what we feel but would never dare say in public. We know that it's all foolishness, that tonight we're just bitchin' a lot and struttin' around. Life has not allowed them to take themselves very seriously, so they have a great laugh when I say to a big, fat, tired housewife sitting in the front row, "Okay, Rosemary, who've you been sleeping around with lately?" Many of these women have given their lives to men and family, but they love to hear me say, "Come on, you old tramp." They want to think their life has been a choice, that they could have had the career, could have slept around with those sailors.

I am telling them that maybe they still have the capacity and looks and style and sex appeal to choose, to be the sexual person they were in high school. There is nothing worse for a woman than feeling no longer desirable. I once went to a birthday party for Jeane Kirkpatrick, the former ambassador to the UN, and there were Richard Nixon, Henry Kissinger, and Walter Cronkite. I mean, it was heavy furniture. Not one of them had read *The Life and Loves of Errol Flynn.* To my surprise, Kirkpatrick was a very pretty woman. So in the middle of all this political power, I went up to her and said, "You're so good-looking. You've got gorgeous eyes." She dimpled and blushed. "Oh, thank you. How nice of you. Thank you." One of the most respected social thinkers of our generation became absolutely *girlish*—what we all are. It was a lovely moment.

I think of myself as a kind of leader in a support group. This is a very, very angry country, and women are thrilled to hear another woman articulating their rage. In my act I am angry at age, angry at men for going for just one kind of woman, angry at what women have to go through in life. I am angry at very beautiful, very rich women who complain that life has short-shrifted them. Princess Diana, for instance: "She is always complaining, 'I'm not happy. I'm not happy.' She married one of the richest men in the world. His mother owns England, Ireland, Scotland, Canada, New Zealand, Australia. By sleeping with Prince Charles, one day she will own—listen to the verb, *own*—England, Ireland, Scotland, Canada, New Zealand, and Australia. . . ." Then I say, "I would screw a duck for Rhode Island. What does she want?"

That is a rough line, but it gets a *huge* laugh—from women who work a whole lot more for a whole lot less. I have another line I am shocked they laugh at. I talk about why I do not exercise. I say, "Jane Fonda had the best body in the whole world—and her husband left her anyway. Thank you, God." Big laugh.

Pretending Christie Brinkley is stupid gets another big laugh. She is so beautiful, and if a woman is sitting there in an over-blouse, fifty pounds overweight, and going back after the show to a mobile home, it is nice to hear that Christie Brinkley may at least be dumb. People come out of my act saying, "Good. Let's hope."

Audiences tell me what they want to hear. I am pushing to see how far they will allow me to go, what new areas I can open, how much deeper into truth and feelings. Sometimes they stop me with a gasp. Sometimes I lose them, and then I need raw courage to stay onstage. But mostly they come with me, giving me tremendous warmth, a camaraderie, a total love going back and forth between us.

At the end of my act I give a woman in the audience a huge ficus tree and as I *struggle* across the stage with it the orchestra watches but does not offer to help. I say, "Fucking liberation. We did it to ourselves." Women love that line. I am raging out like King Lear—Queen Lear—screaming in the wind, screaming for all us women.

My Las Vegas career began in 1969, while I was still in New York. I came out to open for Charles Aznavour at the Flamingo Hotel. I was terrified despite four years of toughening with Carson and Sullivan and the Downstairs at the Upstairs. Dealing with those enormous audiences has defeated great performers. Danny Kaye flopped in Vegas. So did Ethel Merman. Elvis Presley bombed his first time there and was so gun-shy, he waited thirteen years before appearing again. When I am rejected by an audience, I feel total self-hatred. I want to stop the act and spit in my own face. The larger the audiences, the worse I feel.

I took along a security blanket. I brought Melissa and the nurse and transplanted a piece of my Downstairs at the Upstairs cocoon, where I was queen. My accompanist, Rod Warren, came and sat in the midst of a thirty-two-piece orchestra—and Archie Walker, the maître d' who had always introduced me, came also. The loudspeaker announced, "Ladies and gentlemen, Miss Joan Rivers." Then Archie walked on and said—as he had for five years—"Ladies and gentlemen, Miss Joan Rivers." That way I could pretend this was only the Downstairs. So I was crazier then. I admit it.

During one of my stints alone in Vegas, I discovered the companionship of a dog. I was in the beauty salon of the Tropicana

Hotel eating a ham sandwich, and in stumbled a filthy, ragged poodle with bloody paws. I gave it the sandwich and a bowl of water. Nobody knew whose it was, and I decided it was one of the dogs gamblers abandon when they lose everything and sell the van.

I cleaned him up and took him everywhere. He slept in the room with me—the first time I realized how wonderful it is to have something alive you can talk to—"What do you think. Should we get dressed? Should we watch TV? What do you want to do?" I loved him.

I got a call from the tennis pro at the Tropicana—"I hear you have my dog." He came into the dressing room and said, "Hello, Pierre." The dog jumped to the ceiling with joy. Six months earlier the pro had been in San Diego at a tennis event, and Pierre had disappeared. The pro hung around two days looking for him and, heartbroken, came back to Vegas. Pierre must have walked 350 miles across city suburbs, mountains, and desert. It was like a Disney movie—finding his way to the hotel where his master worked. Then this stupid dog missed the pro shop.

For my "triumphal" return to Las Vegas I was "costarring" with John Davidson, which meant that I was opening the show, but more important, on the Riviera Hotel billboard our names were the same size. However, his name was above mine—the arcane intricacies of show-business rank and ego.

Bob Hope, who had just been in a movie with Davidson, was flying out to introduce John on opening night. Edgar and my manager had screamed on the phone, "No, no, no, Bob Hope must introduce Joan, too. She is the costar. Otherwise you are implying that she's just the little warm-up opening act, and here's the real show now with John." The word came back from the biggest comedy star in the world, "No way."

Well, I came onto that stage opening night with my adrenaline pumping—furious that a man of such stature would be so mean. In the front row were June Haver and Fred MacMurray, and on my first line, she fell apart. What joy. I felt the whole audience with me.

Backstage Bob Hope was pacing up and down saying, "Get her

off. She's wearing them out." Angry. Pacing. "Get her off!" When I came off high from that audience, he stalked past me, went to the microphone, and said, "That girl is too funny for her own good," then did a whole routine of his own to make them forget me, to show that he was better.

Nobody wants to admit these great icons are killers. When I dared cross Johnny Carson to go to Fox, he came on like a gutter fighter—and let his representatives do the talking. Bob Hope could not even say my name. To succeed in this rough business, we all have to be killers—myself included. God knows what any of those people came out of and how hard they had to fight, what humiliations they suffered. Johnny Carson once said, "I started in Bakersfield doing magic off the back of a truck to guys standing in cornfields."

I know how Bob Hope must have felt. Here was a funny young woman—and it's known he does not like funny women—doing humor he did not understand, and the audience was having a very good time. Nobody was looking at his wristwatch waiting for Bob Hope. I am sure he was wondering, "Will my jokes still work? Can I top her with, 'I wouldn't say it's hot in Vegas, but . . .' "

I did a show for the Cancer Society last year and was backstage talking with close friends, waiting to go onstage. Suddenly I stopped and turned and listened to the opening act, a twenty-six-year-old girl who was terrific, the way I was twenty-five years ago, fresh and still a surprise. Here was somebody who was going to take over. The Dauphine is born. My body tightened. I was *totally* focused on her. If somebody had cut off my hand, I would not have felt it. You smell the threat. It is animal. And it is very hard to be gracious.

But I smiled and went out and said, "Wasn't she fabulous." The little bitch. Then I took off. A-1 material came out. Oh, did I work hard. She stayed and watched me. Afterward we talked together, and she was exceedingly nice—but she knew she had done well. I complimented her and told her she was wonderful—because I knew I had won.

I really hate to be admired by young comics. I am not ready. I am still one of you guys. I have not peaked yet. I do not know my full potential—maybe stage or movie acting, maybe directing or writing. I suspect no star, no matter how big, wants to be put on a pedestal. Then you are a monument to yourself, by definition part of the past. I still think of myself as absolutely the present.

As I grew stronger onstage in Las Vegas, my contract time went from twenty-five to thirty to thirty-five to forty minutes. When the hotels wanted me to move to closing act, I refused. I did not care about the glory. I was getting headliner money, equal billing, three quarters of the perks, and none of the pressure. If I walked onstage and the room was full, I thought, Gee, it's me. If the room was empty, I'd think, Poor So-and-so, he's slipping.

I was enjoying myself so much onstage, playing with my fans, loving my audiences, I began to feel an obligation to them and stretched my time longer than the prescribed forty minutes. The hotels were using me with stars who needed support, so I knew a lot of people were there to see me, and they should not get shortchanged.

The smart headliners like Neil Sedaka did not care because I could bring in that extra five hundred people. Andy Williams was a great gentleman to me. Robert Goulet was wonderful, and spent a dear, sweet Christmas with us in Vegas because his marriage had failed and he was alone. Lola Falana was so sweet backstage and always came over to say, "I'm enjoying your show." One closing night Helen Reddy brought a chair out onstage and watched my act, laughing and applauding. Another time, at the end, I joined her chorus line.

But a few stars treated me as a threat, hard to follow. Paul Anka must be about three foot two, and when I came offstage filled with excitement, there would be this little man screaming into my chest, "Too long! Too long! Too long!" I never saw anything but the top of his head.

Shirley MacLaine used to pace backstage complaining over and over, "She's going long. She's wearing them out." This was the first time two women had been booked together, and her act, singing and dancing, was wonderful. But I found her a cold, strong, driven woman. One night my dressing-room door opened, and it was Shirley. She stood in the doorway and said, "I just came in to say hello." She looked me over for a second and left. Didn't even say good-bye.

After the engagement her tips to the stagehands and band were not the usual envelopes containing fifty dollars. Instead, she handed out tiny pocketknives inscribed LOVE, SHIRLEY. So with my envelopes I passed out stainless-steel knives from the coffee shop, with LOVE, JOAN printed in nail polish.

When I opened for Tony Bennett at the Sands, I wanted no trouble about stretching, so I had forty minutes written into my contract with Walter Kane, the head of entertainment for Howard Hughes's hotel. But Bennett was constantly late, and I would have to keep stretching until I saw him backstage. Then he would do only twenty minutes and come off. So I stretched even more to give people their money's worth.

Tony noticed. During this time my father was ill after a heart attack, and I would leave a Do Not Disturb notice at the switchboard—unless it was an emergency call from my husband or father. So in the middle of the night when the phone rang, my whole body clenched. I picked up the receiver, trembling. It was Tony Bennett. "Joanie. Tony. Hey, babe, you're going way over. I'd appreciate it if you just did what you're supposed to do—twenty-five." I said, "I'm supposed to do forty." "Well, I'd appreciate it if you just did twenty-five." Click.

Edgar called Walter Kane, who said I should do as long as I wanted. I did my forty. In the middle of the next night the phone rang again. "Joanie. Tony. I'm not pleased. You're not listening. I want twenty-five." Again Walter Kane said, "Do what you want to do." I decided Tony Bennett needed a lesson. I called him and said, "I promise you, I'll be off in twenty-five." "Thanks, babe."

That night I came off in twenty-five. He was not even in the theater. Our dressing rooms were ground-floor suites, and we had to walk through the kitchen and the coffee shop and across a sort of garden. Ann Pierce, my beloved dresser, and I reached the coffee shop—behind us in the showroom a drumroll was sounding—"Now, ladies and gentlemen, Tony Bennett"—the longest drumroll in the history of Las Vegas—it should be in the *Guinness Book of World Records*—and through the coffee-shop window we could see Tony Bennett, strolling along a garden path, not a care in the world.

Ann and I hid, giggling like two little girls. I went back to doing my forty and stretching and never heard from him again. Much later he performed again in Vegas and was marvelous.

You get crazy playing three weeks in the glitzy limbo of Vegas, no days off, no sense of time. You get giggly and silly. You do anything to shake the cabin fever. I once played a funny trick on Sergio Franchi, a great singer and total gentleman, a class act if ever there was one. Very elegant. Absolutely straight.

I was trying a series of crazy endings to my act. For a long time during Watergate and the Nixon tapes, I went offstage and reappeared pulling a tableau of the famous painting of George Washington crossing the Delaware. George is staring toward the shore, and I would say, "He's looking for the missing eighteen minutes." One of several chorus boys who played George Washington left after the first week. Shortly thereafter a man came to see me from the Board of Health and said that this young man had the clap, and anybody who was with him sexually should come downtown for treatment—"Tell them to call me and I will be *very* discreet. Just say they're from the MGM."

We penciled *Please call me* on the health officer's card and pinned it to Sergio Franchi's dressing-room door. Now you know the officer said, "Yes, Mr. Franchi, this is something we had better discuss privately when you come downtown." And when Sergio, this European gentleman, got there, the man said, "Mr. Franchi, I understand you slept with George Washington."

During the 1970s, Vegas was VEGAS. Until the end of the 1970s there were at least fifteen showrooms at the hotels, each with major stars at their height doing two shows a night. Vegas even attracted Marlene Dietrich, Tallulah Bankhead, Noël Coward. Edgar researched a book, never published, on night life, and interviewed several dozen performers, including Dan Rowan and Dick Martin. They opened for Jane Russell, who got twenty-five thousand dollars a week for a nonact that began with her being carried onstage lying on a couch. They came off the first night and told her, "The audience was great." Jane said, "Fuck 'em." You've got to love her.

The hotels wooed stars for promotion. Movie-studio publicity men set up star junkets. Jack Entrater brought Humphrey Bogart, Judy Garland, Lee J. Cobb, and Sinatra to Joey Bishop's opening at the Sands. One evening Jayne Mansfield got into an elevator stark naked under her open mink coat. Later that night a doctor was called to treat her for a cold.

Stars mingled with civilians in the casinos. When Joe E. Lewis took Eydie Gorme gambling, he said, "Boy, I hope I win tonight." Eydie said, "I hope I break even. I need the money." Grace Kelly could be seen playing 21. Woody Allen used to deal poker sometimes, and I liked to deal 21. The dealer would let me go behind the table, and I changed the cards for people; they laughed, and a crowd gathered, and it was fun for everybody—publicity the casino could not buy.

Elvis Presley, when he was young, came up to see the shows. He never drank and asked people with him not to smoke. When he did start performing regularly, he was king of the Strip, the first to have guards with walkie-talkies.

During Elvis's show, he had two bodyguards on each end of the stage, to deal with the girls who would be trying to get close to him. They'd climb up onstage, and the bodyguards just threw them off, whoppo, tossed them back into the audience like rag dolls—and they came right back.

I did not particularly like Elvis's music, but what magic, what charm, what self-mocking humor! Elvis knew it was all a crock of shit. When stars begin taking themselves seriously, begin thinking they really are the image they present to the public— that is when they start to slip.

Elvis came to my show and afterward backstage. First six men arrived and said, "Elvis is coming. Elvis will be here in a minute. Please don't go anywhere." Then there was *buzz buzz buzz.* "Elvis is coming. Elvis is coming." Then in he walks, very much the star. Still, he was being a charming country boy, so much a part of his allure—in a black velvet Prince Valiant cape. "Ma'am, how nice to see you. Enjoyed your show. How's Melissa?" He knew we were all waiting for him. And we were.

When Elvis left, the energy went out of the room. Vegas was where I learned about energy. I started there as the Young Turk feeling superior to the golden oldies. But Edgar cautioned me, "Don't smirk at Dean Martin. See why he's been able to hold that stage for thirty years." After my act I would pile into a car with Edgar and run through the casinos to see those great performers with years of experience walking on a stage and dealing with their audiences. I saw that the one thing Martin, Elvis, Trini Lopez at his height, and Wayne Newton shared was energy.

I learned. Onstage I got up off my stool, got myself a cordless mike, and stalked that huge stage, making sure those people over on the side saw me up close, working the audience, letting people know I was killing myself for them. If you take a breather in those big rooms, a thousand people are restless. The act became a little like music, a kind of dance. It was the same for all those men.

Every show puts your reputation on the line. Those people are going to walk out there and talk about you to seven other people. I think one reason I am still around is I have known the ground rules—no coasting, no saying, "Here I am. Aren't you lucky." I have never had the great talent, the sparkling wit. Jokes take me forever to write. So I try to work as though each performance is my last show on earth.

In Las Vegas then, gaming made all the profits and everything else was to attract the gamblers, especially the high-rolling Texas and Oklahoma oilmen who sat behind stacks of black hundred-dollar chips. Regular folks paid twenty-six dollars for a round-trip plane ticket and flew up from Los Angeles for an evening. Pit bosses gave big losers a bus ticket home, and free drinks were handed out at the slot machines. Rooms were cheap. The shows charged little or no cover or minimum, only the price of food and drinks.

Each hotel was run by one man who had a personal relationship with the performers. At the Frontier, where I was opening for Juliet Prowse, I mentioned to Walter Kane that there was no shower in the opening-act bathroom, and he put one in overnight. Hotels gave out presents—one gave a mink coat to Judy Garland. A Rolls-Royce was wheeled out onstage for Anthony

Newley. Diana Ross received a pair of diamond earrings and returned them for a larger size.

Diahann Carroll was opening at Caesars Palace for Sammy Davis, Jr., and in the middle of his engagement he got sick. They asked me to fill in for headliner money that night, and I just made the airplane. The Caesars head of entertainment met me in Vegas, and as we were hurrying through the airport, he said to me, "Diahann Carroll won't open for you. She feels she is a bigger star [which she was]. If you don't want to go on, we will understand and pay you anyway." He was wonderful.

I said, "Put me anywhere. I don't care." I opened the two shows that night. After the second one a fifty-dollar gold piece surrounded by diamonds arrived in the dressing room with a thank-you note. That was why stars loved to come to Vegas.

Las Vegas was like a town-sized, all-night house party. After the second show Edgar and I almost always went out. I loved the sight of him, in his English suits, enjoying drag shows, physique contests, talent nights, nude shows. Suzie Midnight made my hairdresser eat a marshmallow stuck on her nipple. There are certain times in your life when you let loose, and Vegas was that time for me.

We spent most of our early morning hours listening to the comedians in the hotel lounges that had shows at 4:00 A.M. There was Totie Fields, terrific, Don Rickles at his height, and Shecky Greene, wonderful. I learned so much from Shecky about being free onstage. He had no fear. He lay right down on the stage and stayed there and did jokes into the microphone and sang.

For a comedian, that is the ultimate trick. That is saying, "Invisible control is now taking over." That is telling the kids, "I don't want you to move for an hour while Nanny takes her nap." Shecky could not translate onto television, and I do not see his name much anymore—but put him on a stage and he is fantastic. He gave me the courage to see how much of a lion tamer I could be, how far I could go putting my hand into the lion's mouth.

Don Rickles was in the Casbah Lounge, and if he roasted you, that meant you were somebody. Sinatra—who once chartered a train to bring his friends to Vegas—was there one night with a beautiful girl. Rickles hurled at him, "Do you think she likes you for yourself? Tell her you're bald. Tell her you're poor."

Don was and is fabulous and supremely outrageous. He would see a table of blacks and go into a shuffling sort of dance and say, "Gotta show'm we're friendly. Show'm you got rhythm, then they don't bother you." People insult Don when they call him an insult comic. Like Lenny Bruce, he is a truthful comic—and they both broke that ground for me. When I say, "Elizabeth Taylor wore yellow and ten schoolchildren got aboard," people laugh out of embarrassment and out of the truth of it and because they also are thinking the unspeakable—the unspeakable that some comedians dare to say.

I am delighted to be called outrageous. That means I am still blasting people out of their comfortable complacency. I think to survive well, to have some happiness, we must face the world as it really is, face the truth about what we are and what we want. I know that now. Then we can go forward working from that truth—which I think really does set you free even if only for an hour at Caesars Palace. If Blanche DuBois took stock and said, "This is where it's at, and I'm going to get rid of these *schmatte* clothes and get me a nice pants suit and look smart here, with a pocketbook and hat"—she would have been all right.

If a mother has been telling her chubby daughter, "You're very pretty, and anyway, looks don't matter"—that is lying to make things easier. When I say onstage, "Looks count! Forget 'inner beauty.' If a man wants inner beauty, he'll take X rays"—that fat girl knows that is the truth. I want to help her realize she has to pull herself together. If she keeps the delusion that life is going to be beautiful, everything will stay wrong. I was a fat tub of lard—was the whole front row of my class picture—but my mother kept reinforcing those myths. I am still waiting to wake up pretty.

Our whole society is so uptight, so puritan. What is so terrible about saying, "I would like to be wealthy," about admitting, "I hate my brother," about saying, "My baby was ugly"? We are so afraid of our real feelings. When I ask a lady if she would sleep with Onassis for $58 million, how dare she say no? I want to slap her. Fifty-eight million dollars in one night! I tell them, "For a hundred thousand dollars I'd jump in with Big Foot." That shocks them into thinking.

Of course, I am using very silly things to try to crack people's armor, attack their hypocrisy. For instance, I love getting a lady in the audience to admit that she would be a cannibal. What a taboo subject! But if you are lost in the snow and have not eaten for twelve days and were about to die of starvation, you are going to eat Shelley Winters. No question about it! You are going to have her knee for lunch.

I am particularly disgusted that the public buys the hypocrisy of the men revered as national institutions. I want to scream, "Everybody, grow up!" Bing Crosby, his son wrote, was always drunk. The public wanted Bing Crosby as a grand old man, but everybody knew he was a drunk who screwed around and beat up his wife. Another beloved American has a nest full of blondes in Vegas. That is his choice, but do not do family specials and talk about "My bride . . ." A famous actor came on *The Tonight Show* and carried on about his happy marriage. I wanted to say, "Wait a minute! Everybody in the industry knows you can't be left alone with a plant!"

I am furious at the comedians who do an hour and a half of filth and then close with talk about God. One grand old man tells the filthiest stories, but always says, "This one was told me by my friend the monsignor." He gets away with it because he has a sanctimonious manner. With my persona, I cannot say, "Here's one that my dear friend Rabbi Schwartz told me, and I hope you will enjoy it with me. A nun met a traveling salesman and . . ."

I am doubly furious because I consider myself a clean act, and the critics regularly pretend I am too shocking. I never read a discouraging word about Sandra Bernhard, who reaches inside her blouse and fondles a breast because it "feels so, mmm good." Roseanne Barr ended her act with, "You don't like what I say? Then suck my dick!" Whoopi Goldberg does an hour and a half of "motherfucker," "cocksucker," "fuckin' bastards," and people say, "Oh, the language is intrinsic to the performance art." Go figure it.

Maybe part of my problem comes from walking onstage in a designer black dress, a piss-elegant woman who should be talking about the latest sale at Christie's, doing Cartier jokes. And then watch out for what comes out of my mouth. But that is one reason why I am funny onstage. I think my commonness turns off the men and the real piss elegants, but turns on the regular people.

I *am* tasteless. If you are a current comic and do not offend somebody, you are doing itsy-bitsy cutesy-wootsie pap. If 10 percent of the people hate me, I will be fine. I always want to have one couple that gets up and leaves. That means I am still on the cutting edge.

However, my whole humor is actually based on the loneliness and hurt of being left out, of being thrown over—which I always fear and dread. I feel sorry for everybody and everything. I am upset about the guy waiting for the bus, for the old cleaning ladies coming out of office buildings at dawn. To me, every inanimate object has feelings and is full of pain. I keep sets of dishes, clothes, shoes, because, if you throw them away, you break their hearts. When I cut flowers, I never leave one alone on the bush, always leave behind a friend—or I cut them all so they can come into the house together. In my pain, in my upset and anger, I am railing at the world.

After a night of touring the Las Vegas shows, Edgar and I ended up at dawn with the other performers in the Sands coffee shop, which served great Chinese food. We felt part of a very special fraternity, hanging out and playing trivia games and table-hopping to listen to Milton Berle or say hello to Sinatra, who knew who you were and said hello back. "Hello, Joan. How's it going? How's the kid?"

When I was at the Desert Inn, I got all my food free. But my whole group—my road manager, Billy Sammeth, Ann Pierce, my hairdresser, Jason Dyl, anyone who was visiting—would all sneak like naughty kids into the empty bakery kitchen and take pie plates and fill them with goodies still hot from the oven and laugh hysterically and, if anybody came, hide under the counters.

At the Sands the bellboys delivered guests to the bungalows in carts that were left charging at night in front of the golf-club pro shop. Edgar and I and Billy Sammeth would swipe them and have races across the fairways just at dawn, crackling through the fall leaves on the ground, the pale light slanting against the red and gold trees. We never got to bed before 6:00 A.M. Once somebody telephoned Edgar at three in the afternoon, and we were very annoyed.

Melissa loved Las Vegas. We put her in a nursery school to be with other children. At the Sands I sometimes had the star's bungalow with its private pool, and I could swim with Melissa without people watching and eat on the terrace and really be a family.

There was no class structure. The stars and chorus girls and dancers were at all the parties—at Sammy Davis's opening-night party, at Siegfried and Roy's opening, with lions walking around, at Cher's roller-skating party in Caesars sports arena, at the celebrity softball games, Sinatra's birthday with Italian food shops built for the occasion around the ballroom walls. At the Caesars fifth-anniversary party fifteen hundred guests in formal dress sat at flower-heaped tables among reflecting pools. Live butterflies were released. Two specially built summerhouses were hung with orchids, and the base of a fountain was covered with chrysanthemums, gladioli, orchids, and gardenias.

Edgar loved all of that, and he also had empathy for the grubby end of the business. He heard that the lead nude dancer in a show had cancer and might lose both breasts. At the Halloween Ball he found the girl and encouraged her and gave her a check to keep her going. She was so touched. He really saved her. He had a kind side that, in his shyness, embarrassed him, and he covered it up with gruffness.

He often did secret acts of generosity, was always ready to lend money. He was really full of sentiment—and embarrassed by sentiment. When he got up to make a toast, he would choke up so you could not hear his voice. And every time Melissa and I wrote that we loved him, he kept the note forever.

Around 1979 our Las Vegas world was transformed. Hughes and his Summa Corporation bought more and more hotels, and ran them like aircraft factories. Other huge, soulless, bottom-line corporations followed, and soon cost accountants in four-button suits were in charge everywhere, figuring profit per square foot. Now every department—the shows, the rooms, the coffee shop— had to be money machines.

The cover charges in the showrooms went up, and the stars were replaced by cheaper revues performed to taped music— shows named things like Boy-lesque, Splash, and Beach Blanket Babylon. Ultimately there were only three star showrooms—at Bally's, the Hilton, and Caesars Palace. Performers had to pay to see other acts like everybody else. The paternalism was gone.

To increase profits, the corporations began targeting the broad public, marketing themselves to tour groups and conventioneers, who come with expense accounts and have to get up for meetings. Regiments of slot machines catered to the small-time gamblers, the men and women who save all year to come to Las Vegas, their glamour capital.

Simultaneous with Hughes, there began to be fewer and fewer stars who could fill a showroom. Everybody's acts had already been seen on television. Costs soared. For many years twenty-five thousand dollars a week had been top, and then in 1955 Liberace opened at the Riviera for fifty thousand dollars. Eventually $100,000 was commonplace, and the next big leap was Dolly Parton, who demanded and got $350,000 a week. I hear Sinatra now gets $500,000.

You never hear anybody scornfully call such people "Vegas singer," as though there were something disgraceful about the place and the money. But when newspapers want to dismiss you, they say, "Vegas comic," which in their mouths means a crass, second-rate comic telling raunchy jokes for rough, blue-collar drinkers mainly interested in nude women and gambling. A businessman I was interested in for a time frowned and told me, "My friends keep saying you're a Vegas comic." That makes me crazy. Johnny Carson has taken millions out of Vegas. Bill Cosby. Jack Benny. Bob Hope. Sam Kinison. Robin Williams. Go sneer Vegas comic in *their* faces.

9

ooooo

I picked up *People* magazine, and there was Elizabeth Taylor on the cover, fat as a house. I realized that nobody had dared say about this icon, "She's a blimp," dared admit you could stamp Goodyear on her and use her at the Rose Bowl. I did not realize that this moment was going to skyrocket my career.

Since my job has always been to tell the world that the emperor has no clothes, right away, that night at Ye Little Club, I did an Elizabeth Taylor joke: "I took her to McDonald's just to watch her eat and see the numbers change." That got such a reaction, I went on, "I had to grease her hips to get her through the golden arches." When I tried those two jokes on *The Tonight Show,* the reaction was an eruption of laughter way beyond anything I had ever experienced. I had hit a vein.

Audiences have always dictated with laughter what they want to hear, and they were telling me they wanted to hear about Elizabeth Taylor. The women loved having somebody else say the truth so they could go, "That's terrible! Isn't Joan Rivers mean to say that! Ha, ha, ha." Increasingly audiences waited for me to tell them that when Elizabeth Taylor went to Sea World and saw Shamu she asked, "Does he come with fries?" or that she had more chins than a Chinese phone book and loved to eat so much, she would stand in front of her microwave and yell, "Hurry!" When I eventually tried to drop such jokes from the act, people called out, "What about Elizabeth Taylor?"

We women were furious when the most beautiful of all women let herself go. As long as she was sexually viable, I could be viable. If she became a slob, there was no hope for any of us. I felt betrayed—and so did women across America.

These jokes became part of my reputation. But if Taylor ever told me they *really* upset her, I would have dropped them from the act. I once asked her through Roddy McDowall whether the jokes hurt her. The message came back, "They don't hurt me where I live."

I admire Elizabeth Taylor because she is still here and still famous. She did not turn out to be a child star in the category of Peggy Ann Garner. Malcolm Forbes's date was not Margaret O'Brien. There is a lot of steel there, the strength to plow through life and achieve what she wants. She is a killer. We all spot each other.

I first met Elizabeth Taylor in 1973 at Roddy McDowall's house and found her to be a man's woman, uninterested in me and my talk about children. Years later Elizabeth and I were asked to cohostess a dinner benefit for battered children at Spago. I knew that people would pay a thousand dollars a plate to see Joan Rivers and Elizabeth Taylor walk in together—and so did the benefit chairman. And so would every newspaper and magazine in the country.

Edgar phoned Elizabeth's assistant and said we should arrive together. She said, "Fine, we'll meet you there." That smelled fishy. Taylor was always late, so the little peon, Joan Rivers, would be waiting around for the queen to walk in.

Finally the assistant agreed to send one of her guards to Ambazac with a walkie-talkie. He would tell us when Elizabeth left the house. I said, "They're not going to tell us the truth. We'd better find out when she *really* leaves," and I staked out Elizabeth Taylor's house with *my* security man. When Elizabeth's man came, he told us her limo had left and we should go, but *my* man radioed, "The limo is not even at the front door." "We'll wait," I said. Her man went crazy.

An hour later I got the word from my stakeout—"Her limo has pulled up to her door." I got into my limo and made her man ride in a lead car. We set off. The lead car turned right and drove into the hills, taking him far beyond the range of his radio contact with Taylor. I turned left and proceeded down Sunset Boulevard.

My stakeout radioed that Taylor still had not left. We pulled to the curb and waited. Finally we spotted her limo and pulled out ahead of it, driving in tandem to Spago's restaurant, where the dinner was to be held. I stopped at the door and got out. Taylor's limo zoomed past up the hill. Dressed in an Oscar de la Renta black velvet dress and about $3 million in sapphires lent me by Winston, I ducked into a little alley and waited beside a row of garbage cans. In about ten minutes Elizabeth Taylor arrived ready to make her solo entrance. I scooted out to the sidewalk and said, "Liz, hello." We went up the steps side by side, the Bobbsey Twins together as camera lights popped.

I thought it was all amazing, ridiculous, hysterically funny— and classic Hollywood. An international superstar, who will go down as one of the biggest stars of the century, is playing games so she can make her own entrance into a restaurant.

While Elizabeth Taylor jokes registered me with the general public, my partnership with David Brenner, that wonderful co-median, elevated me to a new, heady level within the entertain-ment industry. He and I had always admired each other's comedy. The son of a former vaudeville song-and-dance man, David had been a television writer, producer, and award-win-ning documentary filmmaker, but chucked it all to follow his heart and be a stand-up comic. By 1981 he had become one of the other substitute hosts for Johnny Carson and a friend.

David suggested we tour together. Everybody worried that ninety minutes of uninterrupted comedy would wear audiences out; they'd stop laughing. But David and I were two separate shows. His stage persona is clean-cut, low-key, and mild, never offensive, a storyteller-observer describing the lunacy of life—the flip side of me. And we all know what *I'm* like onstage. It was a perfect match. We sold the idea to the Diplomat Hotel in Florida and broke the attendance record set by Liza Minnelli. As a result, our lives were booked for the next two years.

Edgar and I and David went on the road together—the happiest time I ever had performing. We had such fun—playing tricks and games, one always trying to outdo the other. David hated to be recognized, so we would do things like scream at him out the car window—"DAVIIID! DAVID BRENNNER!" We had everybody in a restaurant applaud him when he came out of a men's room. We had pizza delivered to him at 5:00 A.M.—and he pretended it never arrived. "What pizza? I didn't see any pizza."

We were in Chagrin Falls, Ohio, and went into a terrible antique shop full of knickknacks to kill some time. As we were leaving, I said, trying to be nice, "You have a lovely store, but I have an appointment now, so I'll come back later." David immediately said, "Excuse me, Joan, but exactly *when* are you coming back? I don't want to buy anything in this store and I will *not* be back, but we all heard you, Joan, say you are coming back, so let's find out exactly what time." I was dying. *Dying!* "Three-thirty," I murmured. And I did it, too. I came back and bought something. I had to.

Edgar loved joining in. Once David's limo pulled up parallel with ours and David pointed at our front tire, acting as if we had a flat. Suddenly Edgar rolled down our rear window and, bang, mooned him. Everybody was flabbergasted. For Edgar to do that was like watching Winston Churchill drop his pants. But David won that game in the end. When we got to the theater, he said, "You shouldn't have done that, Joan."

Everywhere we went, we sold out in theaters seating three and four thousand. Finally in 1982 the Riviera Hotel in Las Vegas decided the format worked and booked us. This was the turning point for me. The show opened with the audience hearing us on the sound system tossing a coin backstage to see who went on first. The show was better with the easiness of David coming first, so we agreed I would always win the toss and go second. I became, *ipso facto,* the closing act. A headliner.

• • •

By 1983 I had reached that state I describe so enviously about others. I was white-hot. The first inkling came that February. A promoter sold me on a performance in New York at Carnegie Hall early in a national tour I was planning. I was overwhelmed. I do not like playing my hometown, because if the audiences don't like me, if *The New York Times* hates me, I still have to walk those streets again, feeling unwanted.

But Carnegie Hall was Carnegie Hall. As a child I had been dragged there by my mother for an injection of "culture," walking in with my hand in hers and looking at the huge posters of Jascha Heifetz and Toscanini with a slash across them saying, SOLD OUT. I had gone there with dates, with Robert Sherman to hear Nadia Rubenstein, with Edgar to hear Leonard Bernstein. I knew that row of doors in the back, the awful ugly plants on the stage, the cream-colored paint and moldings.

At that time very few pop acts had played Carnegie Hall, so its aura of class was far more imposing than today. It was still the pinnacle of music—where every major name in that world continued to perform. When Mischa Elman was asked on the street how to get to Carnegie Hall, he answered, "Practice, practice, practice."

And New York is New York. For me this city was the scene of years of frustration and failure. I knew those audiences, people who had seen it all, done it all, who were cool and smart—the Catskills with a B.A. If I bombed, I would be confirmed as just a Vegas comic. If I hit, I would have a new, subtle definition on the East Coast, touched ever so lightly with "art."

The second inkling that I was white-hot was a call from Calvin Klein, asking me what I was planning to wear. I said I had no idea. So Calvin designed the most wonderful tight, tight, tight, tight black satin dress with a square neck and a square back, a slit up the side, and a wide cinch belt to die for. It was stunning. The press loved it; *The New York Times* put it on the cover of one of their fashion issues. I even wore it on *Saturday Night Live*—and so did Joe Piscopo. Calvin designed an identical dress for Joe for a skit called "The Dueling Joans." Hilarious.

I systematically guarded against getting all worked up. I scheduled Rochester the night before, so New York City would be just another stop on the schedule, another one-nighter doing two shows—even though co-owner Steve Rubell was giving a major party in my honor at Studio 54. I deliberately booked a show the next night in Syracuse to get me out of town quick, before the reviews could hurt me. Was I terrified? I guess I was, deep down, but somehow I succeeded in blocking the fear. If it had come to the surface, God knows if I could have even got through the stage door.

Billy Sammeth went in a day ahead. He called me in Rochester with the news that both shows had sold out the morning the tickets went on sale. People had spent the night outside in sleeping bags. Scalpers were getting up to four hundred dollars a ticket. Now *my* poster had a slash across it—SOLD OUT. The promoter wanted to hold me over for two more shows. I refused. In and out. And don't get excited.

I walked out on the stage of Carnegie Hall, and as I reached center stage, the audience stood up and cheered. I began to cry. The tears running down my face were from longing—the longing requited at last, to be on that stage, to be so validated after over twenty years of my parents saying, "No. Show business is not right for you," after fifteen years of telling bookers and agents, "I am good! I can do that."

The tears were there for my mother. She had been dead from a heart attack for two years—the person I had called every day, the one who listened and listened to all my drivel, always took my side, ready to pick up the sword and kill the enemy next to me. She was the person I did my tricks for. How I wished she could have known her daughter was somebody.

I did my act, the same one I did in Las Vegas, the same one I did in Rochester. I am what I am, and that was what I thought was funny. I did all the tried-and-true routines—stewardesses, nurses, gynecologists, marriage—"On my wedding night Edgar wanted to make love with the lights on, but I said, 'Shut the car door.'"

I gave lots of good advice to ladies who wanted men. I told them, "Don't cook. Don't clean. No man will ever make love to a woman because she waxed the linoleum—'My God, the floor's immaculate. Lie down, you hot bitch.' " I told them, "Education doesn't count. Only looks. No man ever put his hand up a dress looking for a library card." I said, "If you break up and he wants the ring back, swallow the stone. No man will look through shit for a diamond." Pause. "Nancy Reagan told me that." Everything worked. Tremendous laughter. Applause. For the first time I really felt what it was like to be a star.

That night the Studio 54 crowd came to celebrate, but for me it was just another version of Jim Nabors's party when we first arrived in California—we knew hardly anyone. David Geffen of Geffen Records. Bianca Jagger. Barry Diller, then chairman of the board of Paramount. The press was everywhere. Guards had to wedge the two of us through the throng. Inside, Calvin Klein and I stood on a high catwalk and waved down at the crowd. They put me in a private room so packed nobody could move. Andy Warhol was there. Truman Capote. I didn't know any of them—not Steve Rubell, not Halston, not anyone.

The next night I was in the kitchen of my Syracuse hotel suite reading the New York reviews, which were all bouquets. My hometown had welcomed me back with huzzahs. But the room had no heat. So the toast of Carnegie Hall was sitting in Syracuse with her feet in the oven to keep them warm. Show business is so insane. People think celebrity performers lead glamorous fairy-tale lives, but the only real fairy tale occurs when we're performing onstage.

Something had clicked in America—partly because something had clicked in me. I had always loved clothes. But I was conservative. Basic black with a circle pin. I was the Edith Piaf of comedy—the audience shouldn't be distracted from my mouth.

When Edgar and I were first married, I went to Saks and bought a tiny summer silk dress, very pretty, with a black-and-white boa. Edgar hated the boa. He said, "You look like a chicken. Like a Mafia wife."

I did listen to Jason Dyl, my hairdresser, one of those men who know if you put a diamond pin here, a bow there, something ordinary becomes truly glamorous. He kept telling me I looked too plain, and I put myself in his hands. He put everything together for me. Jason had found his Barbie doll.

He sent me to Bob Mackie, the biggest theatrical dress designer in the world. I must have been the first person in history to walk into Mackie and say, "I want a dress but I don't want a bead on it." This was during the height of the bead. So Mackie designed a dress with one beaded sleeve. Onstage I felt like the whore of Babylon—but everyone loved it.

So I figured, if I can wear beads, maybe I can show a little cleavage. Within six months there were plunging necklines. And so many beads in my closet, you had to wear sunglasses when you opened the door. Then it became, what the hell. Let's have a good time. Add a boa.

Look at all the stars. Look at Lily Tomlin, at Bette Midler. Barbra Streisand. Look how they change, get prettier with more money and assurance. And with help from the great photographers. Diana Ross. Ann-Margret at her height. Their mouths open, eyes flashing. I was always an ugly duckling, never the one to look seductive, but Harry Langdon took pictures of me with the hair and wind machine that Edgar and I could not believe—a shot for a comedy album cover in a full-length black mink with nothing underneath and just a leg coming out. Glamour was coming into my life.

When I became Johnny Carson's permanent guest host, all the designers began to call me. It was a lot of Oscar de la Renta, Perry Ellis, Yves Saint Laurent, Trigère, Mary McFadden, Donna Karan, Anne Klein. The only one who wouldn't lend clothes to me was St. John Knits—unlined St. John Knits.

I was asked by ABC to go to London and cover Fergie's wedding and Amen Wardy of Newport Beach offered to bring clothes to me. I looked outside that morning, and down the street was one of those huge, huge moving vans, too big to get in the driveway. In the truck was the whole fashion world, everything my size. Dresses, four. Shoes, six and a half. Heaven in a truck.

It was the first time I had seen Valentinos, couturier Chanel, Galanos, Ungaros—all in one afternoon. I chose and chose and chose. Bill Blass. Geoffrey Beene—skintight as if it's water on you.

I'm talking two thousand, three thousand dollars a dress. Every handbag in the world. I went to the royal wedding and looked better than the Queen. "Where *did* you get that hat?" she said to me, touching her crown—"I'll trade you."

Now came the Fox show. Who was going to dress me? I called Saks. I wanted them to lend me clothes. They didn't call back. Then Amen called and *volunteered.* So one day every three weeks Jason Dyl and I went down to Newport Beach, to Amen Wardy, one of the great stores on earth, and Amen would pull out everything for me. He'd scream things like, "No, not this belt with that dress! I have a much better belt"—and the belt *was* much better.

He once put me in an eighteen-thousand-dollar Valentino dress—and my joke was, "Should I buy this dress or a new car?" All the Valentino people tuned in to the show to see this dress on. Well, the show was built around the swallows coming back to Capistrano. We couldn't find a swallow, so I appeared in the eighteen-thousand-dollar Valentino dress with a pigeon attached to my head. The Valentino people almost died. They made me return the dress that night.

Dissolve. When I was fired from Fox, everything stopped. My clothes were gone. Jason was gone. I never had to think about clothes before. Jason put everything together . . . down to the gardenia in my hair on New Year's Eve. It was all gone.

When I began my present daytime show, I thought, Well, I'll have no problem borrowing clothes. Saks turned us down again. Macy's turned us down! Bergdorf's. So we called Barney's, which turned out to be a magical store like Amen—so nice to me, so smart. Everything I wear on the show walks out of the store the next day.

But the point of all this was still the career. The glitz made me feel glamorous, and therefore I looked glamorous—which made me into more of a star—which made me realize I was a star— which made me feel better about myself—which gave me more assurance—which made audiences accept me more—which made me more relaxed—which made me more assured—which . . . it was all wonderful.

Maybe, too, my kind of audacious humor came into vogue. I

had become wilder on television, doing more of my nightclub act on *The Tonight Show*. Before, I was doing routines about how my husband doesn't like cooking. Now I was saying, "Yoko Ono is so ugly. John Lennon saw her naked on her wedding night and said, 'Yoko. Oh! No!' " The press loved it. And maybe everybody had got used to me, had figured out that I was not serious, that I was just laughing.

My new comedy record was a great success. It went gold. I wrote a book for mothers—*Having a Baby Can Be a Scream*—and it became a best-seller. I was guest host on *Saturday Night Live*. In April of 1983 my first *People* magazine cover called me "The First Lady of Comedy." One critic wrote, "Ignorance of Ms. Rivers' rocketing ascendance into the ether of hype virtually amounts to contempt of one's fellow man."

The signals of stardom were all around me. Money was flowing in. We had to hire an extra secretary to handle the fan mail. When I performed, major stars wanted to meet me. Young people were in the audiences, screaming right along with me and coming up to me later as though I were a contemporary. I went from never being a presenter to hostessing the Emmys. Suddenly Brandon Tartikoff, then president of NBC, was sending me flowers and coming to see me at the Improv, the local comedy club.

You know you are white-hot by the change in the world's attitude. Restaurant owners are friendlier—lines melt away, wine is sent to the table. Hairdressers would come into my dressing room admitting they were nervous about doing my hair. Perks were given to me—hotels would upgrade my rooms for no extra charge. In Toronto we were put in a Royal Suite—for nothing.

In Hollywood Edgar and I leaped from the "F" to the "A" list. We went to one of those "just close friends" parties given by Swifty Lazar, and there were Cher, Neil Simon, Dolly Parton, Rock Hudson, and Neil Diamond. When David Geffen began courting me for a record, suddenly he was my best friend in the world and invited Edgar and me to a party at the Beverly Wilshire Hotel. It seemed to me the entire world of show business was there. Mel Gibson. Jane Fonda. Jack Nicholson.

That night Barbra Streisand was simultaneously having a fight with her boyfriend, Jon Peters, and dickering to buy a diamond ring from Diane von Furstenberg. Jack Nicholson got so high he went to the ladies' room by mistake. "Jesus, I'm really whacked out tonight. I gotta sit down," Jack said to a friend of mine, who answered, "You are sitting down." Jack said, "Then I gotta *lie* down."

I kept telling Edgar and Melissa, "Be aware that these are the wonder years, and they can go away at any moment." In show business people get spoiled so easily. You assume your name will always be stenciled on the studio parking space, assume the gate will always go up for you at NBC. You assume that people will keep on buying tickets and dressing up and getting themselves out of the house to see you. Your people around you assume these things, too, because the phone never stops ringing with other people bringing fresh ideas. I kept reminding myself of Jack Benny, who stood in my dressing room one night at Ye Little Club and said, "They used to line up for me, and now they don't. But I still love my business. Take the money now, because nobody will care when you are gone."

Since childhood I have had this constant insecurity that I will suddenly be back in Greenwich Village making ketchup soup. Long after I was well established, I used to pack up everything in the dressing room—makeup, clothes—and take it all to my hotel room every night in case I was fired. I always buy classic clothes so they will not go out of style, and all my miniskirts have huge hems so they can still be worn when the style changes. If I am wild about a dress, I buy one for now and another to put away so I will still look nice when my career has come to an end.

I'm crazy.

10

·····

I don't know how much of the next stage of my career I owe to Bill Cosby, who was also one of Johnny Carson's guest hosts. I do know that Bill telephoned Freddie De Cordova, the executive producer, and said, "Why are you rotating guest hosts? You should use Joan permanently." And in August, once again, *The Tonight Show* lifted me to that degree of celebrity that only television can achieve—lifted me to the level of a household name. In August of 1983 NBC anointed me as the permanent, sole guest host of *The Tonight Show.*

The job did not come to me with a lit candle on it. That year they did not invite me to Johnny's annual party, so I had no sense of any new, special status of being taken into *The Tonight Show* family. Freddie De Cordova and Peter Lassally, the producer, told me they were simply tired of scheduling a series of names and wanted to have one, predictable host.

I was proud to be the first woman allowed to host a full week at a time—a major trust—but I did not understand what it meant within the industry. My primary reaction was worry—how was I ever going to find enough new material for all those opening monologues? When NBC invited me to a lunch introducing the affiliates to the fall shows and their actors, I, amazingly, did not understand the significance of all the hoopla.

Backstage all the performers were lined up, and I was put at the end of the line. I thought, Well, okay, I guess it's because I don't have a real show on NBC. After everybody else was on-stage, they announced, "Joan Rivers!" and the whole place stood up and went crazy. I thought, That's nice. Everybody likes me. I had never allowed myself to "believe," and still saw myself as just an up-and-coming television personality, still on trial. I had not been told the ratings for my guest-host shows. Peter or Fred-die would say, "They were fine," or "You didn't do well in Tampa." I didn't care because I never bothered to understand what those numbers really meant—and Edgar was kept at arm's length by the Carson people. So I did not realize my importance to all those stations, how much money I was making for them. I did not realize the significance of the Cartier watch NBC sent me afterward for doing a few minutes of jokes. In retrospect, it's almost impossible for me to believe I was so passive about the fundamental numbers of the business. I was so naïve.

From then on my career became performing comic and televi-sion interviewer—who still hoped to be a legitimate actress. But hosting *The Tonight Show* for eight weeks a year was the final boost that took me into the big, big time. Though it was not prime time, not *The Cosby Show* or *Cheers,* I was still seen by 30 million people. *The Tonight Show* was the Tiffany of talk shows, the one show that had true meaning in my career and everybody else's career. If I had done nothing but *Hollywood Squares* during the day and Carson at night, I could have floated in my career for-ever.

I was the guest host of *The Tonight Show* for nearly three years. I loved walking into NBC, where everybody knew and liked me. I loved going into the wardrobe room with my dresses hung and labeled for the week, seeing the three armoires, side by side, labeled JOHNNY, ED, and JOAN. Those dumb symbols are very important in show business; they reassure you. When I said, "Gee, I wonder if we can get some black thread?," a spool of black thread would appear. "If it's not too much trouble, I would love a Diet Coke." A Diet Coke would miraculously appear.

Edgar looked forward to those days, too. He liked to sit with me in the dressing room while I went over my notes. At three o'clock, during makeup, Freddie De Cordova and Peter Lassally would come in, and for an hour we would laugh and gossip.

Freddie was marvelous-looking, big, still a dynamo in his early seventies, perfectly tailored, immaculate, always seemed to have on a different wristwatch, always had the meanest mouth in the West.

He had a gay man's vicious humor in a straight man's body and was witty and bright and smart and sharp, and he had seen it all and done it all and done it first class. I adored him.

Freddie's social world was on the fringe of the Hollywood "A" list—the older, legendary names. We heard how Jack Benny's wife, Mary, never loved Jack, heard that Cary Grant was cheap and that Jimmy Stewart was getting gaga. He said Billy Wilder was wealthy, but his wife, Audrey, had to make her own clothes. He claimed Alfred Bloomingdale's widow was holding out on the cuff links Alfred left him in his will. Michael Douglas's wife ruled everything, and he was a puppet in her hands. Bill Cosby was mean. I don't remember a good word about anybody, dead or alive. He even put down the guests I was about to interview on the show. Before I went on with Joan Collins, he brought in a magazine story to show how old she looked.

The only person from the show I miss is De Cordova—but when he was in my dressing room, I didn't dare leave, not even to go to the bathroom—because the minute anybody's back was turned, he might make one of his wicked remarks. But what I loved: when Peter Lassally, a thin, serious, straight-arrow Dutchman, forced to be always deferential to the executive producer, made his own sardonic remarks about Freddie.

And showtime was such a high. I loved walking out to the center of the stage with the orchestra playing the theme we've all heard for twenty years, with the big audience, invisible behind the lights, revved up, the excitement, the tension coming at you, the love and anticipation. Inside me was a great swelling up and a joy at being there. My whole body felt awake and ready, as though I had just walked five miles on a cool morning.

I loved sitting behind the desk, pushing the show into any area I wanted and seeing it bubble. When everything was right—the guests were good, being sassy right back at me, and the audience was right on the same beam—the show took control of itself and became bigger than its parts, and I was in the middle of magic.

Some guests were wonderful—Rita Moreno was full of energy and knew she was there for performance, so if I said something, she said the opposite. Betty White was terrific, coming on and playing bitchy and man-hungry. Lily Tomlin worried terribly about being good and called again and again to go over what she'd say, and then what I'd say, and what she'd answer—line by line, every nuance, every aside. I work spontaneously, Lily works totally controlled, but when she gets on camera, she is some package. Tyne Daly came at the last second from the *Cagney & Lacey* set with no time to change, so she brought the dress she was supposed to wear on a hanger to show the audience. When she came on my present show, she wore the same dress.

Orson Welles—this astonishing, huge ruin—had to be brought onstage in advance in a wheelchair. He came on the show to please his wife, who loved to watch me, but playful was not his middle name. I don't think he ever in his life went for funny ladies. By then there was no greatness left, just that remarkable voice we remember from *Citizen Kane* and *War of the Worlds*.

The best guests know they are booked to entertain, and they have eight minutes to score—like a civilian going to dinner with the boss—to be their most charming, deliver the three great stories that have carried them through life, perform their public persona.

Sometimes guests were not the brightest. Or they were terrified. Or drunk. Or egomaniacs. Or mean. Some guests, otherwise fantastic people, just have off days. Michael Landon came on angry, and I never knew why—unless he was mad that he had me and not Johnny. But he was a reluctant talker and subtly antagonistic. He did not like me and let it show—and finally threw me a zinger, saying that selling door-to-door as a young man he met a lot of obnoxious people. Then, looking right at me, he said,

"And you certainly tend to meet them in studios, sometimes." I came right back at him, saying, "And you meet such rude guests, sometimes." What makes you good as a host is that you stay human on camera, but I always regret encounters like that—and, of course, I regret that one doubly now that Michael is dead. I'll never have the opportunity to see him again. Such a brave, brave man.

Larry Hagman came on at his peak during all the brouhaha over "Who shot J.R.?" At showtime he had not arrived, but we announced him as a guest, and I kept getting the word, "He's on his way, he's on his way." Well, he never arrived, so I had to stretch the other guests and vamp with Ed McMahon to fill the time. As I came off at the end, Hagman strolled in looking for his dressing room, saying he thought the show was ninety minutes, not sixty.

The rock star Elvis Costello sat there on camera sweating and nodding off to sleep. I mouthed to the audience, "He's asleep." I thought it was hysterical and kept talking loudly to wake him up. I was so naïve then. I could not figure out what his problem was. After all, the man had just sung a song.

Vanna White used to come over from *Wheel of Fortune* night after night and hang out behind the rear curtain with the makeup people and the sound technicians, hoping somebody would spot her and have her on as a guest. Finally a slot did open up, and I put her on, a nice, bright girl, eager to play on camera.

I never did well with the old-time stars, Freddie's contemporaries he would put on from time to time. Their brains had been studio-washed; they were always so careful. Everything in their lives had just been marvelous, everybody so lovely. Lana Turner came on and said, "I'm not here to promote my book. I'm just here to meet you." I said, "Good," and threw her book over my shoulder. Thank God she laughed.

But I tried never to go too far with guests because I was, in fact, a hostess, and my obligation was to make them feel they did well. I watched their hands to see if they shook and looked for the sweats. I listened to what they said during the commercial break because I never wanted a guest to be truly uncomfortable.

. . .

Steered by Freddie De Cordova and Peter Lassally, *The Tonight Show* had become a stately ship gliding on an even keel through unruffled seas. The show was the embodiment of Johnny's cool tone, his ease and charm, his familiarity. By 11:30 P.M. most TV audiences are lying down, and they want to watch—but not *watch.* You can do your nails to Johnny because you know he will bring the ship in smoothly, no surprises. Jay Leno is cut from the same cloth. You can be alone in a hotel room in Sioux City and know that if you turn on *The Tonight Show,* you will find family companionship.

Now into this placid sea steamed Joan Rivers, a hot, mouthy, pushy little tugboat painted pink. I was Johnny's opposite. Compared to years of unruffled sameness from Johnny, I must have been like a dash of ginger. I tried not to do the usual plain-vanilla interviews. I wanted to ask the intimate things everyone really wanted to know. I confess I'm very interested in all that cheap fan-magazine gossip. And so is America. I became the *The National Enquirer* of the TV screen.

Victoria Principal was my guest first in 1983 when she was on *Dallas,* and I wanted to know about her break-up with Andy Gibb of the Bee Gees. "Did you keep the ring?" I asked. Well, she denied they were engaged and denied there had been an engagement ring. At that moment the audience and the camera disappeared, and we were like two women at a kitchen table. "But you showed me one," I reminded her. "You and Andy Gibb came to my dressing room in Las Vegas. You had the ring. You'd just gotten engaged.

"Why was it on your left hand?" I wanted to know. "It's my best hand," she said. "For what?" I asked.

After we went off the air, Victoria said sweetly, "I'll get you next time." And she did come back, determined to win—came on all vulnerable and innocent, playing the victim. But she made a big mistake. Early in the show she said this was her thirty-third birthday. Later she told me she was born in 1950, the first American baby in Japan after the war.

Well, I know when the war was over—1945. Let's see, subtract that from 1983 and you get . . . I said, "Victoria, you've ruined yourself again." I teased her, "Okay, I was born in 1950, too." She wanted to know where I bought my birth certificate. "Same place you bought yours," I said.

When the show finished, she stormed off the stage in a fury. But that same year Andy Gibb was my guest. Agreeing that Victoria had claimed it was an engagement ring, he said, "She played with the truth a little bit." I asked him how old Victoria was when they broke up two years earlier. He said, "Same age she is now, I think."

That was great television. That was what Johnny could not do. No wonder it was threatening to everybody.

Johnny pretended that he never watched my shows—but Freddie would say, "Of course Johnny never watches, but he wanted to know if that joke was from us or you."

In Johnny's shoes I would have felt just as competitive. I've yet to meet one person who got to the top with generosity. You have to be very, very strong and push your way through, or people will shove you under. It's human nature. It's survival of the fittest. We may be out of the jungle, but we're still fighting over the one banana.

The whole staff was terrified of Johnny, and rightly so. When the press began writing that *The Tonight Show* was stale—as they periodically did—he would go on a rampage, saying, "We're going to have to clean house around here," and people played hide-and-seek, trying to avoid him in the halls. We all lived at Johnny's whim. Our one-year contracts were with Carson Productions. They paralleled his one-year contract with NBC. Each year he milked the renewal drama for every watt of suspense, playing it right down to the wire—Is this the year that Johnny Carson quits? The producers were men with families. Peter Lassally had two children to put through college, a big mortgage on a big house, several cars, and a maid. And, of course, when Jay Leno finally does take over, who knows what will happen to Freddie and Peter.

Johnny was doubly frightening because as the years passed, he seemed incapable of true warmth and intimacy. When I first knew him, I think we were both terribly shy, both loners. I think show business wore my shell away to raw sensitivity and anger—while Johnny's shell grew thicker and more impenetrable.

I remember while we were still in New York, Joanne Carson, wife number two, invited Edgar and me to Johnny's fortieth birthday party at a steak house. I looked around, and every person in the room was beholden to him—his lawyer, manager, producer, director, Ed McMahon, the head writer, me. I wondered, Where are his friends, the people who just like him for himself? Maybe Freddie De Cordova is close to him, but I wonder if that would be true if Freddie did not work for Johnny. Certainly around town, Carson has the reputation of being a solitary man.

That party was the first time I saw what stardom can do, how easily you get entrapped within a little group of dependents, and I felt sorry for Johnny. Eventually the same trap happened to me—and I escaped only when I moved back to New York, my career in shambles. Without realizing it, a star becomes surrounded by people who say, "You're the best. You're the brightest. You're the funniest. You're right and I'm wrong." Such an atmosphere is so gratifying and safe, you are tempted to hide out in your little group and never grow, staying exactly as you are, becoming more and more closed with no need to reach out to anybody else.

Odd as it may seem, during the times I was permanent guest host, I had almost nothing to do with Johnny personally, because he was not at the studio. In fact, my New York relationship with Johnny had never ripened into a friendship. That was a myth created by our amazing comedy connection on camera. During commercial breaks, when the red light went off, we found we had nothing to say to each other beyond, "How's Edgar?" and "Gee, the band sounds good." Even those banalities lapsed after thirty seconds when Johnny would fall silent, drumming his pencil on the desk.

In New York Joanne had invited us occasionally to large parties. It was heady being there with Mayor Lindsay and Truman Capote. But when wife number three, Joanna, took over in Los Angeles, those invitations stopped. She was pursuing the "A" list. I stayed on the Christmas-card list and once a year received a phone call. "Joan, this is Joanna Carson. How are you? Joan, I saw you the other night on the show. You were wonderful." Right away I would be feeling guilty—Oh, hell, I should have invited them for dinner Thursday night.

I'd say, "Oh, Joanna, thanks. You know, I've been so busy with Melissa and . . ."—thinking maybe we could have them to our house for dinner on Wednesday. "Joan, the reason I called, I'm president of SHARE and would like you to perform at our annual fund-raiser." That happened for five years. After the third year I was always busy.

I believe my relationship with Johnny was permanently shaped by his feeling, on some level, that I was his creation and so could be taken completely for granted. Indeed, I played that role, catering and kissing and thanking—and staying loyal beyond reason.

After I became the permanent guest host, I was offered talk shows opposite Carson by two huge conglomerates, Orion and Viacom—but I had sworn never to go up against Johnny. ABC wanted to make me the queen of daytime TV, and in the days before 1985, when Oprah came on the scene, it might have happened. I was wooed by the president of ABC, Tony Thomopoulos, in a secret meeting and offered obscene money. After stuffing myself on Danish pastry, I declined.

Johnny had been the one person who said, "Yes, she has talent. Yes, she is funny." He was the first person who knew what I could become. He handed me my career. I could not make myself leave that man. There was still an umbilical cord. He was JOHNNY CARSON, and he believed in me more than I believed in myself. I always thought that somewhere behind his shell, he was the one person in the business who understood me and really wished me well.

Looking back at these years, I can now see that beneath the joy and the camaraderie with Peter Lassally and Freddie De Cordova there was a tension that slowly built to a crescendo during my eight weeks a year as host. I think they eventually saw me as their baby who had grown away from them.

But I also know that Freddie and Peter, each for his own reasons, were glad when my shows were terrific. They wanted me to succeed. Their careers were involved with me. Peter particularly was an ally. Though I constantly struggled against his taste, he was still a close friend Edgar and I saw socially. He had considered himself my champion and enjoyed my success personally.

Freddie, however, considered me rude and crude. After he was hired in New York, he demoted me from occasional host back to a mere guest. Three years later, at the urging of Peter Lassally, I was reinstated. I wanted to believe that Freddie had changed his mind when I became permanent guest host, wanted to believe in all the dressing-room bonhomie. And Edgar and I saw the De Cordovas socially, for dinner on many occasions. But then Freddie wrote an autobiography that was a valentine to Johnny Carson, and I was virtually the only person in the book who was not "wonderful" and "marvelous."

Neither man wanted me to do so well that I challenged Johnny's preeminence. Peter especially believed Johnny had a proven, wildly successful formula, and any violation of it—by anybody but Johnny—would be perilous. He had a crystallized vision of *The Tonight Show* audience and what it expected. And I was sitting in for Johnny Carson on his show, and nothing should alter that show—which in justice to them had been the dominant late-night show for more than a decade. It will be interesting to see what Jay Leno's formula will be.

I think in their view of me, they believed a Marshall McLuhan theory about cool and hot TV personalities: Carson was cool and therefore welcomed into homes night after night. I, on the other hand, was hot, and people could only tolerate me in short bursts. The more comfortable I became, the bolder, the hotter I became—the more I was somebody to be kept in control. Nobody from Carson's staff ever walked into the dressing room and said, "God, the ratings were terrific this week." They always found the one failure. "Jesus, you lost Detroit." And we would think, Oh my God. We lost Detroit. That kept us off-balance, and for a long time I was quiet, not wanting to cause any trouble.

The primary way Freddie and Peter could keep me—and any of the other previous guest hosts—in line, was in their choice of guests. There were what we called "Lassally rules": No authors or politicians were allowed. Hard news was out—no relative from the KAL plane shot down by the Russians, not Corazon Aquino, now running the Philippines, not Christine Craft, the newscaster fired for being too old. A singer had to sing—so we could not have Cher, who had begun an acting career and had temporarily stopped singing. I wanted Brooke Shields, but knew we could not ask a teenage celebrity to fly from New York alone. Too many people would approach her. But it turned out there was a Lassally rule against paying for two tickets, so Edgar and I offered to pay for the second one.

Certainly my panels should not include anybody Johnny might want himself—or who would embarrass him. I remember one of my guests brought on a Yorkshire terrier dressed in a tuxedo— apparently too weird for *The Tonight Show*. Afterward, Freddie De Cordova hunted down Billy Sammeth, who booked the guests we chose, and yelled at him, "No surprises!" They wanted my segments to be safe, uncontroversial entertainment. Edgar used to say, "They don't want Italian opera, they want Strauss waltzes."

But, of course, when the guest is terrific, the host is terrific. I keep pushing to do better, which probably makes me an annoying nudge. But I am terrified of coasting. I believed on *The Tonight Show* that the more I could be myself, the better I was, the better the show. Edgar and Billy Sammeth in particular spent hours wringing out their brains trying to think of names who were unfamiliar on the talk-show circuit and would volley with me on camera—take a question and make it into a joke, a game, hit the ball back into my court.

Joan Collins, one of my favorite guests, is a pro at playing the game. One night I asked her, "Besides your husband, who's the best man you've ever been in bed with?"

"Your husband," she answered.

I shot back, "Funny, he didn't say the same about you."

So the lineup of guests was a constant issue between us and them. While they doubtless resented our second-guessing, we resented their choices. We felt they were feeding us Johnny's castoffs. They were alarmed by the unknown, by anyone who was unpredictable. Of course, those were exactly the guests that I and a younger audience liked, and once they had been on, they were fine, and, ironically, coveted by Johnny.

When we wanted Pee-wee Herman, Peter said, "He's a Letterman guest," which meant he didn't have *The Tonight Show* type of humor. When we finally got permission to have him, I heard that Johnny called up and said, "How come we haven't used Pee-wee Herman?" I really cared about Pee-wee—and I still do. I'm so sad for him. They were also nervous when I asked for Howie Mandel and Arsenio Hall, both of whom became regulars. When we were finally allowed to have Cher, they said to her right in front of me, "We want to bring you back for Johnny." That wonderful woman refused.

In our constant campaign for the right guests, Billy Sammeth was our buffer. He was brilliant dealing with Peter, with whom he had a nice father-and-son relationship, and was marvelous at persuading guests to come on the show. As well as being a professional, Billy is the best playmate in the world. Everybody loves him. He could get through to anybody and talk anybody into anything because he is charming and nonthreatening and very funny.

Peter complained, jokingly, that Billy was like a little Chihuahua at his ankle. Billy would say, "Yes, Boy George is really strange, really odd, and probably your audience won't like him. But, Peter, think how funny it could be." He would say to Peter, "You had a great show last night. Speaking of great shows, have you thought about Howie Mandel?"

If Billy struck out, then I would step in, playing the same game of "Please, Daddy, may I?" I would say, "Please, please, it's my birthday. The present I want most in the world is Bobby Goldthwaite. Come on." When David Lee Roth was really hot, I asked for him for Christmas. I think I finally got him for Passover. But everything has its price. After prostrating myself like that, I would hang up angry—at Peter and at myself. But stubborn as he was, he was still a friend, and we usually got what we wanted by relentless wheedling.

This jousting with Peter over what were known as "Joan guests" was kept jovial and joking. That was very important to us

because the Lassallys—Alice and their son and daughter—were
the only family that ever in our lives became intimate friends.

We met Peter while we were still in New York and Carson was
married to Joanne. Peter worked for the Arthur Godfrey radio
show, and Joanne Carson brought him over to *The Tonight Show*.
Joanne liked intrigue, liked being involved in the show, promoting ideas, and she wanted a producer who was her guy, who
would report to her—but right away Peter discovered he had to
be Johnny's guy. He had survived a Nazi concentration camp,
and he survived the Carson show—got in nobody's way, made no
enemies, ruffled no feathers, made sure the powerful people
were happy. When Edgar and I moved to California, the Lassallys were new there, too. I liked them, and they were the only
couple we met who liked being a family and doing things with
their children. We went on vacations together—unheard-of for
us: skiing in Vail and Aspen, day trips up to San Simeon and down
to San Diego, stopping in La Jolla to play on the beach. We took
a house together in Hawaii. Their daughter traveled with us to
Europe.

They were the one current of normality, of suburbia, we ever
had—the friends we called on a Sunday and said, "Come on over.
We'll order a pizza and make a salad. You bring the wine." They
were the only couple who ate in our kitchen. We discussed our
children—major decisions like should their daughter wear cork-
soled shoes in her high school graduation. They were the family
we piled into the station wagon with for a trip, letting the kids
go to sleep in back on the floor. It was a neighbor kind of friendship, as ordinary as we could get in a high-powered world. In the
middle of a universe of deals and networking, they made us feel
grounded in reality.

But the glue in the relationship was the friendship between
Edgar and Peter. Edgar had more in common with Peter than
with anybody else in Hollywood. Peter was Dutch, so both had
European backgrounds, both were displaced by Germans. Both
loved European food. Both loved show business and gossiping.
Both had the same outlook on life and were very dramatic and
Prussian about their authority. I remember Peter making a fed-
eral case about his daughter's boots, forbidding her to wear them

because they looked cheap—and there I was standing there wearing a pair myself.

With Peter, Edgar did not feel like a star's husband. When I was out of town, the Lassallys had him to dinner alone. The friendship worked partly because the power was equally divided. Edgar could feel superior because Peter had to butter up Freddie De Cordova and let Edgar pick up most of the checks. But Peter held my Carson career in his hands.

I was grateful to have Alice in my life. She was a reader like me, very much a New Yorker, but we were never friends to the point where we did anything alone together. I think she felt too different from me. That is a curse of celebrity—friendship with a star must be extremely hard. This affected Peter as well. Everywhere you go with me, there is a fuss—"Oh, Miss Rivers, right this way"—and everyone with you becomes a tagalong. If somebody takes me to that favorite restaurant where they've been going for years, suddenly the chef is coming out of the kitchen. For a man like Peter Lassally, who had major clout on his own, that could be a subtle putdown, especially if he felt he had made my fame and fortune possible.

When nobody is allowed to forget that I am Joan Rivers, relaxation and naturalness are hard. Alice Lassally once said to me, "You always dress like a star, don't you?" And simultaneously I am wondering why people really want to be my friend.

Trust is hard. I cannot relax. There are so few people with whom you can take the second step, because celebrity makes you four times more vulnerable. I feel constantly scrutinized and am terribly careful what cards I put on the table. But I trusted the Lassallys, and they were very important to me; I opened up to them more than to anybody else in the business.

In 1984, after my first year as permanent guest host, the Lassallys introduced us to the NBC vice president for special services, Jay Michelis. Jay became a friend who was willing to educate me in reality. He was a man bigger than life, full of energy, with a barrel chest, a booming voice—and he was absolutely outrageous. He had come up through the ranks at NBC and was a key figure in charge of relations with the affiliate stations. At a meeting he would join the portly, proper wife of the owner of a station in North Dakota and say, "Well, Martha, gettin' any lately?" and she loved it. "Ooooohhh, Jaaay!!!!" He was full of the devil.

The first time we went out to dinner, he totally embarrassed me with his language. Then I told myself, "Stop being such a prude and sit back and just enjoy him," and soon there were evenings when he became a real person who talked quietly and seriously. During one of those evenings he told me that, in fact, my ratings were higher than Johnny's. This information, Jay said, was kept from Carson for fear of upsetting him. *People* magazine confirmed this in a story, quoting the Nielsen company that in my three years as permanent guest host, Carson averaged 6.5 in the week before my guest-host shots, and I averaged 6.9.

Because advertising revenues are based on ratings, I was far more successful than I had been allowed to know.

Then, around March 1984, an event occurred that began the long decline to the end of my relationship with *The Tonight Show*. My memory of the details are of course from my point of view, but remembering, I am saddened again by the silliness of this tragedy on all sides.

Each afternoon when I arrived, I gave a secretary a copy of my monologue for the censor to review. On this particular day Lassally came to my dressing room and directed me not to use a certain joke in the monologue, one so insignificant, I can't even remember it. The censors had nothing to do with this; Peter just considered the joke not funny.

I told Edgar that I could not take it out—"It's wrong for him to ask this." Lassally was already in control of my guests, and this meant to me that he considered himself a judge of my comedy as well. I was already being driven crazy by the show's censor on questions of taste, and if I let Peter start editing my monologue for humor, he would be another door to fight through before I went in front of the camera.

Everybody in the business thinks they know comedy. Everyone has theories about what makes comedy work, except that the theories don't work. People will tell you what type of person is a television-comedy personality, and then along comes Roseanne Barr, or Whoopi Goldberg. Neil Simon has a wonderful line about this: "If we all knew what was funny, we wouldn't have to go out of town." When people interview me about comedy, I'm hard to pin down because I don't know what makes people laugh at a joke. But when they do laugh at one of mine, I fall on my knees and say, "Thank you, God."

Ordinary people say a joke to themselves, and it doesn't feel right in their mouth, doesn't sound funny in their head—so they think it must not be funny. They don't realize two things. First, only 50 percent of a joke is the words. The other 50 percent is delivery—whatever makes a comic funny, what lets him say "hat" so you laugh—and when anybody else says "hat," it's nothing. Comics have their twist on the ball, something they are born with. You can teach dramatic acting, but you cannot teach comic delivery.

Second, just because ten guys don't laugh doesn't mean the next ten guys won't laugh. No one person can decide what will be funny. Nobody. Not Neil Simon. Not Bill Cosby. Nobody. You can only guess what may work for you. Comedy, the only thing I know that is truly democratic, is for five hundred people in an audience to judge.

I have learned this truth the hard way, writing jokes on pieces of paper and putting them on the floor and saying them out loud. Sometimes you do try a joke on a comedian friend you respect. When Gary Shandling was my opening act, I would say to him, "Do you think this is funny?" He might say, "Yes, very funny"— but thoughtfully, a professional opinion, no laughter.

Peter, from time to time, brought me comedy ideas. I tried a few and they were good, and I still do them. He suggested that after a joke about a celebrity, I should look for her in the audience. "I met the Queen of England. She doesn't look anything like her stamp. For example, she's not all one color. Is the Queen here? Look for a woman in a housedress and a crown."

But most did not feel right for me, so I would swallow and say, "I'll think about that." This time, however, he was directing, and I was very upset.

His veto of that joke tripped every switch. It released the fear that comes when I feel constricted on camera, when self-consciousness inhibits the spontaneity that keeps the audience in suspense about what's coming next. Worst of all, Peter's veto released the hurt I feel when yet again the core of me becomes vulnerable, the center of where I must believe I am funny, my comedy instinct.

Peter returned to my dressing room with Freddie De Cordova. The instant I saw them, I lost control. I fled into my bathroom and locked the door and ran water in the sink to drown out their words and make them think I was preparing to go on the air.

Edgar stayed behind to handle the crisis. He did not consider our friendship with Peter. He stood my ground—doubtless with the same lack of finesse I had displayed. He refused to remove the joke. He said to Peter what he always said in those moments: "Joan doesn't respect your judgment on comedy. She doesn't respect mine. She doesn't respect anybody's."

Peter was helpless and furious. What he heard was "We don't respect your judgment on comedy." Period. So his best friends— the woman he felt he had promoted and protected—had humiliated him in front of his boss, a man he had to pretend to like and who would soon be adding this insult to his store of gossip. By the time I decided to emerge, fourteen years of friendship with Peter were gone.

A few nights later, Edgar and I met with the Lassallys to patch up the relationship. The four of us sat at our kitchen table, tears were shed, but ultimately they wanted an unconditional apology. Perhaps I did not appreciate how much we had humiliated Peter, because telling him I was terribly, terribly sorry was not enough. It was like that wonderful *New Yorker* cartoon of the wife saying to the husband, "It's not the egg rolls, Harry, it's the last twenty years."

It was such an unnecessary break, such an ego thing. From then on, Peter was correct and professional—but the tension was now just below the surface. He had to deal with us, and we had to be nice to him. We all pretended that everything was all right. We still met in the dressing room before the show and laughed. But all of us knew deep down that the relationship was not working.

I remember one week in particular that summer when America was having Olympic fever. The games were held in Los Angeles and Mary Lou Retton had just won the Gold Medal for gymnastics. We wanted her on the show. They said, "She's only sixteen. She won't be able to talk." But after a lot of arguing, they finally agreed, and Billy got her. She was adorable. The audience ate her up. "You know what I'm going to do?" she told me. "I'm going to get a red convertible with Dolby sound."

Once we realized everybody wanted to see Olympians, Edgar suggested we assemble all the winners on the show. Freddie and Peter said no because the show would have to pay them. We said, "We'll pay them." Freddie and Peter said, "How are you going to get them here?" We said we would pay for a bus. Freddie and Peter said, "They can't talk." Then how about opening the curtain and showing them? No, we could not do that. Edgar suggested putting them in the audience. Finally that was okay.

Billy and Edgar got on the phone and arranged an open invitation to be posted on bulletin boards and around the UCLA campuses where the athletes were staying. About twenty young team members showed up, swimmers, gymnasts, wrestlers, basketball players, almost all Gold Medal winners. One by one these extraordinary young men and women, the cream of the country, stood and gave their names and sport. Seeing these wonderful kids, feeling so proud to be an American, I had to fight back tears.

I guess I felt that current events, what was on America's mind, should be recognized by *The Tonight Show*. When the *Challenger* exploded, I was adamant that a comic monologue would be totally inappropriate. I pleaded with Peter to let me drop it, and he said, "You must do the monologue. That is our format." In his head the monologue was sacred.

Freddie backed him up, of course. "What is all this shit? Of course you're going to do a monologue. You're contracted to do a monologue." I told him I could not go out there and make jokes when men and women had just died in a national disaster. I was sure in my bones that right now America did not want to laugh. Peter and Freddie were just as sure that the Carson show was an entertainment show and existed to make people forget their troubles. If people wanted to hear about the *Challenger*, let them tune in to Ted Koppel.

I finally obeyed my inner voice, and out-and-out refused to do a monologue. I went onstage and voiced my feelings. The reaction from the audience was that we were all the same person. That we all shared a common experience in grief. It was incredibly moving.

Though I am easily hurt, my need to think the best of people, my desire to have everything work out, is powerful. Deep disillusionment comes hard and slowly. The knowledge that Freddie and Peter did not respect my instincts was a profound blow that amplified much milder slights that would ordinarily have seemed unimportant. Increasingly, reluctantly, during those last few years, Edgar and I recognized a pattern of disinterest.

In all my years as a guest host, I had never received a note or a call from Carson about a show of mine. Not thinking of me as part of the Carson "family," the chief executive officer of NBC and chairman of the board, Grant Tinker, bought a table at a benefit dinner honoring Billy Wilder and invited the whole Carson group—except me. When I had Bill Cosby on as a guest, Brandon Tartikoff, the president of NBC-TV, sat with him in his dressing room—which was right next to mine. Brandon never bothered to step next door and knock and say hello to me. He escorted Cosby to the set and stood with him in the wings till Bill went on—and again did not bother to come over to me during a commercial and say hello.

I know this sounds silly now, but then I felt humiliated, which was stupid and sentimental, an uproar in Lilliput, but I so wanted to think of that show as a place where I belonged. Everyone told me that these were corporations, and they are cold, and I had always said, "No, no, no. This is my home base." So the golden-haired girl was having problems! "Nothing is perfect," I told myself. "You'll survive the problems because the show is good." As I entered the summer of 1984, I still thought my heart and best interests lay with Johnny Carson.

11

ooooo

Since the success came from doing what I had always done, my life changed very little. I worked the same hours with the same intensity, still sat on the bathroom floor organizing my comedy, still went each night to some little club to get new material for the Carson show. There was really only one difference—my comedy lines now brought forth a *tremendous* reaction, and were picked up all over the country—*The Orlando Sentinel* quoted me about Jackie Onassis's marriage to Aristotle Onassis: "That's why God gave women sex, so we can shop the next day." Or *The National Enquirer* was quoting me on my lack of sex appeal—"Rapists tap me on the shoulder and ask, 'Have you seen any girls?' "

On the other hand, I was being inundated with decisions about publicity, bookings, offers, investments, contracts, tax strategies—and Edgar was constitutionally unable to relinquish control, unable to trust the managers and agents who become necessary to the smooth running of a celebrity career. Proudly quoting his favorite aphorism, "God is in the detail," he was unable to stop obsessing about the minutiae of our life.

Feeling responsible for each move, fearful of a wrong step,

trying to double-check every person, Edgar was running without a stop. He would call two people at our accountants and ask for the same information and see if they had the same answer. He would assign a task to a secretary, and then, if she delayed, make the call himself. At night he woke repeatedly to make notes on a pad kept on the bedside table. When he tried to relax, he was distracted, nervous. He completely lost his sense of humor.

In December of 1984, his fifty-ninth year, Edgar's overextension, his stress, came to a culmination. He went to a routine meeting at the office of my career consultant, Bernie Brillstein, who told me later that Edgar was crazed, ready to explode, twitching, talking a mile a minute, pacing the room, smoking without cease.

He arrived home at around six, poised to blow sky-high. Just at that moment Melissa came into the office and told Edgar and me she had decided not to go East to college; she wanted to enroll at UCLA a mile away and live with a California girlfriend. Both Edgar and I—especially Edgar, who was a stickler for good education—were determined that she get away from home and have the experience of an eastern education. She had been accepted at the University of Pennsylvania, so we thought this long-playing, ugly argument had been settled.

Melissa is a good fighter—a chip off both old blocks—and suddenly we were in one of those operatic teenage uproars that happen in every family. Edgar and I erupted. Melissa ran upstairs to her room, and Edgar, losing all control, ran after her. In her room Melissa yelled, "Mommy's a bitch!," and Edgar yelled, "Don't you call your mother that!" A random motion of his hand made her think he was going to slap her, and she yelled, "That's it! I'm leaving home!"—and ran down to her car—with me behind her shouting, "You're not going anywhere!" and wrestling her in the car and grabbing the keys out of the ignition.

Dorothy Melvin, our assistant, later told me she heard Edgar calling softly, "Dorothy. Dorothy." She went into the stairwell and found him leaning on the railing of the landing, his face a dead-man's gray. "Please call the paramedics," he said calmly. "I think I'm having a heart attack."

She ran along the hall screaming for me. While she called 911,

I raced upstairs. Edgar was lying on the bed. I could not believe that this was serious. With a heart attack nothing shows—no blood, no guts on the floor, no death in front of me—just Edgar having a pain on the bed in his nice gray-flannel slacks and his impeccably tailored Dunhill blazer. But that was classic Edgar—the English gentleman who, when told, "Well, old boy, the blighters got you this time and we'll have to cut off your leg"—answers, "Pity."

Our marvelous houseman, Jacob Bjerre, who had been a medic in Denmark, laid Edgar on the floor, and I ripped a blanket off the bed and covered him and held his hand and kept saying over and over, "It's all right, honey. You're going to be fine. I love you. It's okay."

The paramedics arrived in minutes, hooked Edgar up to an IV, and ordered me out of the way, but I kept sneaking back through Melissa's connecting bathroom, saying, "There's no reason I can't be in the room. I'm not in your way. I'm up against the wall." I needed to be with him. "I don't think he's going to make it," I heard one of the medics say. I had to let that go right past my head.

We could hear Melissa downstairs crying hysterically. "Quiet that girl," the paramedic said. Dorothy took her outside, but she grew even more hysterical, screaming, "I killed my daddy! Don't die, Daddy! Don't die." Finally, to shock Melissa silent, Dorothy slapped her face.

I told Edgar I was going to ride in the ambulance with him. As I left the room, I overheard a medic say, "Over my dead body." My husband looked up from the depths of his terror and said, "You don't know my wife."

I climbed into that ambulance ahead of them and tied myself down with the safety belt and sat there gripping my pocketbook like a club. Nobody suggested I move. As they loaded him into the back, Edgar said, "Tell Melissa I love her."

I sat there saying over and over to myself, "Please, God. Please, God. Please, God," and calling out to Edgar, "I'm right here, Edgar. Right here in front."

Dorothy, who followed with Melissa, tells me the ambulance, its siren on, flew through the streets. In my memory the ambulance crawled, and, grasping at straws, I thought this was a good sign. They must not be very worried. When we arrived at the UCLA Medical Center, we rushed right past the red tape. The hospital grabbed one of the top Los Angeles heart men literally out of the elevator. That is what celebrity is all about. Anybody else, there would have been a dozen forms to fill out and the surgeon would have gone home and let his assistant take the case.

Now Melissa became very strong, stronger than I was. We were put in a small room off the emergency room, and along the wall were computer screens showing the heartbeat of the cases inside. All of the lines were jumping around, except Edgar's. His was almost straight. He was dying in front of us, but I did not understand this then, and the ignorance *was* bliss. "Look how good Daddy's line is," I kept saying. "He's going to be all right."

The doctor told us the operation would not be done until the next day; he wanted Edgar to stabilize. We should go home and get some sleep—"Everything's fine. No point in your staying here." I took that to be a *very* good sign. In actual fact, it was the first time a doctor lied to me; I found out later he thought Edgar would not last the night.

At home I was back into my normal life, taking a bath and luxuriating in its hotness, and thought, Edgar's going to be all right; life will continue. Melissa and I slept in my bed. I really thought the worst was over, and he would be sitting up in four days. I woke at dawn, called the hospital, and got an orderly too inexperienced to lie. He told me, "It's touch and go."

In the car rushing back to the hospital, my body was clammy, my fingers numb and tingling. I felt I was living underwater. I could not believe that this was happening. This was not the way it was supposed to be. *I* was the one people told, "Take care of yourself." And doubling the tragedy, Edgar's death would maim the person he loved most in the world. To Melissa, beyond me, he gave his totally unselfish devotion. He adored her.

I just left the car with the keys in the ignition in front of the emergency entrance and hurried to Edgar's bedside, where, as I arrived, he was having another heart attack. The doctor asked him, "Tell us the pain, one to ten." Edgar answered quietly, "Ten."

I was torn by a bizarre, schizophrenic tension. It was inconceivable that his body was racked with pain, because I couldn't see him suffering. When I go to a doctor for a simple tune-up, I say, "Doctor, don't let me die." Here was Edgar saying conversationally, "Ten."

I could not let him see my panic.

After the doctors pulled him through, Edgar was conscious, and I pretended that the previous night had been the dangerous one and told him, "Thank God you didn't die last night, because I couldn't go on without you. You are my everything." I told him, "You've got to get well. No one else is going to buy me a Fabergé frame." That little joke was enough of a good-bye for me. He knew now how precious he was in my life.

That evening the doctors told me that if they didn't do a triple bypass immediately, there was no hope. Even then, there was only a 20 percent chance he would pull through. Melissa and I went back to Edgar and pretended he had options. "It's up to you," we told him. Meanwhile the surgeons were scrubbing.

He said, "I've been thinking—after nineteen years, we are finally gathering in the harvest." But I was not going to indulge myself with a deathbed scene. I refused to change into Mrs. Maudlin, all weepy, so I did what I always do when I am tense: I began making jokes. Edgar agreed to the operation, but sensed the odds. He said, "I want to donate my organs." Very sassy, I said, "Who'd want your organs? I feel sorry for the guy who gets your eyes." A wonderful last thing to say to your husband, right? But it meant to him that I thought he would be okay. He would not believe I was shallow enough to make jokes at his deathbed. Little did he know.

As the white-coated orderlies moved him onto the litter, he spoke to Melissa: "Take care of Mommy." Then, trying to comfort me, telling me he was fine, he squeezed out an Edgar joke. "If I don't make it," he said, "give Billy Sammeth a bonus. But not too big."

That was our way, a taproot of our deep affection—the willingness, the ability, to cover pain with black, ironic humor. If you can laugh at something, that says you're superior to it. See, I'm laughing, so it's serious, but I'm really okay. The day of my mother's funeral, I told the hairdresser, "Make me look good or else you'll be doing my mother's hair this afternoon."

I watched the litter disappear down the hall. I had never imagined life without Edgar, had always thought I would go first. He was the one remaining companion in my little nuclear family. Melissa had one foot out of the nest. "Hi, Mom," she'd say as she changed her clothes for a date. "Good-bye, Mom," she'd say as she left.

At such moments, with death in the wings, the past conflicts, the old frustrations and tensions that strain a marriage, become nonsense. I saw them in a new perspective. They were like a broken fingernail—you say, "Ugh, damn"—but never think to be grateful that the fingers are working.

I was very, very grateful that in my own way I had told Edgar how much I loved him. It is tragic when people have no chance to tie up loose ends and never say even three sentences to somebody they love before the person dies. The last time I spoke to my mother, we had an argument on the phone, and the next day she was dead from a heart attack. I never said to her, "You're wonderful and you're my mother and you're my friend and I love you. You've done a great job." The regret has never left me.

I went home for an hour to distract myself. In the bathroom I went down on the floor, flat out, no knees, like in biblical times. I said, "God, what's the deal? What do you want?" I said, "You won, God. Here I am on the floor." In *The Ten Commandments*, when Charlton Heston lay down, God spoke to him. So I waited for the lightning and thunder and the big voice telling me, too, "Do this." Finally I had to accept that God wasn't into theatrics that night. There was peace in that—getting back to fundamentals, back to the simple faith of "I believe in you, God. Please tell me what I must do."

Much later, when I told Edgar, our joke became ". . . and God said, 'No more Elizabeth Taylor jokes.'"

In the hospital we waited eight hours in a room, and I tried to reassure Melissa that nothing was her fault. Edgar, I said, was a heart attack waiting to happen—and we were lucky it happened there with help all around him. In a way she had saved his life.

When Edgar came out of the operating room, he was weak, but essentially fine—until five-thirty that morning when his lungs began to fill with fluid. Gradually he slipped into a profound unconsciousness the doctors classified as an ICU psychosis—a violent coma. The operation had been a success, but Edgar was lying strapped to the table and barely alive. The roller coaster began—hope and despair, hope and despair.

Every time I had gone home, something terrible happened, so I moved into the hospital. I decided, right or wrong, that Melissa should not live there. She belonged with her friends; the people she could freely talk to. I was trying to spare her the awful atmosphere of a deathwatch by letting her think that things were going okay. Each day at noon she phoned. Each day after school she insisted on coming to the hospital until long after dark when I would force her to go home, saying, "Daddy is on the mend."

At the hospital I had a room on Edgar's floor and shared it with Dorothy Melvin, who unselfishly stayed with me through most of the nightmare.

But still I felt utterly alone, utterly helpless, no source of strength but myself—and I was empty. I believe that one draws strength from others, and I had not realized how much I drew from Edgar.

The ICU was a long, narrow room with eight tables, side by side. On each was a naked figure draped in a hissing, gurgling, pinging ganglion of life-support systems. Otherwise the room was eerily quiet, the special nurses moving surely from patient to patient in a sort of choreography.

Edgar lay on his table looking like Dr. Frankenstein's monster, an oxygen cup over his nose. Tubes ran to his lungs, to a balloon under his heart, to bags of pus and bags of urine, to plasma bags and IV bags and to every machine known to man.

I thought, If Edgar is going to hear a voice, feel a touch, smell a smell, it should be mine. Something in all that confusion and pain and madness should be telling him through his coma that it's okay. Day after day I stood by his head, holding his hand, rubbing his shoulders and face. A nurse said maybe he wasn't coming back because he was afraid, so I kept telling him, "Edgar, it's Wednes-

day morning. The doctor said the operation was a *success*."
"Honey, it's Friday afternoon. Everything's *fine*." He liked winning, so I told him, "Honey, you're a day ahead of schedule." I
would appeal to him, "Edgar you cannot do this to Melissa." I told
my good friend Treva Silverman what I was doing, and she said,
"His first words are going to be, 'Will you shut up! I'm trying to
get some sleep.'"

I would lose my nerve and decide that what I was willing into
him was not enough. I had little faith in the doctors. They were
not ones we had investigated and gathered from the four corners
of the earth. They were the ones we found in the elevator on
Thursday night. They turned out to be wonderful, but we could
also have found Schwartz the Butcher.

I would go back into the hall, pacing up and down, sure Edgar
was going to die. "What have I done?" I wondered. "Is this God
saying, 'Thought you had a good year, did you? The joke's on
you.'" I wondered how I could ever again put on the beads and
the feathers and hit the stage screaming nonsense about big rings
and first wives. It was the first time I had ever felt my determination was not going to be enough.

My own heart doctor advised me that if I didn't let up, I was
going to be lying right beside Edgar. So now I was walking
around in my hospital greens with a portable heart monitor and
electrodes fastened onto me while I wept, my face wet and hot,
pockets filled with tissues. At good news and bad, tears were a
reflex I could never control.

I did not care that people saw me. At first I thought maybe I
should be embarrassed walking around looking ninety years old
with swollen eyes and a red nose, but a camaraderie had been
formed in those halls—a camaraderie of fear and sorrow but also
of comfort. During times like these, patients, relatives, and
friends are in pain, and they all know when to look away and
when to come over. In the entire month I spent there, only one
person had the insensitivity to ask me for an autograph.

Two couples asked me to talk to their terribly ill children—one
time when being a celebrity helped because comforting them
lessened my own anguish and gave me strength. It gave me back

my old facade: See, I am in trouble, but I can reach out to you and your sick child, so I must be a strong person, not this bag of tears.

People reached out to me. One night in the hall outside the ICU, a poor woman connected to a pole draped with every machine in America rolled it all the way down the hall to me and just said, "Don't forget that Jesus loves you"—and turned and wheeled her pole all the way back. Another man I had seen in the ICU was now ambulatory and rolled his IV holder up to me and said, "For what it's worth, none of us remember what went on in there." That was one of the big things that got me through. When Edgar's veins were collapsing and they didn't know where to give him another injection and he was so sick but fighting—I hung on to that.

After a week by his bed one of the nurses said, "If I hear, 'Edgar, it's going to be all right' one more time . . ." I was so hurt. Soon afterward, I was pushed aside as a corps of nurses, interns, residents, swooped down on him. I stood in the hall looking through a tiny window, watching outside my feelings, watching myself watching them—as five doctors and nurses bent over his inert body like a human tent working on him, pushing, pumping, socking, injecting. Afterward, I learned they were trying to bring him back to life—that his heart had stopped, that he had died.

Finally the doctors stood up. They had pulled him back. And that nurse I had annoyed came to me and said, "Come in and tell him some more, 'Everything is going to be all right.' " Everybody wanted to pull him through. The resident spent most of three nights watching the numbers on the monitor.

I did everything I could think of to wake him. I brought in a tape recorder, hoping his favorite music could strike home. Gershwin, Linda Ronstadt, Ella Fitzgerald. I wore heavy perfume so maybe he would smell me. I thought perhaps if I made jokes, he would come to and laugh. I pretended his heart monitor was Nielsen ratings and told him, "Edgar, your numbers are terrific." I said, "If you really want to die, wake up and eat the food here," and, "I'm going to call Sunny von Bülow and see how things are on the East Coast." I called into his ear, "*Edgar,* if you don't answer me, I'm going to pull the plug." Nothing. "*Edgar,* do you hear me? One. Two. Three. Okay, I've pulled your plug. Damn it, I pulled out your razor."

A nurse said to me, "He's going to make it. He's like a turtle," and I started to cry. Edgar had given me a diamond turtle pin because my career had always been like a turtle—ugly little struggling steps—so right away I put on that pin and never took it off—and did not worry that people would think, Mrs. Rich Bitch wearing diamonds while her husband dies.

One night at 2:00 A.M. I was there beside Edgar, and Billy Sammeth came by. We began helping the nurse make cold packs by filling rubber gloves with ice. Then we got silly and blew up the gloves into balloons. With people dying around us, the long, shadowy room lit only by a light at the nurse's desk and the green glow of computer screens—Billy and I laughed hysterically as we hit five-fingered balloons back and forth across my husband's body. Totally macabre.

When a situation becomes *really* awful, I get silly and laugh, make it absurd. The laughter helps me convince myself, "I can get through this." I feel a lightness, a release. I suppose that is why I am a comedian—I can do that for myself and for audiences.

Another time Billy and I were riding down in an elevator crowded with doctors. Suddenly Billy turned to me and said, "They sued him and they won. The man doesn't have a house, a car, doesn't have any practice left." The elevator became very, very quiet. "I would be a witness all over again after what that butcher did," Billy went on, "and I actually enjoyed lying on the stand." You could hear a stethoscope drop. I tried to remember everything funny that happened so I could make Edgar laugh when he woke up.

Even humor could not defend me in the second week when I came into the ICU and found a crowd of doctors around Edgar's bed, bringing him back after his heart had stopped for the second time. When I went home for a few hours of rest, Melissa asked me if there was anything new. "Nothing," I lied. She said, "Tell me the truth." So I took her arm, and we walked up and down the long hall the length of our house. We must have walked a mile. I told her what she already knew, that Daddy might die.

It was the first time we had actually verbalized the truth of what had happened to our nice little life. We were saying out loud to each other, "Okay, we can never put it together again the same way, so let's see if we can step into the next chapter."

We kept walking, up and down, up and down, arm in arm, talking about everything—what I wanted for her, what Edgar wanted. I talked about the importance of family, how sad it was that Edgar and I never had other children so there would be a crowd walking together, not just the two of us. Suddenly Melissa said, "Mom, I've got to say it. Maybe this is Daddy's time."

Melissa saying this was a tremendous comfort to me. I was struggling so hard to get him through, to keep it from being his time. But how much pain do you put somebody through? Maybe we should accept the worst, she was saying, so that if it happens, it will be easier to bear.

Without realizing it, we were preparing ourselves mentally. Nature does that for you. We were constructing in our minds a future without Edgar, which was very important at that moment. Until that Thursday, I did not think I could go on without him. Now, with Melissa's help, I knew we really *could* go on, no matter what. I drew a great deal of strength from that.

I wrote Edgar's obituary that night. If he died, I wanted it to be correct and complete. Nobody knew Edgar's history, the important jobs he had held. People thought of him only as Joan Rivers's husband—and I was sick of that. When I finished the obituary, I felt peaceful. I had faced what had to be faced.

After two weeks of coma, doctors began warning me there might be brain damage, and we talked about letting him die. I think I could have done it, but nobody was giving me a solid judgment; it was always maybe.

I had a performance scheduled at the Century Plaza Hotel, and Billy Sammeth persuaded me to keep the date for my own sanity. I was amazed to go through traffic and see living people and realize they had been there all this time, while my whole world was the UCLA hospital. Daily life had been continuing full throttle, and here I was up onstage in front of people who had come here to be happy, and *could* be happy. Nobody in the audience was thinking about tubes in the throat and watching heart monitors. Everybody was alive and having a good time and flooding the room with an energy of *life*. I soaked it up—but it had nothing to do with reality. It felt like a movie. The only place that felt real was the hospital, those halls, that bedside, that air sounding with gurgles and pings and the whoosh, whoosh of respirators.

One day, weeks after Edgar was first admitted to the hospital, a nurse was holding his hand, and suddenly his hand moved, felt her fingers and worked down to her fingernails, which were short. "Where's Joan?" he said.

I rushed to his bed—but he was gone again, the same silent body of the past weeks. I was devastated. "*Edgar*, open your eyes!" I yelled. "Enough of this! Open your eyes!" He opened them and then slipped away. I felt then that I was getting through, but the neurologists talked to me again about brain damage from oxygen starvation, preparing me for my husband drooling in a bed, preparing me for the terrifying possibility that he, in tremendous pride, might *want* to die.

The next day I persuaded those wonderful nurses—they really saved Edgar's life—to use a child's oxygen tent instead of the oxygen mask that had clearly been irritating him. They were adjusting it over his head and torso while I was taping it to the wall, barking out instructions to anyone who would listen, when suddenly I heard Edgar's voice say, "Joan, stop trying to run the hospital." He had come back.

Of course, *I* wanted his first words to be, "Joan, I love you." But the first time he could really talk, I asked, "Okay, what would you have done differently in your life?" He said, "Nothing much." I was thrilled.

In a few days Edgar was moved to an ICU transition room. When he learned we had installed an electric seat to carry him up the back stairs, he picked up the phone by his bed and called his accountant, Michael Karlin, to be sure that if somebody was hurt using it, we were covered by insurance. That cheered me up. Edgar was himself again.

I felt excited, but not on the tremendous high I would have expected. I had somewhere in those weeks stopped allowing myself the luxury of hope. Whenever the doctors said Edgar was out of the woods, he was not out of the woods. When you are on that roller coaster of hope and laughter, despair and horror, lifting yourself back up becomes harder and harder.

After six weeks, he came home. Our room was full of flowers. The best linens were on the bed. He sat down on the bed and said, "It's good to be here." On his table were his books and magazines. On his pillow was a sign made by Melissa with dozens of colored Magic Markers, saying, WELCOME HOME, DADDY. I felt a great calmness. We had come through. Everything was going to be back the way it was and *should* be.

One night during the hospital ordeal, I had talked to a woman outside the ICU door whose husband was back in the hospital after a second heart attack. She told me, "Get ready. This is not the worst. The worst is when he comes home and his personality is changed." Of course, I thought, Not in my case. I'll bring him around.

How naïve I was. The man lying on the bed, twenty-five pounds thinner, moving gingerly about the house, looked like my husband, but Edgar was no longer inside that body. He was like a jigsaw puzzle, painfully put together, but at the end one piece was missing in the head.

I rented him Woody Allen's *Broadway Danny Rose,* and Edgar hardly smiled. Depressions plagued him, and he retreated to his bed for hours—or he was swept by mood swings. Some emotional governor was missing. The rage that reached back to his childhood was now on a hair trigger—and almost encouraged by a psychiatrist Edgar saw to pacify his doctor. This man, a South African all too happy to sit around discussing books and the old country, told Edgar the cause of the heart attack was his habit of locking up emotions. He must start speaking his mind, start unloading his stress.

Melissa and I would even encourage him, saying, "Tell us, tell us. Don't hold it in." Melissa, looking back years later, wisely said to me, "Daddy thought if he didn't let everything out, he'd just explode. But once somebody gets used to blowing up, it must be very hard to put things back in check again—and his whole life got sort of crazy."

So the cap was off the bottle. He became agitated over nothing—"Get the dogs out of the bedroom"—"This soup is cold"—raging if his suit was not back from the cleaner. He could not concentrate and changed TV channels incessantly with the clicker—and was furious if I wanted one show and he didn't.

He tried to take charge of the business right away, so the accountant brought him checks to sign. He came down to the office to go through his mail—and was upset when he found a clean desk, found that the accountant and Dorothy Melvin and Billy Sammeth and I had done very well without him, found that the water had closed over and the flow continued.

Part of his anger was at himself, a rage of frustration. Before the attack Edgar's mind was an immediately accessible card file. He matter-of-factly remembered every name, every date, could tell you the author and publisher of every book he had read, knew what each person in a meeting had said, knew every comma in a contract.

He came out of the hospital with his mind muddled, distracted and forgetful. I still think his brain might have been damaged during those episodes when he was brought back from death. He had trouble grasping complexities and remembering details. His memory was so undependable, he carried his own phone number in his wallet. When he did stumble mentally, his embarrassment and self-disgust were profound.

I have been told—and believe it—that anger is not a basic emotion. It is a symptom, a way of cloaking and expressing feelings too awful to experience directly—hurt, bitterness, grief, and, most of all, fear. For both of us death was now a palpable presence, waiting just out of sight.

Edgar was frightened to be alone, particularly at night. For a year he kept a nurse with us twenty-four hours, hiring the pretty young girls from the hospital ICU during their off-duty hours. He had never exercised in his life, but he began a program with a treadmill. He ended his four-pack-a-day smoking habit—and I told him if he started again, I would pull out pictures I took of him in the ICU with his 185 tubes and bags of urine and pus and plasma.

He had always been the stoic British type about his health, never a hypochondriac. Now, he worried about every little pain and went to doctors constantly. I think the only moments he felt truly safe were the four times a day when the nurse was taking his pulse and blood pressure.

But there were two Edgars, one that frightened child, scared that any ripple in his life might signal another attack, and a second Edgar asserting his independence, fighting to prove that he was as good as ever, that he could still perform, could still be the keeper of my flame.

He began defying us all. The doctor told him not to drive for six months, and he got right behind the wheel. I refused to drive with him, and we had awful fights about that. When I performed in Lake Tahoe, the doctor told him not to go with me; the air was too thin. He went anyway. At the time I thought it was a death wish. But I think now he was in part, like so many other invalids, using illness as a power play—"You better watch out for me very carefully. Put me at the center of your life." I was a patsy for that ploy.

Soon after Edgar returned from the hospital, we began living by unspoken rules. All of us were careful not to upset him and cause another heart attack, careful to walk on eggs and keep him calm—do what he wanted the way he wanted. When we broke those rules, Edgar found ways to remind us. When I snapped, when I could no longer stuff my feelings of anger, when we had a fight—Edgar twice checked into a hospital.

I think that under the pressure of a life-altering crisis, a husband and wife revert to type, each losing the small conscious stratagems that have kept them in balance: My need to be the nurturer took over, Edgar was another baby to take care of, and I was the little mother—cheering him up, making sure he received perfect care and was getting better.

The keystone of Edgar's character was the need to keep himself and the world around him in control. So any loss of control—helplessness—left him vulnerable and terrified, put him in a downward spiral. His sense of impotency fed his fear, which increased his frustration—which came out as anger—which increased his loss of control—which multiplied the fear and anger—which made people avoid him—which made him even more isolated, and angry. He was driving himself crazy—and driving everybody around him crazy, too.

The one element that gave him a sense of power, even manhood, was money. He had gone into partnership with Tom Pileggi on several housing developments and made several million dollars. Now, convinced that he did not have long to live, he acted out his dream of wealth.

Edgar redid the house lavishly and bought an eighteenth-century breakfront for over $100,000. The antique Oriental rug cost more than our governess made in a year. He bought all new luggage from Louis Vuitton, one suitcase just for shoes. He sat in our study bidding by phone against Malcolm Forbes for a Fabergé frame. When we went to London, he went to Wartski's jewelers and bought me a pearl choker with a big black diamond in it—and Marie of Romania's necklace of Fabergé eggs. When you are buying Fabergé pieces five at a clip, the clerks are on their knees to you.

He came back to the hotel with boxes of Fabergé animals and set them out on the desk and asked me to help him decide which to buy. I never asked the price, but made my stock speech: "This is nuts, why are we doing this? It's stupid"—and then picked the pig and the rooster.

Of course, I enjoyed money and buying—that was one of the bonds with Edgar. But I never, never wanted to spend *big* money. Part of me has always been my father the doctor, who pinched every penny and taught me to be terrified of poverty. However, there was no way I could control Edgar—nor did I want to have that battle. He was already emasculated by his condition, and I was still terrified of the effects of a major fight. And there was a second side of me that watered down my resolve, the part that took after my mother, who wanted to live like a duchess on no money and prayed for whooping-cough epidemics. So I went along with Edgar—and once the money was spent took pleasure in the luxuries I had always denied myself.

Edgar bought me a Fabergé pin once owned by the czar's sister. He just handed it to me—"This is for you." I screamed, "Take it back! Take it back! Are you crazy?" He said, "If you don't want it, I'll never buy you another thing." I thought, Well, wait a minute. He said, "Wear it. Put it on. You work so hard. You deserve it." It was madness.

When we were in Atlantic City, he would take a helicopter up to Bucks County in Pennsylvania to see Tom Pileggi, who teased him, called him "Onassis." When we were in London, we stayed in the Royal Suite at Claridges—which I loved—and he had a car and driver waiting for him all day at the curb. He spent days at his London tailor, and clothes were delivered by the dozens. He wanted the respect he no longer received and he got it by playing the rich man.

This man, fighting for his sanity, still searching for a source of ego and self-respect, was the husband who would soon be leading us into the jungle of the Fox Broadcasting Network, a place populated by men able and willing to kill us.

I had taken the reins of my life during his illness and did not release them for two years. He was a man too unstable to be the "rock" in command of my impulses, persuading me with pros and cons and practical consequences. His natural caution had increased to paranoia, and his priorities were reversed, details becoming more important than fundamental issues.

After he had talked to the agents and lawyers and the manager, I would call them privately and second-guess him—tell the agent, "Just get the best money you can, and I'll take it"—all the while trying to give Edgar back his self-esteem, his feeling of importance in my life, without really giving him control. And Tom Pileggi was there to keep me from making mistakes.

My independence from Edgar was not entirely a lack of trust. After running my own affairs for a while, I was feeling my oats. I was beginning to trust myself, feeling terrific on a new level of confidence. Everything was being handled just fine.

But of course Edgar knew he was being shunted aside, and sometimes we *had* to tell him the truth—that a contract was wrong or somebody had tried to cheat us—and I was terrified that such incidents would bring on another attack. And, indeed, often during a moment of pressure, he would feel a pain in his chest and go upstairs and lie down.

We no longer had totally happy moments, none of the highs we once had shared. The one exception was at Melissa's coming-out cotillion. Edgar escorted her in the processional—while I sat sobbing because after all our despair, against all odds, there he was, his daughter on his arm.

What helped me survive this life-threatening blow to our marriage was constructive denial. I made myself believe that this horror would pass, and we would come out the other side stronger than ever. I had this romantic image of us—two old crocks laughing at the absurdity of these times.

But in the spring of 1985 I was performing in Virginia, as usual without Edgar, who was frightened of making long flights. I was with my little entourage of Billy Sammeth, Ann Pierce, and Jason Dyl. We had a free day and visited the reconstructed Colonial town at Williamsburg. The weather was poor, Williamsburg was deserted, and we felt *in* Colonial times—in a time capsule, not tourists, because there were no other tourists.

Our guide was an elderly, thin-lipped DAR type who treated us like children. She said she had seen me once before and didn't like me much, and disapproved of Jason, who was wearing a woman's colonial mobcap that we had bought at a souvenir stand. Ann and I did not have warm clothes, so we borrowed coats from the limo driver's wife. Ms. DAR refused to take us on the tour until we had watched a little movie about the town. So four grown-ups sat in a row on a bench and then were tested to see whether we had paid attention to our Colonial history. She thought we were the dregs of show business and hated taking us around—and we thought it was hilarious.

During the day I realized how silly and loose I felt, and for the first time since the heart attack I consciously thought, I'm having fun. And I'm having fun because I'm away from Edgar.

After twenty years of marriage I was happy because I was not with my husband. That is a terrible, terrible truth to admit to yourself; I was barely able to face it and felt guilty and frightened, and pushed away the thought because there was nothing I felt I could do to change the situation.

I understood then that my life was the last place he belonged. It was too hectic, too pressured, too fast-forward. I was doing *The Tonight Show* and *Hollywood Squares,* Las Vegas, and weekend concerts around the country, I had begun to write my book *Enter Talking.* I was living the life Edgar used to love, used to describe as an Italian opera. But now he craved calm and companionship. He needed somebody with a picnic basket.

I also understood—selfishly perhaps—that for self-preservation I needed something to balance all the intensity. I craved free moments filled with air bubbles, with silliness and giddiness. When I had an hour of my own, I wanted to drop water bombs.

I began looking forward to going on the road alone. Edgar would telephone and say wistfully, "You sound wonderful," and I would say, "I miss you, I miss you"—while a little corner of me was glad he was not there. I would be speared by guilt, thinking, What a terrible, terrible, disloyal way to feel. But when I came home to that pressure chamber, the house loomed like a prison.

I was frightened. Melissa was leaving the nest and going to college in Pennsylvania. I was living in a place without cheerfulness, with a husband in bed every night at nine o'clock holding the TV control wand. Feeling he was *really* a star's husband, knowing that whatever power he still had came through me, Edgar was resentful and competitive. He would not let me read *Time* and *Newsweek* until he had read them, even if that took him a week—so I had to take out duplicate subscriptions. Any book he bought I could not read first—so two copies of the same book sat on our bedside table.

When we did go out to dinner, he wanted to be the star in social situations and would cut me off in the middle of a story and tell one he thought was funnier and better. At the table, as though it were a joke, I would say to him, "Hey, we're on the same side," but then I would step back. He was still my husband. I was glad that he could have even that place in the sun.

12

°°°°°

T_he Late Show Starring Joan Rivers_ was a self-contained saga of the folly, the infantile behavior, the ego exercises, the fear and ambition, the pain and delight, that pervade backstage show business. The plot was driven not by business considerations, but by the characters' needs and compulsions and terrors. Nobody in the drama rose above the foolishness. Not me, not Edgar, not the chairman and CEO of Twentieth Century–Fox, Barry Diller, not any of the lesser executives. To this day, so much of what happened makes no sense to me. All I know for sure is that when the curtain on the tragedy descended, the smartest man in Hollywood was the dumbest, forced to give five nights of late-night programming back to Fox's affiliated stations. I was so deeply wounded, I nearly did not survive. And my husband was dead.

The story begins in July of 1985. Flying back from London after a successful series of talk shows on the BBC, I was asleep and Edgar settled into a _Newsweek_ cover story about the British publisher Rupert Murdoch.

Murdoch had bought the Twentieth Century–Fox Film Corporation for $325 million and spent $2 billion buying outright six Metromedia VHF television stations in New York, Los Angeles,

Washington, D.C., Chicago, Dallas, and Houston, covering 22 percent of the country. With those as a core he planned to add affiliated independent UHF stations and form a quasi–fourth network that might eventually be broadcast globally on his Sky Channel satellite.

Edgar realized that they needed a high-impact name like mine to launch this network, to give them credibility with those stations they were courting around the country. I was Johnny Carson's replacement, the number-one comedienne–talk person at that moment in America. ABC, to get me, had offered two specials, one of which was Barbara Walters's time slot before the Academy Awards. Fox, with somebody like me as the lead ship in its fleet of programs, would no longer be dismissed with, "Yeah, right, a lot of *Leave It to Beaver* reruns," a station you pass by on your way to the show you really want to watch.

Also, Edgar knew Johnny Carson had signed a two-year contract with NBC. Our contracts with Carson Productions had always matched Johnny's. But this time when we opened negotiations with Carson's lawyer, Henry Bushkin, he offered us only one year. Suddenly the rules had changed. Why did I have one year to Johnny's two? Was I on probation? I had once asked Peter Lassally how many nights he would allow me if I stopped being funny—"seven or eight?" He succinctly answered, "Three." If my ratings had dropped at NBC, someone else would have been in, and I would have been out with no place to go.

When Edgar broached the idea of approaching Fox, I said, "If you think it's right, do it." I was not really expecting anything, and happy that Edgar would have a deal to push that would engross him. I thought this would stabilize him, get his mind off the pills, the gallstones, the gout, the fear. But I did not take the prospect seriously.

The day after we arrived from London, Edgar phoned our lawyer, Peter Dekom, and asked him to approach Fox. Peter had lunch with Murdoch and Barry Diller. Their interest was immediate and enthusiastic.

Discussions began, slowly at first, but then they began to snowball. Something that had started in my mind as going along with Edgar suddenly became extremely serious. Now I had to decide if I really wanted to take this major, major step—and I was torn.

"Joan," I would tell myself, "if you can do well at Fox, then sooner or later Johnny is going to leave, and your show will inherit those ratings. You'll be a huge profit center, and treated accordingly."

On the other hand, what if the show didn't work out? I would never be able to go back on NBC. What if Fox folded? I'd be left with nothing.

But leaving Carson was having my security taken away, being told I had to grow up and stand on my own two feet.

"When Johnny is gone," Edgar said to me, "so are you." Do you think anybody who takes over is going to say, 'Let's keep Ed McMahon and Doc?' " He pointed out that ever since my very first contract, NBC had never bothered to make me exclusive to NBC; I could have appeared opposite Johnny on any network. I said to Edgar, "They think nobody will ever want me."

Then a friend—a real friend, Jay Michelis—smuggled me a list prepared by NBC naming the ten successors if Johnny retired. My name was not on it. I almost died. When we confronted NBC, the president, Brandon Tartikoff, denied such a list ever existed. But we had seen it. Edgar said, "There's no future for you there. You've been deluding yourself."

The negotiations with Fox continued until early in 1986. Edgar and I were very clear and simple about what we wanted. We required artistic control. After all those years of fighting for guests at NBC, we wanted autonomy. And since everybody wanted a show competitive with *The Tonight Show*—one that would immediately seem to have been on the air for several years—we required an equal studio, equal staff, equal budget.

We also wanted major money. If the show did not work, we would be destroyed, so we wanted to be destroyed with enough money in the bank so we would never have to work again. Edgar called it "fuck-you money." Money that would let me go to the summer theater in Williamstown, Massachusetts, and work for $125 a week if I wanted to.

And we required three years. Edgar was savvy. He knew that talk shows take forever to establish an audience. The host has to become a friend, a habit, somebody people want to visit with every night for an hour. A new show has to take friends away from some other host—and people feel guilty for abandoning their old pal. These friendships come very gradually.

People try you out once from word of mouth, or because of a particular guest, or by mistake on their way to Johnny Carson—and they don't pay a call again for weeks. We would be going up against an NBC habit that started not with Johnny Carson, not with Jack Paar, but went back over thirty years to Steve Allen's original *Tonight Show* in 1953. Edgar used to say, "If Jesus came back on another network, they'd still turn first to Channel Four."

Our need for a three-year deal became a major sticking point. Diller wanted two years, not long enough to make me give up the power base I had built on *The Tonight Show.* And at a deep, visceral level, I was terrified of leaving Carson. There was still that umbilical cord of loyalty and gratitude. He still represented safety to me. The Tiffany exposure of *The Tonight Show* was keeping me hot in my comedy-show career. Fox was the great unknown. The network might not even exist in three years.

I kept waiting for the NBC people to give me some reason to stay with Johnny. If they had offered me a two-year contract, if they had offered me a role in a *Movie of the Week,* some specials, a series pilot, anything that said, "We want you," I would have broken off with Fox.

At one point I called Peter Dekom and told him I could not leave Carson, I could not take the gamble. A show-business career is like riding a shimmering soap bubble, beautiful almost because of its fragility. If you are a television personality, the bubble is kept filled by visibility, reputation, freshness, currency, celebrity, excitement—what Carson provided. Without *The Tonight Show* I would be floating free in show business, a world of knives. Even the biggest stars have no shield. We are all piece-workers, always anxious and supersensitive, knowing that our only resources are talent and smarts.

Never in our relationship with *The Tonight Show* were we allowed to speak directly with Johnny Carson. That was forbidden. He was kept under a bell jar. Everybody had to deal with Henry Bushkin, his personal lawyer and mouthpiece in all business dealings. He once called and said, "We want you to go into this deal on a TV station," and when the man who runs Carson says that, you go in. A lot of people—including David Letterman and Neil Simon—lost a lot of money, but Bushkin got out whole.

For a while we had to use Bushkin as a "consultant" when we negotiated our contract with Carson Productions. Peter Lassally told us Bushkin negotiated all of his contracts. Now whom do you think Bushkin is going to favor, us or Carson Productions? But none of us had any choice. He could say to Johnny, "They're no good. Get them out." I've always heard that Bushkin was a major factor in Carson's breakup with his third wife, Joanna.

In January of 1986, Billy Sammeth telephoned Henry Bushkin to discuss renewing our contract. Bushkin never returned the call—and later claimed that Billy never made it. That told us worlds. Edgar said, "You've got to get out while you're on top and go somewhere else."

At the beginning of March everything was still stalled. The negotiations between Barry Diller and Peter Dekom were hung up on the length of the contract, and there was still no communication at all from NBC or Bushkin, not even to close his offer of one year. On March 13 Billy Sammeth phoned June Baldwin, the director of business affairs at NBC. She was leaving the network and referred him to John Agoglia, executive vice president of business affairs for NBC. Billy phoned him repeatedly. Agoglia never called back.

On the twenty-first Billy phoned Brandon Tartikoff, who took no position on renewing me but did prod Agoglia into calling back. Billy told him we wanted to renew—which was still true. But Billy also asked, "Does Joan have a place at NBC to hang her coat when Johnny isn't there anymore? She wants some feeling that NBC really is her home." Agoglia said I should sign for a year with Carson and *then* talk to Tartikoff about the future.

Simultaneously Barry Diller asked to make his pitch directly. He came to the house. Until then I knew him primarily as the best friend of my former manager Sandy Gallin. Sandy, David Geffen, Barry, and Calvin Klein shared a friendship legendary in Hollywood, a place not known for enduring intimacy. Barry had been to the house a couple of times with Sandy for dinner, but he had made no particular impression on me. I knew him mainly from the few times a year I performed at a bar named Studio One, when he, among others, would come to the dressing room after the show.

At the house that day Barry's performance was virtuoso. He was charming beyond charm, warming us up with wonderful stories—about driving around Beverly Hills with Katharine Hepburn and jumping over people's fences and swimming in their pools.

Barry talked about playing poker with Carson and said Johnny was getting old and tired—like his show. Barry said, "I promise you he'll be gone in one, two years." He said there was no way NBC would make me the replacement, and only the Fox show could give me what I wanted. Movies would not do it for me, even if I had a huge hit. He told me, "You're a television star." If we could not work out a deal, he wanted to keep the door open and stay friends—but he might not need me by next year. We still insisted on three years. I told him I would not give up everything for a two-year contract. Finally he caved in and agreed.

A few days later we met for lunch at Barry's house. Billy Sammeth came with us, and Barry had Jamie Kellner, president of Fox Broadcasting, who the previous year had tried to get me for his syndication company, Orion. It was another charm meeting to warm us up to accept the contract Diller would now work out with Peter Dekom. Barry took me on a tour of his house, and kept pointing out pictures of his ex-girlfriend, Diane von Furstenberg.

Diller and Kellner talked about their deep pockets—$100 million committed to launch the network. They discussed the show in broad strokes, promised any guests we wanted—"It'll be totally up to you. We will give you the show." They said they would not look at ratings for at least a year, were not expecting big numbers. Fox was in it for the long haul and knew the show would need a long time, even years, to find itself. If we had a terrific show, the numbers would come eventually.

Barry and Jamie were like two psychiatrists. They understood everything. Jamie had my Carson numbers in front of him and agreed that Carson and NBC were not treating me right. Barry and Jamie were my two champions. I wished I understood then that to operate in their league I needed a vinyl raincoat. When they told me they were my best friends, the words would have rolled down my arms, down my fingers, and hit the floor like drops of rain.

I suddenly wanted the show *so* much, I was completely taken in. I thought, This time the words are true. These people are different. I've made friends here. I liked Barry that day. He had a wicked sense of humor, he was up on everything, and I thought *I* had charmed *him.* I thought the exchange was real when our eyes met across the room and we would laugh. I thought all the bad I had heard about Diller—that he was a cold, ruthless businessman—was not true.

Now, Rupert Murdoch joined the romancing. On March 24, before we all went to the Academy Awards ceremony, we went to Barry's house for drinks to meet Rupert Murdoch and his wife—just folks getting to know each other. We talked about the show and the excitement of forming a network and how pleased they were to have me aboard. He wanted to start in October and do the show live—which we agreed to try in a six-month test.

Mrs. Murdoch had written a novel; we discussed her book. She was wonderful. Murdoch was being a nice, regular man who just happened to be a billionaire and a press lord. We talked children. We talked about his mom and her garden—all warm and family. We talked about decorators to do their house; they were moving to California, and I thought, Well, I'll help. By the end of that meeting I was afraid we were going to have to spend every Sunday night with the Murdochs. Later, after the show started, his mother, Dame something or other, visited from Australia, and they brought her to meet me. Mrs. Murdoch told her, "Joan's my very good friend"—so when I never heard from her again, I first thought maybe she didn't have my right phone number.

Shortly thereafter, we all attended Swifty Lazar's traditional "A" list party following the Academy Awards ceremony—and pretended we did not know each other. At a table across from us, seated with Johnny Carson and Freddie De Cordova, were Barry Diller and Rupert Murdoch, smiling and laughing and palsy-walsy. Hours earlier they had been telling us, "Carson's old, he's tired, he can be taken, he's a has-been, it's over for him"—and there they were, kissing up to him. That's Hollywood.

I wanted to tell Johnny what was afoot. Despite everything that had gone on, I wanted to believe that he of all people, so totally at the pinnacle, would understand. I told myself that if I went to him, maybe that old spark that was there in New York would rekindle. I thought maybe he would be the same man who had done the pilot of *That Show* and let Melissa hold his finger. I wanted him to say, "I don't blame you, kiddo. I'll be on your first show."

But my advisers said I would be an absolute moron to act as though the Carson people were civilized and generous. The moment I told Johnny we were talking with Fox, I would be out of the studio in twenty minutes. I was there at *The Tonight Show* when David Brenner told them, "I'm going to have a show in the fall." Produced by Motown, it was to be mainly music and musical personalities, with comedy mixed in. It was not direct competition to Carson, but David was instantly persona non grata at NBC. When I wanted him on during my weeks, the network said absolutely no, and Johnny did not have him back as a guest until long after his show failed. Even then he had to come on bowing and scraping and saying, "Boy, Johnny, there's no one like you."

So calling Johnny meant leaving the show immediately in March, and the angry, defiant side of me was saying that by this time I owed Johnny nothing, that I had a right to make the necessary business decisions. The Fox deal was not certain until the contract was signed, and my career has been ninety-nine disappointments and then one thing happens. Moreover, with the Fox deal I knew I would not be back on TV for five months, and my career required exposure on Carson for as long as possible. This was just a fact of life.

On April 4, 1986, Peter Dekom sent Barry Diller a letter of understanding that stated the negotiated terms that ultimately became our Fox contract. It gave us everything we wanted.

In the letter Diller agreed, "The show will be produced with production quality and staffing equal or better than that of *The Tonight Show*." We had approval rights of staffing, format, guests, and the producer. In matters of taste, *Saturday Night Live* would be the standard. The paycheck was $5 million a year for three years. That was a total of $7 million after taxes.

I'm told Johnny makes $8 million-plus a year. But much more important, he owns his own show. Even the Letterman show is owned by the Carson company. Carson gets half the profits. While Letterman is rich, he's rich because he's careful. He will always be an employee.

Nonetheless, this incredible amount of money would finally put my fears and frights to rest. That's what Murdoch had said, that's what Diller said—and Edgar—and our accountant, Michael Karlin. A girl who had lived with nothing but money problems from the time her eyes were open—had lived in a low-grade panic of scraping and getting by and then insecurity—was being told she didn't have to worry about money anymore.

There was no downside. With my own show, I had made the final step in my career. I would be getting the fun and respect Johnny had at NBC. I could devote eighteen hours a day to the show because Melissa was now at college at the University of Pennsylvania in Philadelphia. Edgar was slated to be the executive producer, and I believed that would save my marriage, would pull Edgar out of his unpredictable anger, level out his highs and lows, renew his mental acuity. Already he was beginning to be the old Edgar, happy to get up in the morning, happy to go to work, happy to go to all the meetings I thought were boring then. The possibility that the show would not work never crossed my mind.

In the second week of April Billy Sammeth received a call from Joe Bures, the vice president of program acquisitions at NBC and the first executive to voice any interest in extending my contract for another year. He was referred to Peter Dekom. By then it was too late.

Our first business meeting with Fox, the first shared decision with Barry Diller, took place in late April, when we met to discuss the press announcement of *The Late Show Starring Joan Rivers*. In retrospect, I see that all the psychological dynamics that would destroy the show surfaced that afternoon in a sunny conference room in the Twentieth Century–Fox tower in Beverly Hills.

Barry and the Fox press agent planned to announce *The Late Show Starring Joan Rivers* at a press conference of selected reporters, including me along with other new developments, like new stations, new plans. We knew they had a front-page news story that would take TV America by surprise, and they should launch the show with a gigantic press conference.

Looking back, this was the first signal that Barry Diller was inexperienced in the daily, dirty machinery of station-level television. His colossal success must have made him confident of his judgment about starting a show from scratch—the details of staff and the content of the show. But as we discovered, he did not know what the affiliates wanted, was unrealistic about ratings, had no feel for the late-night audience, and little understanding of the necessary staff.

His experience was movies. As a young man hooked by show business, he bypassed college to work in the mail room of the William Morris Agency. At age twenty-five he was a lesser executive at ABC, where he revolutionized programming by inventing the made-for-TV *Movie of the Week.* The man who hired him at the network, Leonard Goldberg, has described Barry seated at his small desk across from such studio heads as Lew Wasserman, Charles Bluhdorn, and Joe Levine, who fought with this boy while they ate egg-salad sandwiches and their limousines waited downstairs. Goldberg said, "Here was this rough, tough kid who wasn't afraid of them and had class and style."

At age thirty-one—in 1973—Diller was hired by Charles Bluhdorn to be head of Paramount Pictures. With Michael Eisner, now the CEO of Disney, Barry chose movies that brought in nearly $3 billion. After Bluhdorn died in 1984, Diller left Paramount to work with Marvin Davis, running Twentieth Century–Fox, which was in terrible shape. After Diller brought it back into the black, Davis sold a controlling interest to Rupert Murdoch.

When I became directly involved with Barry, people told me he was the smartest man they had ever met—a terrific manager, decisive—but inscrutable, a man both social and antisocial. At the dinner to introduce my show, he made one tour around the room and then left. When he traveled on commercial airliners, he sometimes bought the seat next to him to keep it vacant.

I heard he was a man who reduced issues to black or white, unconfused by gray—and once he had made a decision, nothing would turn him around. I rarely heard "God bless Barry." I heard about terrorized underlings and survivors who got promoted. I heard he was feared as a killer who finished people off when he sensed weakness or mediocrity, a man of shadows, filled with secrets.

I suspect most people who get to the top are ice-cold when it comes to business, and take all challenges personally. To rise to the top, you have to step on people, destroy or be destroyed. There's room for just Barry Diller and nobody else.

At the announcement meeting I left the talking to my publicist, Richard Grant, and Edgar. I didn't even want to be there, but they said they needed me for reinforcement. I was the gun, a role I hated.

Richard Grant made our case very strongly, but Barry was not interested. Then Edgar joined in, explaining that I was a major star moving from a major network show. Being humble was *nuts*.

Edgar was treating Barry as an equal, challenging him. And nobody talks back and forth with Barry, except maybe Rupert Murdoch. Suddenly Diller lost his cool. "Shut up," he snapped at Edgar. Though Barry immediately apologized, he had done the unforgivable.

It was awful. Winning Barry Diller's respect was Edgar's fantasy. To Edgar, Barry represented the Hollywood establishment that had denied us our breaks. Also, the show was Edgar's ticket to being important to himself. So when Barry turned on him, particularly in front of me, the hurt and humiliation must have been unbearable. From that moment forward Edgar's attitude was, "I'll show you."

That "Shut up" was a flash of Diller's contempt for Edgar from the very beginning. If Edgar had been my manager, he would have had a status. But to Barry, he was merely a star's husband, superfluous, an unnecessary evil. Barry considered him another Gary Morton, Lucille Ball's husband, a Catskill-mountain comic made head of comedy development at Twentieth Century–Fox in order to get and keep Lucille. Gary was laughed at, ridiculed behind his back, never taken seriously. Maybe Gary Morton *was* smart about comedy, but nobody will ever know.

I believe Sandy Gallin encouraged Barry's scorn. Sandy felt Edgar was responsible for my leaving him as my manager. Edgar had been very upset when Sandy had tried to launch his own television career by hosting a star variety show called *Live & in Person.* "Why do we have to pay Sandy fifteen percent when he's never there?" Edgar kept asking. The last straw came when Edgar phoned him backstage somewhere and was told, "Mr. Gallin is unavailable. He is doing camera rehearsal."

We fired him and hired Billy Sammeth. Billy was our road manager and was employed by Sandy's firm. Katz, Gallin sued us for $90 million for breach of contract—but finally settled for a token amount. When Barry became involved with us, I am sure that Sandy did *not* say, "Oh, boy, you're going to love working with Edgar. He's smart as hell and really mellow."

So at the start Barry and Edgar disliked each other. Whatever one did was annoying to the other. Issues that might have been resolved amicably were escalated to the moon. After that first argument Edgar set out to prove, *mano a mano,* that he was just as tough and smart as Barry Diller. Diller simply overlooked him, froze him out. In the few meetings he allowed after that day, Barry talked only to me.

I think Barry and Edgar were destined to collide, partly because their natures were so alike. I think both were unhappy men, insecure at center but very intelligent, and fighters who used fear to keep their antagonists off-balance. Both had to be right, both had to be important, had to win—and everybody should know they had won. Both were control and detail freaks. When events were out of their control, both of these perfectionists were deeply disturbed.

At that meeting my husband lost whatever clout he might have had. When I heard Diller tell Edgar to "shut up," I stiffened— along with the whole room—and thought, Uh-oh, wait a second. I realized we were not all on the same side. We were adversaries. We were going to do the press conference *his* way—so the fact that I, the gun, was sitting there was not enough. We were never going to have an equal voice. Well, if I was going to be the gun . . . I said, "Obviously then, my presence will not be needed."

This initiated a pattern. In addition to the terms of the contract, the threat "She won't show up" became one of Edgar's weapons—the same ploy he used against Irving at the Downstairs at the Upstairs. Edgar was fighting for our side, but creating confrontations that I had to follow through on.

As graciously as he could manage, Barry gave in. After we left, we were told, he rolled his eyes at his lieutenants and said, "Okay, go ahead and make it a zoo, make it a circus."

But I was stupid. Our position was right, but you do not fire the gun on the first day. You save it until the very end, when you are desperate.

Everything seemed so important at that moment, but it wasn't. No single thing like a press conference makes or breaks a business relationship. So what if our show had been part of a list? We still would have made all the papers. Another pattern was begun: victories not worth the trade-off of anger.

The threat to stay away is only effective once, because you can surprise the producers only once. After that, they begin asking themselves how much they need you, and begin preparing in some way, including getting rid of you. After the first surprise, threatening becomes a grandstand play, crying wolf, and one day they will call you on it, which later happened to us.

The next decision was how to break the news to Johnny Carson. I was forbidden by Fox to tell anybody until the day of the press announcement, which was scheduled for 11:00 A.M. Tuesday morning, May 6. The secrecy was so great, when the contracts were written, the only four copies were locked up in Barry Diller's safe. Even the flowers he sent me had an unsigned card.

My last Carson show with Johnny—on Friday, April 25—was tremendously sentimental for me. I knew it was the end, rounding out the circle. I went on camera with such a feeling of warmth and sadness—really that I was leaving my childhood now, going off on my own. I had sent a copy of *Enter Talking* over to Johnny in advance with a warm note expressing my gratitude—and the book was dedicated to Edgar, "who made this book happen" and to Johnny, "who made it *all* happen." I was hoping that when he read the dedication he would call, and that maybe then I could ease into the Fox deal on the phone—if it was possible to ease into that. But he never responded.

On the show I wore the original plain black Lanz dress that I had kept, and I found a feather boa like the one I wore in 1965. I opened our segment by giving him a second book and showing him the photograph of us together on the show in 1965, and he just said mildly, "Isn't that great." Off camera Freddie De Cordova held up a copy of *Enter Talking,* pointed to the dedication, and called out, "Read the dedication." So Johnny had not even riffled through the book and had not received my note. I thought, I've been so loyal to Johnny? I've been loyal to a stone wall, to a bunch of buildings."

After the show I sat in the car clutching the feather boa, and cried and cried. In spite of the turmoil I was feeling inside, I loved Johnny that night. Everything was still there between us, the relationship on camera, the rapport, breaking each other up, the ESP—it was all there as it had been for twenty-one years. I had just closed the door on the best comedy team since Gracie Allen and George Burns—and I think closing that door hurt him, too.

My regular one-week stint on *The Tonight Show* came up the following Monday. It ended on Friday, May 2. During those weeks I had been taping *The Tonight Show* in the afternoon and flying up to Vegas for Caesars Palace performances. On Monday afternoon, May 5, the day before the announcement, I was in the hotel suite writing jokes, doing mail. About three o'clock Edgar called to say that word of the announcement had leaked. The radio columnist Rona Barrett was going to use the item that night. In a conference call with Barry Diller, he agreed I should call Johnny immediately.

By then it was too late. Brandon Tartikoff, hearing rumors, put two and two together and called the Fox head of programming, Garth Ancier, who used to work for him, and asked if I had signed. Garth Ancier was evasive, and Tartikoff made his deduction and phoned Carson.

I telephoned Johnny's beach house, and the secretary, very

friendly, said, "Oh, yes, Miss Rivers, one moment, he'll be right here. Hold on." After a pause she came back and said, "I'm sorry, I don't know where he is." I made a joke. I said, "He lives in an all-glass house and you don't know where he is?" I knew I had received my answer—Johnny was furious—but I left the message that I would call the next morning. I was still dreaming that after a night's sleep, he would wish me well.

I telephoned Freddie De Cordova. He was shocked. I phoned the Lassallys and had to leave a message on their machine— "Please call me back."

I flew to Los Angeles late Monday night and was so excited and frightened by this career move, I slept only a couple of hours— was up at seven-fifteen Tuesday, nervous, nervous, nervous. I called the NBC executives but had to leave messages with their secretaries. I called Johnny at his office, but there was no answer, it was too early. I had to leave for Fox, but in my dressing room I again tried to reach Johnny. Barry Diller was impatient. I was holding up the press conference, and he could not understand why I refused to go out until I had spoken to Johnny. My secretary, Jeri, kept calling NBC, but Carson was not there. Finally I had her call his home, and he answered. She handed me the phone. I said, "Johnny, I . . ." Click. The moment he heard my voice, Johnny hung up. I put my forehead against the cold wall and wept.

The press coverage of the announcement was terrific, but there was a nearly permanent downside. When I arrived home from the press conference, *USA Today* called. The Carson/NBC broadside had also begun.

Johnny himself maintained the dignified silence of an abused innocent—except to say to the Associated Press, "I think she was less than smart and didn't show much style." But Carson's hired mouths were out in force, assuming a moral tone as though I had committed some kind of sin. They wheeled out the usual "unnamed source" who said that if I had given him the news first, Johnny would have "dropped by her show as a guest." Johnny is very shrewd. I admire that tremendously. I admire anybody with such longevity. Staying at the top requires what he did to me, takes saying, "This girl is going up against me. Let's kill her."

. . .

I think the way Johnny found out was a shame. He should have heard from me, and I like to think that I could have made him understand. It must have been a huge shock. Nobody had said to him, "Rivers's contract is up. Do you want to give her one year or two?" Nobody had said, "The Rivers people have been calling for five months, but we're stalling them." Everybody was afraid to go up to Louis XVI and say, "The peasants are restless." Of course he was astonished.

I think I was always the one discovery Johnny found who did not stray. Cosby is now bigger than Johnny is. Johnny discovered Richard Pryor—who was a good-bye. They became equals. I never became equal in his eyes. I myself always relate to people on the level of how we first met. Johnny was always the boss. I think he did not allow himself to see me grow and would have been surprised to learn I could have sold out a five-thousand-seat house.

I think, too, Carson and his people felt I was being ungrateful. My evidence is what Jim Mahoney, Johnny's representative, told *USA Today:* "He put her on the show. It was probably the biggest break she ever got in her life. You don't treat people that way." I wonder if they would have talked that way if I were a man. I'm sure if Eddie Murphy had screeched "The Star-Spangled Banner" the way Roseanne Barr did on that baseball field, the crowds would have cheered.

Finally, I think the real thorn was that somebody else wanted me. Nobody at NBC ever imagined that I had another place to go. I believe it was the old dynamic in which familiarity breeds contempt. I still like to think that somebody at an NBC board meeting turned and asked, "Why didn't you renew her contract?"

I wasn't surprised to learn Jay Leno was anointed. One, he earned it. Two, we know and like him. And three, his name was already on the list back in 1985! When people ask me, now that Johnny has decided to retire, if I'm sorry I left the show, I say no.

I realized then there was no way in hell I would have succeeded Johnny Carson, so my disappointment would have been thirtyfold if I had stayed. Instead, I found out so much about myself. Remade a life. In a way, leaving was a blessing.

None of us see ourselves as mean or cold-blooded—but we all protect our kingdoms. Sure, Carson felt terrible—and I believe a lot of it was because something that helped his kingdom was being taken away. There was no longer friendship. I see now that there never was.

In the press there were headlines: NOT FUNNY! JOAN UPSETS TV JOHNNY—JOAN GOES AGAINST HER OLD PAL JOHNNY. There were prejudging digs: "Can Rivers create the kind of atmosphere that will make her weary cavorting less wearying?" I was frightened. If I was treated that way now, what would the reviews be like when my show opened in the fall?

As long as I wore Carson's mantle, they loved me. When he turned on me, they all turned. Part of the power wielded by a major news source like Carson is access. Carson had recently begun to mellow toward reporters and was being somewhat available. Anybody who did not take Johnny's side would never have any access to him.

But much more important, I had publicly bucked Johnny Carson, something nobody had ever done. There are certain men in Hollywood who are sacred. George Burns is one. You cannot say anything negative about Bob Hope. I had stepped on the American flag, and when you do that, the old-boy system will kill you.

I think many of the male press have never understood what I was doing and were basically offended by me. I was the woman who broke the stereotype of what they thought a woman comedian should be. I was feminine in a beaded dress, talking about falling breasts and contraception and faking orgasms. Men do not identify with such jokes.

The Carson people announced that I was fired as of Tuesday, and Garry Shandling was given the remaining two weeks. I adored Garry. I thought he was hilarious. I used him on the road and in Las Vegas as my opening act and booked him constantly on *The Tonight Show.* Now I phoned him and said, "Anything you need, call me. I'll help you. This is a great break for you. I'm thrilled." I have never heard from him since that day. I guess that's show biz.

On May 22, two weeks after the Fox announcement, I took Melissa to lunch at the Polo Lounge in the Beverly Hills Hotel. I had not heard from anybody on the Carson show, but there was Ed McMahon. He gave me a big kiss, wished me well, and we made jokes—"Hey, no pictures." Ed turned out to be the one person on the show with real class.

On June 8 I received a birthday present of a VCR from Jay Michelis at NBC accompanied by a note: *A Very Happy Birthday from your only friend at America's Number One Television Network. I wanted to get you a car, but this was all the financial people would approve. They said something about "a bunch of pricks." I assume they meant cactus.*

13

ооооо

In those days, Fox was a gamble. There were no Simpsons then. It was not a place that could lure top-notch people from the networks, so Barry Diller ended up hiring young executives in their twenties who were brand-new to late-night television. "They don't know what late night is," Billy Sammeth joked. "Now they can watch it and stay up for it, too."

All of them were frightened—terrified that they had left secure jobs for a network that would not work. So everybody was under pressure you can't believe—including Barry Diller. To protect themselves, all the Fox people wanted control, wanted to have input into the show, wanted to take over. They became like a sorority that would not let me in.

The more they tried to control everything, the more petty the fights became, everybody grinding private little axes. Maybe the most frightened was Edgar, who right from the beginning was nitpicking: "I insist on this. I insist on that." So right away the show became Edgar versus Barry—which included Barry's chain of command: Kevin Wendle, vice president of prime time/late night; and Paul Colichman, who was directly in charge of our day-to-day operations.

Reluctantly, we agreed to Murdoch's request to have the first show in early October, which gave us and Fox just five months to set up the smoothly running machine NBC had assembled through decades. It was a herculean task: ready the studio—build the set, install the lighting, the sound system, the seating—hire a staff with top bookers to corral the guests, get excellent segment producers to preinterview and handle each guest, find first-class writers to think up the nightly monologue and the stunts, recruit a skillful producer and assistant to manage the show.

The first problem arose over the area assigned for our offices—two thirds of a floor. The space was also used by a school for children acting in a sitcom. Edgar said, "We'll need the whole floor; you'll have to get the school out of there." Kevin Wendle said, "The school has to stay."

Edgar was adamant. The Carson staff filled four buildings on NBC's Burbank lot. Edgar told Kevin Wendle again, "We're going to need all the space." Kevin repeated, "You don't need that much space"—which was like saying, "You're not going to need that much staff." Edgar was now worried and impatient. "I'm telling you," he said, "we're going to have at least eight writers. Where are you going to put them? And where are we going to put the segment producers? They need offices. They're on the phone all day. Where will the producers be? The music department? The bookers? The secretaries? Where is the Xerox room? The research library? The kitchen?"

Then Edgar went to see the studio planned for the show. It was much too small. This studio's audience would sound like one hand clapping. We had been promised the same-size studio as *The Tonight Show.* He said, "There are three studios here on the Fox lot. Why aren't we getting the big one?"

Well, Diller wanted to hang on to the big stage because they were renting it for a lot of money. Edgar protested, "You want us to give you a *Tonight Show,* but with a little audience. You won't get that dynamic feel, that excitement."

We needed a Rolls-Royce, and you cannot make one out of Ford parts and the wrong tools. If you have a little show that's operating on a shoestring with a drab little set, the audience smells that you're a loser. Nobody wants to spend his late nights with a loser.

The ink was hardly dry on "Carson standards or better," and the Fox people were planning to give us what *they* thought we needed. I suspect that Barry Diller figured, "Promise her the world. Get her. Then we'll do it our way." So he must have budgeted the show according to his own judgment, and his estimates were too low. He ended up counting pennies. And all the time he must have felt that I was disposable. I later heard that the president of Fox Broadcasting, Jamie Kellner, was telling affiliates, "If she's no good, she'll be out in nine months."

Edgar never dealt directly with Diller. He bucked him by being brusque and superior to his lieutenants. Edgar was brilliant on ideas, brilliant on follow-through, but his missing chromosome was diplomacy. Getting a job done right was more important to him than finesse. And since the heart attack his patience had been stretching tight.

While Edgar was arguing with Fox about production facilities, we were also pushing to find a producer. According to our contract, we had the right to approve all staff. Fox began offering us people to interview, and I was open to all possibilities, but there was nobody we were wild about, no one arriving in a silver Rolls-Royce with a laurel wreath on his brow. Most of them were big names from the past, but now so worn-out and rumpled you wanted to iron them.

One man we liked was on drugs. Another turned us down. Another wanted creative control. One had a ponytail, and we laughed, "Wait till Barry sees him." And Barry did hate him. I saw at least eighteen people, and we could not find a producer everybody liked, one I could work with who had fresh ideas. And maybe both sides wanted a person who could be "theirs," somebody they could control.

In mid-May Bruce McKay was hired as the producer. He was Billy Sammeth's suggestion and the man Barry disliked the least. Considered our man, he was forever tainted. Bruce hired Courtney Conte as an assistant, and with Edgar they assembled a list of necessary staff based on *The Tonight Show.* When Edgar and Bruce picked candidates for these jobs, Fox vetoed them and tried to put in its own people who cost less.

With nothing settled, Edgar and I left for a week in Europe on business. While we were still on the Concorde, Barry Diller was in Bruce's office asking, "Can't you produce this show without all these people, without all this space?" And Bruce was saying, "Well, I guess I *could* do it with less." Bruce was a fine producer caught between two bosses who were fighting and wanted him to stand up to the other guy, both sides telling him, "You're too weak." Bruce wanted to be liked by everybody. His lips had a hard time forming "no."

When we returned, we were presented with a staff list good for a small daytime show like *Hour Magazine,* not for what Fox wanted, not for a slick, professional sixty minutes that looked like a long-established network show.

Wielding the power of the purse, Fox made us get permission for each move we made, while never giving us the breakdown of the budget. Courtney Conte, who wrote the checks, was forbidden to discuss the budget with anybody. I never felt I was dealing with just straight, cool businessmen; there was always a mysterious agenda. The struggle for control continued.

We chose Mark Hudson as the orchestra leader. He was the right age and had the right contemporary look. Fox said, "He wants too much money." We asked, "Well, who can you suggest?"—and a lot of names came back that made no sense. When we wanted a certain-sized orchestra to give us the same sound as Carson, Fox said, "Too many musicians." The head booker we chose was "too expensive." The inexperienced Fox executives wanted to give the writers the title of segment producers so the pay would be less. We had to explain that the Writers Guild would notice if members were getting eight hundred dollars a week instead of two thousand.

When we did settle on a staff, Fox could not seem to close the deals—dragging everything out during weeks and weeks of haggling and reneging on promises. We suspected Fox was stalling because the later people started work, the less time they had to be paid. Part of me thought all the fighting came from growing pains, but the insecure me was frightened. I had said good-bye to Carson and ripped up my passport and now they were haggling about the staff I *had* to have. I was no longer certain I could land that boat.

Kevin Wendle once told me in a meeting not to get so upset. "If you want somebody cool and rational," I told him, "don't go to a performer, because we are crazy." That is what makes the work wonderful when it is wonderful. And if you ruin our creative climates, you destroy us.

I think Barry never had a clue about Edgar, and never understood the dynamics between Edgar and me. Fox did not understand that such loyalty to the team, the one entity I trusted, was the only kind of security I had. Our life had always been us against the world, and if you were not for us, you were against us. Every challenge was personal—the same as it was for Barry Diller. We were the Corsican brothers. One got stabbed, and a hundred miles away the other screamed, "Ouch!"

Disregarding Barry's instructions that Edgar have nothing to do with the show, Bruce and Courtney continued to consult him. Edgar was the executive producer, and they respected his expertise. In fact, Edgar was coming home happy every night. He was setting up *our* show and doing it well.

In mid-August I was performing for a week at Lake Tahoe without Edgar, who now worried about his heart at that high altitude. The phone rang at my suite at Caesars, and it was Barry Diller. He was calling me, it seemed, to make me his doyenne of taste—but it was Eve and the snake. Would I please go over and look at a house he planned to buy? He wanted my opinion. And, oh, by the way, would I mind asking Edgar to stay away from the show? He was destroying it by causing major problems. The staff was demoralized. "You're the only one who can keep Edgar away," Barry said. "You've got to do it."

On the phone the CEO of Twentieth Century–Fox went on for two hours about his philosophy for the show and how Edgar was being destructive and making everybody unhappy and causing major problems. I kept saying, "I don't understand. I've got to have examples. What major problems?"

Barry never did give me examples. He would say, "You've got to keep Edgar away," and I would ask, "From where? There are no offices." I think the "staff" was Kevin Wendle, who was saying, "The son of a bitch is butting in, saying he has to have this and where is such-and-such."

I tried to make Barry understand the effect of keeping Edgar away, the stress on me if I went home each night to Edgar's frustration and hurt and anger. I tried to make him understand what Edgar wanted—which was what we all want—to be listened to and be included: "Edgar, I've got to save money. Here's the budget. What do you suggest?" Diller could have controlled us so easily by giving Edgar a little respect and me some affection.

Barry wanted me to realize that his men had been picked by him for their enthusiasm—"I wanted people who don't know the word 'no.'" But what he was really asking us to do was to trust an inexperienced staff. This was impossible. There was simply too much at stake.

I never told Edgar about the phone call.

Nobody there except Edgar had created a show from scratch. Having assembled *That Show* from scratch in New York, he knew hundreds of tiny cogs taken for granted on *The Tonight Show.* He was wonderful at all the horrible, boring things that make a show work. Sure, he irritated a lot of people. When Fox tried it later without Edgar, there was nothing but disasters. Do you think Aaron Spelling is Mr. Nice Guy all day long? Is Barry Diller a sweetie pie? Edgar was our man with the whip. Bruce McKay, who is the nicest guy in the world, was not going to be the house bastard. The role of the producer, says top manager Bernie Brillstein, "is to keep everybody happy."

Edgar was the one waking up in the night to write himself a note about release forms for the guests to sign—and what about a mirror backstage so guests can make a last-minute check—and be sure Joan has a long cord for a mike—we've got to lock in a deal with an airline to fly out guests. We would be at a movie, and Edgar would suddenly say in the darkness, "Nobody's working on the hotel rooms."

Those are not the fun things. You want to say, "Let's paint the set pink," not carry on days of negotiations with an airline. Even if Edgar was not the one to do it, he was the one saying, "Did you make the calls? Goddamm it, you were supposed to have it done two weeks ago." Nobody likes that person. But no matter how petty the detail, he was right.

The minute lawyers become involved in a quarrel, the mess is amplified and accelerated, becomes serious warfare, becomes "We've got to build a case, so put it in writing; we've got to watch our backs, and check with me before you talk with them." Throughout the months of forming the show, Edgar won virtually every battle. The Fox people still had to listen to me, and they had to pay attention to our lawyer and the terms of the contract. From July forward, Edgar and I spoke daily to our lawyer, Peter Dekom, and in the fall two litigation lawyers were added to our forces. During the Fox episode, we spent over $300,000 on lawyers.

In mid-July Peter Dekom began sending lawyer letters. In one of them, Dekom wrote a polite warning to Barry Diller that at some point he would have to trust my judgment on the creative side of the show and support me with the staff I felt I needed. The point never came, and eventually Edgar, much too soon, pulled the gun again. Dekom wrote, "Joan being prepared to start the show in October is, of course, predicated upon having all the requisite elements in place to her satisfaction sufficiently in advance . . . to permit proper production values."

In late July Barry came to the house for a meeting. He was not charming. It was the first time I saw the side of him that turned a deaf ear. He said he resented the combative, adversarial letters he was receiving from Peter. Edgar insisted they were not adversarial and got samples. Barry brushed them aside and angrily lectured us about causing dissension and trouble. He gave a little speech about exercising leadership—you give your staff independence. But he didn't seem to realize the only independent person at Fox was Barry Diller.

Looking back, I think we all should have taken a week off. In show business fights always seem to become overemotional—"The color of the cloth must be blue, not red. Don't you understand?" In the arts nobody has answers; the decisions are based on emotional reactions. It's not the Wharton School of Business, where you can say, "The set should be purple because sixty percent of the viewers say purple is the most exciting." We all were caught up in a foolish game that was petty, not playful, an ego version of *Alice in Wonderland*. Everybody lost perspective, became disoriented.

There was a stupid struggle over the rights to the theme music, for example; written by me and Mark Hudson. We were told that Carson and Paul Anka shared royalties for *The Tonight Show* theme 50–50 and NBC got nothing. Edgar wanted the same split and assumed that big money was involved (in fact, it was only about a thousand a month). Kevin Wendle said okay. Then Fox said, "No way. We get it all." Edgar decided that we would set a legal precedent if we did not enforce an absolute duplicate of all Carson arrangements. So he called in our lawyer and made this a major cause.

Finally Kevin Wendle flew to Las Vegas, where I was performing, and sat in a chair in my suite and pleaded for the rights. "This means my job," he said, and burst into tears. I knew this slim blond kid was scared to death. Suddenly I felt sorry for him. "Let him have the rights," I told Edgar. "It's his job."

Kevin wiped his eyes with the back of his hands and asked to go into the bedroom to compose himself. After a few minutes I went in to ask if he was okay—only to find him laughing on the phone, saying, "I got it. I got it from her." That finished Kevin Wendle and me.

On our side, I allowed Edgar to press those buttons that stirred me up—not hard to do when my career was on the line every day. "Those sons of bitches don't want to pay for a fifth camera," he would tell me, and I would go to war, upset, hysterical, and screaming, "We need a fifth camera!" When Edgar did not like something as insignificant as the food the caterer was serving, I made the protest—and was not even eating at night.

Alone, I could have been friends even with Kevin Wendle and done him a needlepoint pillow. I have wooed the devil before. Pride the Queen of England can have, not me. When I suggested letting things pass, Edgar argued me down. He did not understand "Okay, we know we're right, but shhhh, now let's make this work." Nobody was advising, "Edgar, let it pass. Sit down with the devil and schmooze, tell him, 'This is what we need. Let's figure it out together.' "

Most projects in the television business boil down to a succession of minutiae, the daily decisions, few of them crucial but passionately felt out of ambition, ego, pride, fear, or simply caring a lot. During September there were major fights about the number of telephones, about secretaries who could not take shorthand, about catered dinners for the staff. There was a fight about Edgar having a secretary and a big office with the right furniture. Before the heart attack, those symbols would not have mattered. Now, the more Fox refused to acknowledge Edgar's demands, the more important they became. When the champ is no longer the champ, every insult becomes a major insult.

Tom Pileggi watched us from afar and felt compelled to write us a letter: *As much as it hurts, you must be diplomatic and never, never let the other side know how you really feel. The other side may end up being your closest friend. Unfortunately, the whole world is run by the mouth but should be run by the brain. Think before you say something you will be sorry for later.*

But Edgar did not listen. Feeling embattled everywhere, he fought back obsessively to get every detail of our production identical to the Carson show. And I was doing everything I could to build staff morale, create Camp Joan Rivers, to keep Edgar calm, to keep him from having another heart attack.

I could have stopped all the fighting, could have said, "Edgar, you're out of here. Barry, do what you want." But there is no way I could have banished my husband to being at home alone. I did not realize how seriously we were all crippling the future. There are always birth pains in setting up a new show. I thought that once we were on the air, the trouble would vanish. As it turned out, I was surrounded by men who could never let anything rest.

In September came a development that I now think doomed the show. If there was ever hope that Fox and Edgar and I could make an accommodation, it ended when Kevin Wendle hired Ron Vandor, a local NBC newsman he had earlier backed for producer.

Our previous doubts about Vandor were confirmed a few days later when he began his job as our Fox contact. "Just what do you do every day?" he asked Bruce McKay. Courtney Conte then undertook his instruction. Soon Ron was sitting silently in production and writers' meetings, listening and watching. One evening Bruce came by the office late, and there was Ron typing at his secretary's desk. When he saw Bruce, he covered the paper with his arms and asked him to leave. He was writing regular reports to the Fox executives. Barry Diller's vision of our daily activities came almost entirely through the eyes of Ron Vandor via Kevin Wendle, both of whom I think hated us.

In our first encounter Vandor announced he was going to sit in and help pick my writers. Then he introduced two middle-aged men who wrote for local disc jockeys in St. Louis. I said, "You must be kidding. You must be absolutely kidding." Disc-jockey humor! That was the end of him and me. I think that with mature men in those jobs, experienced executives with a light touch and even some humor, *The Late Show Starring Joan Rivers* might still be on the air.

In late September, only a couple of weeks before airtime, another bucket of poison was dumped into the well. The issue was my safety on a live show. The Fox guards were old, retired cops— nice guys who sat at the door and had a Coke. Any nut could run on camera and start shooting. You only need one Sirhan Sirhan. Edgar made this a major power struggle with Barry Diller, even to the point of withholding crucial information from me.

When Edgar asked for the Gavin DeBecker security guards we had at our house, Barry was ice-cold. "This is my lot, and you are my guests," he said. "The tail does not wag the dog." But Edgar would not let up. Barry finally agreed that we could hire guards from some other agency—there was apparently bad blood between Barry and DeBecker. Edgar never told me this. His position was, "If I let them dictate on this, they will dictate on everything." He worked me up to the point where I telephoned Barry and said, "I don't feel safe without my private guards, so I cannot be your guest on the Fox lot."

"Then don't be my guest," Barry answered. He was right.

I called him back, ate crow, and invited him over to the house to talk it over, just the two of us. So two people, one making millions and the other the CEO of Twentieth Century–Fox, argued for twenty minutes over which guards to use—none of whom carried guns. Still, after the meeting, where we discussed many other things as well, I felt we were comfortable with each other, understood each other.

As he left, I instinctively tried to lighten the tension by playing the foolish little girl trying to work her father. Giggle, giggle, giggle. I wanted Barry to go home laughing, wanted to put the fight in proportion, make it seem as silly as it was. I still hoped that Barry and I could turn all this into a game, the affectionate duel I had with Irving Haber at the Downstairs at the Upstairs. I teased, deadpan, "Now that I've been nice, can I have my guards?"

He thought my little joke was serious, thought I was trying to manipulate him. I now know that moment began eroding whatever trust and confidence Barry had in me—he told Alex B. Block, the author of *Outfoxed*, "Oh I knew so quickly. That's the terrible part. I didn't tell anybody but I knew." So Barry, even before the show premiered, decided he could not work with me.

Neither one of us understood the other. When he had originally put on his charm hat with me, all the outward signs had said terrific, funny, flexible. Only later did I discover that nothing in business is ever playful to Barry. Whereas my self-worth came from my audiences, Barry's self-image was "corporate boss" in a battlefield where no prisoners are taken. Of course, I am a strong controller, and I was hoping, hoping—but I knew he had won. I am still amazed that anybody as powerful as Barry would react so totally to such a feeble challenge. He came to me all black-and-white, a Franz Kline. I was not going to win him over with charm and a twinkle.

From then on, I no longer had the full support of the Fox power center.

Those last two weeks before the show aired on October 9 were nonstop struggles. We still had not settled on an announcer. Fox wanted a sidekick who could become a star, a straight arrow, an everyman who would gasp, "Oh, no, Joan," when I was outrageous and fiddle with his necktie. But I did not want an Ed

McMahon. Carson is unable to stand there and just talk to the audience and be intimate. His eyes drop. He needs to talk to a friend who represents the audience. I like talking directly to the audience. It is my friend.

I worked in Atlantic City with a wonderful singer named Clint Holmes who I thought was just right—a black WASP. Fox did not trust my instincts and was nervous about a black man. Barry thought I would have to make him an integral part of the show or be criticized. Fox retained a casting agency in New York and Chicago that sent us endless tapes of confused candidates asking "What do you want me to say?"

A voice off camera answered, "Say, *The Late Show, Starring Joan Rivers.*'"

"*The Late Show, Starring Joan Riversssss,*" they dutifully echoed.

Then I interviewed in person another series of beautiful young men, most of them suitable for casting a couch, blond corn-eaters from Iowa who had not been fully dressed until the day they auditioned. It was like casting for Chippendales. When I rejected them, the Fox executives collectively decided the announcer would be an offstage voice and never appear. The day before we were going on the air, there was a blind audition, just voices on tape. Barry picked Clint. He winked at me. That was nice. His present to me. Good, I thought, everything is still fine between us.

But coming down the home stretch, Fox's priorities seemed backward. The Carson people put the word out that anybody who appeared on my show would be blackballed at *The Tonight Show.* Our friend Jay Michelis, vice president of NBC, told me, "Our job is to destroy you." It was a cold business war. If I cut into Carson, that could cost NBC millions of dollars.

Billy Sammeth and the booking staff worked the phones around the clock. The day before the show aired, Wendle and Vandor, the executives in charge, called a meeting to ask if we should give the guests Hershey's Kisses, mugs, or a jar of fortune cookies. Insanity. Nobody comes on a show because of presents. I wanted to tell them, "Let's first get the guests. Phone Barry and ask him for his friends."

When we heard about Carson's threat, Barry said, "Don't worry, we are behind you a hundred percent. I'll get my friends, and you will have whoever is making Fox films." That meant Jack Nicholson, Barbra Streisand, Jane Fonda, Michael Douglas. All of Twentieth Century–Fox's stars at one time or another. Maybe he called them once and said, "Barbra? Barry. For God's sake I need a favor, honey. You got to do this for me." We needed those calls. The crucial weeks were the third and fourth, not the first. That is what Kevin Wendle, vice president in charge of prime time late night, should have been worrying about, not whether the tapestry in the greenroom worked with the club chairs.

Though the executives had been checking fabric swatches for weeks, the greenroom, where guests would wait to go on camera, was still unfinished a few days before the show, and panic set in. Courtney Conte had sensibly covered the halls and rooms with a serviceable, washable vinyl paper. Kevin Wendle and Garth Ancier decided that Barry would not like the texture, and everything was redone with a perishable paper at a cost of thirty-five thousand dollars. At the very last minute Barry brought in his personal decorator, who furnished the greenroom with seventy thousand dollars' worth of expensive antiques. Their private little executive greenroom was done in English country—tweedy, lots of leather. When I heard they were hiring a bartender, I screamed, "Never mind the bartender! Give us another secretary, a messenger boy."

Three days before we went on the air, I got a call—please come see your dressing room; the decorators are all upset. I had been busy reading stacks of writers' material, watching tapes of comics, going in person to the Comedy Store, and had taken no interest in my dressing room. I had simply asked for two rooms, an outer room for my staff and an inner room with a sink to wash my hair and a private bathroom. I told them, "Just paint it peach."

But they had given me seven rooms, including a little bedroom for naps. The wallpaper in one of the two bathrooms had been changed twice. I found it embarrassing. I never did furnish it with any permanence—just in case I walked in someday and found a stranger sitting at my dressing table.

I wanted to hang my SOLD OUT poster from my Carnegie Hall appearance but couldn't find it, so instead I hung the *Rabbit Test* poster from Sweden, where it was a runaway hit. This gave me courage that maybe I did belong in such a huge suite. On the hall of the outer room, at the center of a line of nails, I hung a picture of Barry and me holding hands at the announcement press conference—but ripped down the middle—my side and his side. This was going to be my Barry-o-meter. When we were getting along, the two pictures would hang side by side, Barry and me holding hands. If something was wrong in paradise, I would move them apart.

I imagined Barry checking the Barry-o-meter every day, and saying to me, "Oops it's a bad day," or threatening me—"I'll move the Barry-o-meter!" Another game. Eventually the pictures were so far apart, I ran out of wall space.

On the same tour I visited the studio for the first time. I had made two specific requests—no carpet under the audience's seats because it absorbs laughter and applause, changing the acoustics—and a steep rise in the audience section so the noise would bounce out to the microphones. I found carpet on the floor and made Fox rip it out overnight. This eventually leaked out to the press as me being capricious and bitchy.

I stood behind the last row and looked down the steep slope of seats to the stage. I knew I belonged there. No doubt about it. What knocked me out, really killed me—I was standing in the same distant spot, seeing the same scene I remembered from the first time I saw a television studio in the early 1950s. I had come on the subway from Brooklyn with my friend Connie Witty to see *Your Show of Shows* with Sid Caesar and Imogene Coca.

That day flooded back to me, my certainty that this business was what I wanted more than *anything* else in the world. I remember that I did not know how I would get from the back row, down all those steps, past the cameras, and onto the stage—but I knew I was going to try, was going to do anything to make a whole theater full of people happy. And now I thought, That girl who was there—this is her studio. I wished I could tell that little girl, "Relax, you're going to have your *Show of Shows.*"

14

ooooo

It took seven months for Fox to kill me off. Every day of my life—since the show debuted on October 9, 1986–I think of those months. But now the anger has dulled. My view is almost clinical, the distant bitterness one would feel about a relative who died five years ago due to medical malpractice.

The night of the premiere was the one moment of unity in the midst of the fighting, the time when we were triumphant and relieved that we had made our deadline, that we were launched. I myself felt terrific. The hassling since January was worth it. Absolutely.

The night of the premiere, standing backstage, I heard the call over the speakers, "Two minutes to airtime. Two minutes to airtime." A red neon sign, QUIET PLEASE, LIVE SHOW IN PROGRESS, kept flashing like a police-light. Out in the studio the audience stamped and clapped. In the middle of a swirl of stagehands, writers, technicians, prop girls, Fox executives, I stood rigid, like a rock in a stream, my heart thumping against my ribs as I breathed deeply, pumping out the tension. Looking at this controlled frenzy, I thought, Everybody's livelihood is on my shoulders. If I don't work, they don't eat. I prayed, "Please, God, let the show work. Let me still be good."

The backstage loudspeaker was intoning, "Three seconds. Two seconds." My hairdresser, Jason Dyl, gave my hair a last touch. The announcer, Clint Holmes, shouted, "Ladies and gentlemen, Miss Joan Riv-ers!"

I plunged forward from the darkness into the brilliant dome of light; the audience was standing, and the applause washed over me. I went over to the audience and found people and shook their hands, I touched them, and even kissed two women. I loved every person there, and they were all telling me that they loved me back.

They made the whole Fox journey worthwhile because they were my family, opening the door for me. I had been waiting for that moment since I had left Carson, waiting through five months of fighting to get to that spot, to get back in front of an audience, to stand in front of people who wanted me to be a winner because that meant they had come to the right show, had picked the right horse.

When I turned and walked back onto the set, all the hassling with Fox fell away. I felt I was walking into the bright future. Fox would see that I had an audience in America and that people wanted me. I silently promised myself, If I have to write every joke myself, I'll make the show work. If I have to beg every guest myself, I'll make it work. If I have to run the cameras, sweep the floors, answer the phones, give up everything else in my life, I'll stay right here.

The guests were remarkable. There was Elton John, who almost never does a talk show. He played "The Bitch Is Back" while I stood with my hand on the piano, almost buffeted by the force of the sound and his startling energy. There was a white-hot David Lee Roth, fresh from his split with Van Halen, wildly outrageous, full of sex, full of the devil. He interrupted a tour and flew out from the East, did the show, and flew right back. We had Cher, who rushed over from the set of *The Witches of Eastwick* to be my friend and sing "The Bitch Is Back." And Pee-wee Herman—long before the tragic scandal—one of the biggest names in America at that time, was there to be silly with me, let me play. I thought, I wish my mother could see me.

That first night was the wedding. Fox never took me on a honeymoon. The bridegroom walked the next morning when he read the press reviews. They said things like, "No need, Johnny, to lose sleep over the new challenger," and called the audience "moronic" and "airheads." Tom Shales wrote in *The Washington Post*, "Maybe Rivers should spend less time at the beauty parlor and more time with her writers. The beauty parlor would appear to be a lost cause for her anyway."

I think those first newspaper columns did irreparable damage. I think they confirmed Fox's distrust of my judgment, of my comedy instincts, and the fear and doubts went all the way up to Diller. When you distrust, you begin following your own judgment. So from then on everybody had an opinion, had input.

There was a second reason the groom walked. Ratings. After being promised that honeymoon, at least a year to find ourselves without worry, the numbers were instantly crucial. They were the fuel for the fire that ultimately consumed Edgar and me. And Fox, either from naïveté or to get the affiliates to the altar, had based the financial arrangements on a guaranteed 6 rating—the number that the Carson show pulled. In fact, a year earlier, when I went to a sales meeting for affiliates in Chicago, I heard Murdoch himself promise a 6. I was amazed—but still believed they knew what they were doing. Later, when stations got 2's and 3's, Fox had to make up the difference by reimbursing the stations with free programming. I believe that, disappointed by the reviews and ratings in those early weeks, Barry Diller wanted to get out of the deal. He had promised me and the affiliates more than he was able to comfortably deliver.

Our ratings in the first week, when the show was competing with the World Series, were 3.2 nationally in 98 markets, each point representing 921,000 homes. Carson's were 6.4 in 202 markets. In the next few weeks, when we began averaging 3.9 in the big cities and 2's in the small stations, Fox panicked. In the third week the president of Fox Broadcasting, Jamie Kellner, told me he pulled his car over to the side of the road and prayed for good ratings.

It is the nature of show business that everybody panics, even at the highest level. Rarely is there anybody who is saying in the face of bad news, "Ho, ho, ho, everything's all right." When the movie doesn't open big at the box office, the reaction is "Oh, my God," not "By God, we'll back this movie till it finds its audience."

None of the Fox executives, including Diller, ever seemed to understand the realities of their network. At that time it was a conglomeration of ninety-eight affiliates, twelve of them established stations in big cities like Los Angeles, New York, Chicago, Dallas, Atlanta. The rest were peripheral stations with short radius signals, the weakest sisters in their area. Des Moines had four stations—Fox's was number four in power; Dayton had four—Fox's was fourth; Chattanooga had four, and Fox's was fourth, and so on. These stations had channel numbers like 29 in Buffalo and 47 in Toronto. I used to joke, "They'd watch us if they could find us."

Most of these small stations were relatively new, formed when FCC regulations eased, allowing more stations. However, as the number of stations increased, the supply of programs stayed the same, and these small stations, unable to afford first-run shows, were broadcasting mainly movies and series reruns. Fox's strategy was to offer a whole menu of high-quality, first-run shows, affordable because the stations were allotted time for local advertising.

Advertising fees are based on ratings, and these peripheral stations had to live on .8's and 1's. Now *The Late Show* gave them a 2 or even a 3 rating on late night. They were thrilled. They were not only getting more money, but also respectability and recognition and the benefit of the national publicity I received. They were suddenly *stations*!

Fox never seemed to realize that in the real market world, my numbers were not only respectable, but probably the best they could ever expect. When the ratings did not climb to 6's, I and the show were blamed—and the fact that the show was a success was never proved to Fox until it was too late.

Moreover, I have since learned an infuriating fact. During all the harassment by Fox, all the arguing about expenses, the show was never losing money. I was told by a Fox executive that the break-even point, no money made or lost, was a 2 rating, and our lowest dip was 2.1 in January. My source said, "Joan Rivers could be on the air right now earning everybody including Fox a good living."

Instead, the show suffered a terminal version of the Bicker-sons—a senseless campaign of executive gamesmanship, cut-backs, penny-pinching, and harassments that must have flowed from the top. Ever since that first meeting about announcing the show, ever since I made that joke about the guards, Barry be-lieved he could not work with Edgar and me. That attitude would then have been picked up by the chain of command, by Kevin Wendle and Ron Vandor, and the story of the next seven months—until I could be moved out—became the struggle by Fox to take control of the show.

In such a situation I am sure that everybody thought he was working for the good of the show—but the net result was that nobody was truly in charge. Fox, with a lot of power and no plan, a lot of energy and no knowledge, ended up with a show that was like the man who mounted the horse and rode off in all direc-tions.

The struggle for control started the very first week. I had been guaranteed by contract control of all creative aspects of the show—essentially what happened on camera. But in those first days I discovered that in his mind, Barry Diller had torn up the contract.

We came up with the idea of a mock anniversary show cele-brating our first five days on the air—a great spoof because Car-son's anniversary was happening soon. We planned all the cliché schticks—put everybody in gowns and tuxedos, run clips of ear-lier shows and say how young we all looked, set up each guest to reminisce, "I'll never forget what you said Tuesday night, Joan." We could not wait to do it.

The idea went up the chain of command, and the answer came back down, "You can't do it." In midweek I encountered Barry in the Fox parking lot and for an hour made a last-ditch plea,

pointing out that David Letterman, before he came up with
stupid pet tricks, tried at least a dozen ideas that did not work.
I argued, "I don't want to be Carson. I don't want to be Letterman. I want to be me, my humor, whatever that turns out to
mean"—which I guess meant silly, acerbic, female-oriented, gos-
sipy, trying anything.

Barry, very cool, just kept saying, "No. It's not funny."

Barry was paying me $5 million a year because I was funny,
and was now overruling my judgment. But I was still trying to get
along with him, so I gave up and got in my car. As I started to
drive away, he ran over and knocked on the window. I thought
he was going to say, "All right. You can do it." But when I rolled
the window down, he said, "You are the strongest woman I have
ever met in my life," then he turned and went back to his car.
I took it as a compliment, but now I am not so sure.

After that night Barry Diller must have thought, Who needs
this aggravation? And from that point forward, I could not get
him on the phone. He had Twentieth Century–Fox to oversee
and prime-time programming to worry about. He did not have
the time or energy to "handle" me, to laugh and say, "Do this and
I owe you. Next time, you win." I suspect day-to-day control of
Edgar and me was turned over to his young lieutenants—the
Iago-ettes, who I believe began whispering in his ear that they
could do a better show without me. Barry sat back, figuring if the
show worked, fine. If it didn't, we would get what we deserved.
So I ended up in a phone booth with a quarter in my hand, and
nobody to call—except my lawyer.

I went about my business, followed my bliss, as somebody once
said. I did have my *Show of Shows,* and loved the challenge of
pulling it together in one day—the suspense of will it work, will
it be on time, will the guests show up? Between 11:00 A.M. and
8:00 P.M. we created an entire hour of entertainment—phones
going, people running around—like a bustling newsroom working on deadline. A nightly, live talk show is so immediate, the
logistics of it so pressured—the rehearsal, getting guests in and
out, making sure they show, what they will say, scripts done—
nothing waits till tomorrow.

When I arrived, I went first to the writers' meeting, where we worked on future ideas and stunts—and that was terrific because when something is good, it's exciting, and comedy writers are funny. After the meeting a file of jokes for that day's monologue was waiting on my desk. I would choose the ones I liked and add my own.

Then I met the segment coordinators, one by one. They would brief me on that night's guests, and we would agree on a list of questions.

My last stop before going to my dressing room for hair and makeup was the bookers' office to look at the board of names on the wall. The bookers, Patti Bourgeois and Saundra Zagaria, each with her Rolodex full of names, sat opposite each other in the middle of the room and worked fifteen-hour days.

Edgar was important to Saundra and Patti, their source for intellectual and real-life ideas—Ralph Nader, Eugene McCarthy, Nancy Reagan, and authors culled from *Publishers Weekly* and *The New York Times.* He talked to Melissa and her friends about who was hot, whom they listened to, what movies they saw. When Patti and Saundra wondered about the chemistry between me and possible guests, they asked Edgar.

In turn he took their advice, listened to their criticisms, fought for them, got proper salaries, the right desks, and when he learned one of them had a crush on Tom Cruise moved heaven and earth to book him. That office was the one place where Edgar felt at home and comfortable and appreciated. Patty and Saundra saved new books for him and teased him, naming a three-foot purple bug-eyed stuffed animal "Edgar." You walked in, and there would be Edgar in his three-piece suit sitting on the couch next to his namesake, wearing a set of Mickey Mouse ears, or what he called his "thinking cap"—a silver-domed replica of a Hershey's Kiss. This was the playful side that Edgar showed only when he felt people really liked him—the side that had rarely surfaced since we left New York.

One end of the long couch became Billy Sammeth's desk. Like Edgar, he had the title of executive producer, but his primary responsibility was the booking board behind the sofa, a square for each night of the month. It was wonderful to listen to him, sprawled there all afternoon, calling managers and agents and studio heads to woo the major stars, pouring persuasion into the phone.

Billy was brilliant at this job, and I loved to hear him say, in his special tone of charming challenge, "Pick a day, Mr. Agent. Let me tell you something. If you don't support Joan, we'll go on being at the mercy of Carson. If he doesn't want your client, you'll have nowhere else to go. Let's make two shows work, with two different audiences. Let's give everybody their six minutes on late night."

Louie Anderson, God bless him, was the first major comic who defied Carson and did my show. So many in Hollywood are scared of their own shadow. Edgar used to say, "They created this monster. By giving Carson first priority, they gave him a monopoly." I was finding out who really had courage, which ones were smart and secure and knew they were big and did not have to worry about being blackballed. That Ted Danson would come on the second night, the pride of the NBC family . . . and Kenny Rogers, who was a Carson guest host. . . .

Nell Carter, a major NBC star in *Gimme a Break,* came to see me in my dressing room in Atlantic City and said, "Honey, you got me." She is warm and generous, smart and funny and a terrific talent. She's been up, she's been down, she's been through it, and she has come out of it. I just love her.

Sometimes Billy would ask me to get on the phone; we were calling in every favor. Lily Tomlin is one of the great guests, so I phoned her and said to her assistant, "I need Lily to come on my show. They're all saying a woman can't make a show like this work. I'm sick of reading that it's a man's world. I need help." She came.

We wanted Roy Orbison, a rock-and-roll name to conjure with, but a man whose manager always refused talk shows, even Carson. Melissa's former governess, Marcia Tysseling, knew the governess of Roy Orbison's child. Through her we bypassed his manager and talked to Roy personally; he was wonderful and said yes.

Michelle Phillips was a guest. She said "tits and ass" and "shit" and talked about safe sex and how she gave her daughter and her daughter's friends condoms—kept a basket of them in her living room—"every color you can imagine." She was a friend of Barry's, and I think they went out to dinner afterward. I heard Rupert Murdoch was watching that night, too. I had to laugh because Fox was always nervous about my tongue.

Robin Givens, long before she dated Mike Tyson, came on the show. At that time she had done only the pilot for the series she later got. Yet this was not a girl saying, "I hope my career is going to work." She had a major attitude—"Here I am. I'm Queen of the World." She also fibbed a bit, told me she had been a medical student, which we now know was untrue.

I had Mike Tyson on another show. He talked about the Lord and showed me a bracelet he never took off, given him by his dead manager and surrogate father, Cus D'Amato. He was very sweet. Eugene McCarthy, another guest, seemed terribly sad to me. He was a fumbler, a mumbler, indecisive, with very little to say. I thought, This is the man we were going to give the leadership of our country? Don King I loved because he and my dog Spike had the same hairdo. Ray Charles was truly an icon—such great joy coming out of his sightless face. Jill Ireland, full of spunk, talked about having only one breast after her operation. She said, "My husband has the best of both. He wants a boy, he looks to my left. He wants a girl, he looks to my right." I miss her.

Nancy Reagan was a guest, and when she talked about her early courtship years with Ronnie, she teared up on camera. The next night Lucille Ball came on. A few months earlier, with huge fanfare and every magazine cover, she had gone into a new series with a contractual guarantee of a full season's run. Then her ratings were poor, and she was canceled. She came on my show reeling. She sat there in the chair, forever "Lucy," a major star, and began to cry. "They don't want me anymore."

When she came onto my stage, she received a standing ovation, but she was living every performer's nightmare. Later, when she was in the hospital dying, fans strung a banner across the street from her window, saying, WE LOVE YOU, LUCY. Meanwhile, nobody wanted to watch her new show. I think you cannot go away from television. Television is a matter of habit. People are happy to grow old with you and tune in as part of their life, but once you've been invisible for a while, the habit is broken.

I found that hosting my own show was very different from being the guest host on Carson, where I was in a brick house, totally secure; people would watch me and wonder, God knows what she's going to say or ask next. *The Tonight Show* was like going to somebody else's party in a great dress, and now at Fox I had to throw the party myself, night after night, and worry whether everybody had a good time.

I did not dare say to a major star, "Oh, come on . . . this is your fourth marriage and he's a hundred years younger than you are, and you're telling me it's true love?" I was praying to get her back—and had been on the phone fifteen times begging her to come to me instead of Carson. Big stars come on your show as a favor and expect thank-yous and flowers. I was constantly torn. Linda Evans refused to come on because she was afraid of me. At the same time Billy Sammeth told me I was being too ladylike. And the press was saying I had far more gush than guts.

But that natural caution was not enough for Fox. The Fox people tried to reach out in front of the camera itself to control me. I think what they really wanted was a Barbara Walters spiced with a few one-liners. Whatever Diller's young lieutenants thought intellectually about the show, no matter how much everybody agreed I had to be different, in the Fox mind-set, mainstream television was still the blueprint for success. I think that, without any feel for late-night content, they were frightened and shocked when they felt the rules were being broken.

From the beginning it was, "Be careful. You can't." They hired me for what I am—dangerous and spontaneous and sometimes tasteless—but the first time I was at all outrageous, they went crazy. During the first two weeks I included an old joke I had used on Carson: "I don't understand country-and-western music. They sing, 'My husband left me. Sheeet, sheeet, sheeet'—and everybody cries, 'Boo hoo hoo hoo.' Now that's deep."

Afterward, Kevin Wendle was waiting in my dressing room, very angry: "How could you say that joke!" I asked, "What joke?"

He said, "That shit joke. You said 'shit' on the air." He began to yell, shaking his finger in my face. "You are never to say that again. Never. Never."

It was Peter Lassally all over, but worse because Kevin was so rude. I yelled back, "I'll say shit all I want! Shit! shit! shit! I'll give you some more! I'll give you fucks! Fuck! fuck! fuck!" He turned beet red.

We were both behaving like children. But I felt like a child who was being kissed and slapped at the same time—who had been hired because she could push the limits of TV and was now being told, "Don't make waves."

After the scene in the dressing room, Kevin, like Diller, disappeared from our view, but not from our lives, and we dealt almost entirely with Ron Vandor, who requested that my monologue be on his desk every day by three o'clock so it could be circulated at Fox. About a half hour before showtime Ron would come into the dressing room and say, "You've got to take out jokes seven and nine; you can't make a joke about Kurt Waldheim being a Nazi." Fox was worried about offending Nazis?

I know now that everybody was allowed to have an opinion about what I was doing, and Vandor was just a messenger boy. He also announced he wanted daily hour-long meetings with me to critique the last night's show. I said no. I felt the whole idea was insulting, and in daily programming you are under tremendous time pressure.

You arrive in the morning and want to know, "Where is my monologue, where are my notes for the interviews?" Somebody tells you, "We lost Meryl Streep," and you say, "Quick, quick, can we get Susan Sarandon?" Or Eddie Murphy is flying from New York and will arrive at the last minute—and the plane is late. "Well, where are the notes for Murphy?" "Well, we couldn't preinterview him because he was unavailable. His cousin is graduating from college." "Well, the writers can't write the snappers without the material."

Meanwhile, you are worrying, "Who's going to be on tomorrow?" And there's nobody good on the booking board for next week—so you put in six phone calls. I should be trying to get

Whitney Houston, not sitting with Ron Vandor—and afterward I would have to report the conversation to Peter Dekom, who would tell me, "You shouldn't have said . . ."

One night early in the show, the pressure, the disappointment, became unbearable. Fifteen minutes before showtime, after Vandor had given me his instructions in the dressing room, instead of going backstage and waiting to start the show, I just walked out of the building and off the Fox lot. I stood on a bridge over the freeway and wept and wept. Courtney Conte followed me at a distance, then led me back and pushed me onstage.

Since I was their *only* show, the executives had nothing to do but sit around and second-guess what we did, tell us, "Too many guests, too few guests; not funny, too much comedy." They looked at each show as *the* show and did not understand that the cumulative impact is what matters, that if you make a mistake now and then, it's okay.

Anything can be pulled apart. You could go through the Bible page by page—"Pillar of salt? Oh, no, I wouldn't ever turn to salt. No, wait, let's make it a pillar of dusting powder. Better. I don't like the use of sandals. I think there should only be Seven Commandments. One for each day of the week."

A big issue between me and Fox was the stunts we did to establish a separate identity—to go for a younger audience, closer to Letterman than to Carson. Some stunts worked. The biggest laugh I ever got on television came after days and days of ending the show by blowing a kiss to Willard Scott, the weatherman on the *Today* show. I never told anybody what I was setting up, not even Edgar. They must have all thought I was being truly ridiculous. But Willard began talking about it on the *Today* show. Finally he came on my show and kept asking why I liked him so much. I said, "We have a lot in common." I pulled off a blond wig—and under it I was completely bald.

When Al Campanis of the Los Angeles Dodgers said black people cannot swim, we reacted immediately. That was the point of a live show. Though Vandor and Wendle did their best to stop us—"It's going to cost too much money. It's not funny"—we had a swimming pool onstage. A black usher and I jumped in and, of course, he swam and I sank. It made all the papers.

Some things that looked funny on paper did not work. Because we lacked the money to travel, we spent a week pretending to be in a different country every night. It was embarrassing. We wore turkey costumes for Thanksgiving. I explained that we were a poor show and could not afford a real Christmas tree, and I brought on a handsome young surfer who stood there and during the week before Christmas we trimmed him a little more each night. So stupid. Such stunts looked to Barry Diller like random searching, but in fact all shows as young as ours take time to find their footing.

Of course, the day came when Wendle and Vandor came up with their own stunt. The wanted to do a mystery show based on the phenomenon of the mystery weekend, a minivacation pastime then becoming popular around the country. I argued against the idea, but went along, thinking, If you don't try, you don't know.

Early in the show our woman saxophonist was "murdered" during a commercial. Then guests and staff dropped clues. The audience and Jimmy Coco, who played an Inspector Clouseau type, were supposed to solve the mystery. But you cannot superimpose nonreality on a real situation. That is too complicated. Nobody knew what the hell was going on. The audience was confused, I was confused, the guests were confused. Backstage after the show Ron Vandor was saying, "This is our Emmy show," and I was thinking, You are out of your mind.

Throughout the fall of 1986 the show was two armed camps with little raids conducted back and forth across battle lines, destructive for all concerned. Almost every day I felt hit by a petty crisis. Nothing had much to do with business. It was like *The War of the Roses.* Everybody had to get everybody. You did this to us, we'll do that to you. Oh, if you're going to do that, I'll do this. Wow! Did you ever dream I could get you that way? Ha! Ha! It was games, but not my kind. It was insane games.

When I asked for a couch in my little office where the writers' meeting was held (everyone had to stand up or drag in chairs), Ron Vandor said there was nothing in the budget for my office. So I had to bootleg a couch. When I asked in October for a week off in December, Jess Wittenberg, the Fox lawyer, wanted more lead time.

Fox was angry that I was flying all over the country to do concert dates. The network thought I was exhausting myself—when in reality my trips alone to Atlanta or Detroit or Minneapolis were revitalizing. I was able to escape and laugh and make contact with real people who kept me in touch with what America thought was funny.

To this day I still wonder why Barry allowed the situation to disintegrate so totally. But who knows how information was translated as it made its way up and down the ladder of command. I remember the producer complaining when Kevin Wendle and Ron Vandor would tell him, "Barry feels that . . ." We never knew whether it was true.

For example, I decided to dress Beverly, the saxophonist, in a sparkly dress to make her stand out—she was becoming a personality. Vandor came into my office and told me no. I had insisted on tuxedos for the orchestra when he wanted short rumba jackets. So his general message was, "You wanted tuxedos? Well, then they'll all wear tuxedos."

That was the instant when the months of feeling dismissed and disliked, the months of disappointment, of feeling, It's not fair—all detonated together. I picked up a glass ashtray and threw it at the wall—and it didn't even break.

The next day my limousine was canceled because someone told someone I had trashed my office. I telephoned Barry, and this time he took my call. I said, "They've cut off my limo."

He said, "You trashed your office."

I told him, "I do not trash offices."

He would not listen.

I told him, "Come over and look."

He answered, "I have to believe what my people tell me," and hung up. I went three days without a limo before Fox relented. It was like a Shakespearean conspiracy. An hour later I was onstage trying to be funny.

Barry was not malevolent. Both of us thought we were fighting on the side of right and God. If only he had come over and looked at the office and started to laugh, then I could have said to him, "You're putting all this money behind us, leave me alone for six months. If nothing else, I'm an old war-horse, so give me your stamp and let me go."

Instead, we continued to be the Bickersons in Wonderland. I don't know about other businesses, but when show-business people are frightened, we can behave like children. I think immature people gravitate to show business, people needy for the celebrity, the power, and the love it can bring almost overnight—a life larger than life. In show business we can even act out the fantasies that have been our escape from reality, escape from ever having to grow up.

Supposedly Diana Ross was very angry at somebody at Caesars Palace, so during her entire two-week engagement, nobody was allowed to make eye contact with her. Tommy Smothers wanted only American Indians on their last Smothers Brothers TV show, and when the producer disagreed, he was banned from the set. When a major male actor did not get a good parking space soon enough, he left his car under a tree to be covered with bird droppings—then parked it in the executive lot.

A studio head who shall also be nameless arrived at the Los Angeles airport and found a blue limo waiting for him. He was furious. He had told people a thousand times he rode only in black limos. He said, "Only pimps ride in colored limos. My bags can ride in this car. I'll take a taxi."

I myself reached a helpless point where I wanted to hurt the Fox people so badly that I decided to hide a fish in the posh little executive greenroom, nicknamed "Diller Acres." It would stink, and they would not be able to figure out where the smell was coming from, and that's how I would get back at them. I actually bought the fish. Talk about childish revenge! That's for the third grade, not when you have the house on the hill with servants.

I remember a meeting with Peter Dekom sitting at the head of the table while Jamie Kellner and Barry sat across from Edgar and me. Everybody was shouting and getting personal, and Peter started laughing. "Do you realize what you are fighting about?" he asked. "People would buy tickets to see this."

Jess Wittenberg was constantly on the phone to Peter, who warned us that the network was building a case to break my contract, conducting a campaign to annoy and humiliate me—anything it could devise to provoke me into breaching my contract, into not showing up or doing something horrendous on the air.

Frightened, we brought in a firm of litigation lawyers to guide us—so now two sets of lawyers were checking every decision—"If I do this for Fox, is that setting a precedent? If I don't, is it breach of contract?" There seemed no way to reverse the war of nerves and say to Fox, "Let's stop and start again." If the ratings had gone up and up, the sun would have come out. But the national ratings had settled into the high 2's and low 3's, below Fox's unrealistic expectations.

In November the lives around me—the people I depended on personally and professionally—began falling apart in tragedy. Billy Sammeth's mother developed cancer, and he was hit very hard. He continued coming to the office, but in pieces. Jason Dyl, who for years had selected my clothes and jewelry, given me my look, tested positive for AIDS.

My husband, my partner, was disappearing into his own morass. While I was a moving, slippery target, Edgar was a sitting duck whom Diller detested. If they could not break me, they could take aim at him.

A central issue was Edgar's constant use of the letter of the contract—"Carson standards or better"—to get his way. Finally Wittenberg reneged in writing, saying that *The Tonight Show* was not a "template" for my show. But Fox, too, by God, was going to dot every contractual *i*.

For example, there was a stupid fight about the limousine Fox supplied to take me back and forth to the studio. I liked to arrive at the studio around 1:00 P.M., so I'd have the morning to do household things, write my jokes, and handle personal business. Edgar wanted to get to the studio long before noon. Waiting for me and my limo made him nervous and agitated, and he would chivy me—"Come on. Come on." He could not drive himself because at night he was too exhausted to drive the fifty-minute return trip. In September the limo took him in and then came back for me. In November, Fox said Edgar could not use the limo by himself. So we rode together, and he saved face, but I had to get up early—which I *hated*.

Next Wittenberg passed the word through Peter Dekom that the contract said I was to be given a limo but not Edgar, so he could not even ride with me. It was just lawyers' tricks, so I sent word back that I would drive my own car with my husband, and the limo could follow me. They backed down.

Then the day came when I had to face the fact that Edgar had begun to crack. While the lawyers were fighting, while I was on the phone constantly with Dekom, while the second team of lawyers was riding shotgun, all of us fighting to keep the show on track, Edgar was worrying about his office bookshelves. They had finally arrived and weren't tall enough for him. That was when I knew I was in deep, deep trouble.

At home Edgar kept railing about the shelves, wanting to call the lawyer. I tried to tell him, "Don't worry about the goddam bookshelves. Don't pick on everything. Let it go; let it go." But he was obsessed. This was a matter of principle—"You don't understand. You can't let it go. They promised us . . ."

It was the first time in twenty-one years I could not reach him on a rational level, the first major sign to me that something was deeply wrong with my husband, the first time I thought, Oh, my God, I've got to watch him, too. This was when I remembered what the UCLA doctors had said. They had warned me that during the monthlong coma Edgar might have lost what they called "instinctual judgment." For months every issue had had equal importance, equal weight.

I was so on edge, my exasperation took over, and we had a fight, one so bad, Edgar slept in Melissa's room. The next morning I put my head in the door to make peace, but he was still asleep. I checked his breathing, and he seemed normal—just sleeping late as he always did when depressed.

This was the night Nancy Reagan, then the first lady, was to be a guest on the show, and the Secret Service men were swarming through the studio, checking everything. During a meeting with my segment producers, my secretary rang through to me—"It's Edgar, and he sounds drunk." On the phone, mumbling almost incoherently, Edgar said, "I think I'm having a stroke."

Suddenly at four o'clock I was in a car creeping to the UCLA hospital—forty-five minutes through rush-hour traffic knowing I had to be back in full makeup onstage at eight o'clock. In my head beat the words, "I did it to him. I did it to him. I did it to him." Edgar was in the emergency room, and I rushed to the bed. He looked up at me and said in a horrible, dead voice, "Get out of here. I don't want to see you. Get away"—and then to the nurse, "I want her out."

I stayed until the doctors decided it was not a stroke; they did not know what it was. He said he had taken a single sleeping pill, and they concluded it had been old and toxic. But I think psychologically he was ill with the fear that he was more and more unnecessary, that I was subtly slipping away from him, absorbed by the show.

I got back to the studio in time for Nancy Reagan. After the show, as I walked down the hall to my dressing room, Barry Diller and Rupert Murdoch came out of the private VIP greenroom. They passed me in that narrow corridor without a word.

In early November Fox held a huge meeting for the affiliate stations. In the second week of that month the stations in Seattle, Toledo, and Atlanta increased their late-night ratings 300 percent. Cities like Hartford, San Diego, Spokane, Dallas, West Palm Beach, increased 200 percent, and ratings for places like Mobile, Fort Wayne, Amarillo, Grand Rapids, went up by 100 percent. The average increase of all Fox affiliates because of my show was 69 percent. But Fox did not invite me, the only new show on the network, to the affiliates' dinner right there at Fox Broadcasting.

When I believe I am right, there is no such thing as pride or manners or rules. I'll do anything, stop at nothing. I never want to put my head down on that pillow feeling there was one more thing I could have tried. I decided to crash the dinner.

I arrived feeling frightened, embarrassed, and furious—but when I came waltzing in to the dinner, the station managers were delighted with me as I walked among the tables and shook hands. They told me I was giving them numbers they had never dreamed of. One man said, "You're making me rich."

I was so desperate, I actually thought these men were going to save me, were going to bring Fox to its senses. I thought they would telephone Fox and say, "I don't care what's going on there. I used to get a point three rating, now I get a two. God bless Joan Rivers."

What a dream!

15

ооооо

On November 13 Barry Diller finally called a meeting of the two camps to discuss a solution. I told our lawyers I was so devastated by Fox, I could not look Barry in the eyes—would just sit there and do my needlepoint. Our chief litigation lawyer, Richard Borow, said, "Let me tell you a story. A farmer bought the meanest rooster alive, and it went into the henhouse and screwed all the hens till they were all dead. Then the rooster went into the barn and screwed the cows till they were dead—and then the horses. Finally the farmer came out, and there was the rooster lying dead with vultures circling overhead. The farmer said, 'It's about time, you S.O.B.' The rooster opened one eye and said, 'Shhhh. If you want to screw a vulture, you got to play their game.' "

So I sat there across from Diller and his lieutenants, acting as though we were all on the same team—while Barry did the same.

Barry started out saying that the quality of the show was not the issue. "The on-air show does not seem to be the problem," Barry said. "The show is good."

He said, "We're sure that a lot of difficulties between us have been caused by our actions and by me." If he'd stayed with that thought, had said he wanted to be friends and let us feel listened to, let us vent all our nonsense and take our share of blame, the pain and tragedy and waste that followed might have been averted.

But that was scary territory for Barry. He was unable to deal in feelings and psychologies. Instead, Barry looked for an answer in the bottom line. He suggested we reverse our roles. As overall producer of the show, Fox set the budget for various categories and enforced it, battling us about size and salaries, etc. Barry offered to give us the role of producer, letting us take over administration of the budget, deciding ourselves how to apportion the money. We could decide if we needed ten writers and no set or ten sets and no writers. Well, that was what we had asked for; we were very encouraged.

Then, almost as an aside, came what I now think was the real reason for the meeting. "Frankly," Barry said, "if we're going to live together for a long time, we either feel nicer about each other or we don't live together for a long time." It was a major threat, but aimed at my team, not his boys. They were going to continue living at Fox, even if we died. So the issue with Fox was our relationship with the executives. I still wonder whether, if Edgar and I had really heard that, we would have capitulated then and kept the show.

Leaving the lunch after the meeting, he walked around the table and touched me on the shoulder. With that, I was convinced that, after all, he was still behind us. Even then. But this was just another of the mixed messages Barry had been putting out—taking my side at an occasional meeting, giving me the announcer I had wanted.

In the weeks that followed, if Barry had been serious, he was sabotaged from below. Nobody at Fox ever followed through on what he had suggested. Nothing changed. Ron Vandor was still in the office telling us what to do. No matter how much we asked and assumed, we never received a serious breakdown of the budget, we were never given the power to make independent financial decisions. We called Diller but never got through. I guess Barry just walked away and didn't want to know. And, once again, nothing made sense. The pressure for numbers increased.

On February 6, I received a phone call: "This is Jamie Kellner. Let me just read you the numbers for the past few weeks. They're down—three point two, three point one, three, two point nine." Then I learned from my friend at NBC, Jay Michelis, that Doctor Ruth, the sexologist, had gone on the air with her new show and pulled viewers from all of late night. "Everybody's numbers are dropping," he said, "Letterman, Carson, everybody. Didn't they tell you that?" Was Fox that naïve, I wondered, or just trying to keep us off-balance?

It must have been the latter, because that month a press announcement went out saying that on a network unavailable to one in five households, *The Late Show* had increased its women viewers by 45 percent, a higher rate than any other late show. Moreover, the advertising for the fourth quarter of 1986 had been sold out, and the first and second quarters of 1987 were sold out. The affiliates were making 200 to 300 percent more money.

Nonetheless, on February 26, 1987, Fox made its first overt move to take over the show. Barry's threat from the November meeting came to pass. We were told—without consulting us— that the contract of our producer, Bruce McKay, would not be renewed when it expired April 3. And henceforth Edgar and I were not to deal directly with the staff of the show. Any suggestions we had must be passed through Bruce McKay, now a lame-duck producer. I would be allowed to work with the writers and segment producers, but not "supervise" them, not give them any directions or make any decisions.

That meant I would come in and receive the monologue and do the show. I would become a puppet. Frankly, if I had thought that would solve the problem, I would have done it, but without the imprint of my identity, the show would just be a mishmash. Now the true agenda was coming out in the open—Kevin Wendle and Ron Vandor said openly they thought they could do a better show. Well, later they got their chance.

We ignored the order and operated exactly as we had before, I supervising my meetings, Edgar still sitting with Bruce at the console during the show.

And finally, as I later discovered, Jamie Kellner was talking with Barry Sand, the original producer of the Letterman show, about creating a show to replace mine.

It was during February that my last prop, Billy Sammeth, cracked under the strain. I had counted on his booking prowess to keep the show afloat, to compete with Carson. But because of his mother's illness, he had been growing increasingly depressed, increasingly unavailable. He hated the confrontations on the show. As both our manager and an executive producer, he was constantly in the middle. Fox pressured him to control us, and we were unhappy that the man we were paying as our manager was not taking strong stands.

Billy was also buckling under the pressure of trying to get *Tonight Show*–quality guests without its clout. And like the rest of us, he was physically ground down by the stress of a live show, working all day and then staying on for the show and postshow meetings afterward, never getting home until midnight. For the staff, the show was like house arrest. When Fox research found out that broadcasting live made no difference, we begged to go to tape the way Letterman and Carson do, but Fox refused.

Without Billy's full attention the guest list declined. I began looking at the booking board and saying, "Oh, yeah, okay," and trying to make second-rank guests work—some of them unknowns pushed on us because they were in new Fox series.

And on top of the pressure of an ill husband, the pressure of running my house and mothering my daughter away at college, the pressure from the press shooting at me, the pressure of Fox trying to fix the show when it was not broken—there was the pressure of putting on a good show each night.

To this day I work best when I am relaxed, when everybody loves me, when the staff, the advertisers, the people who put up the money, are all happy and affectionate. I am not relaxed when I pass Ron Vandor on the stairs and we do not say hello, when Kevin Wendle turns away from me as I go onstage, when every night I have to call my lawyer. I no longer went in front of the cameras feeling, This is my show, my kingdom. I never stopped monitoring myself, never was truly spontaneous. That had to affect the show, no matter how hard I tried.

Nevertheless, in front of that camera was the one time in the day when I was safe and could find some joy. After all the awfulness and anguish, I could go out there and, because the show was live, nobody could touch me. I loved walking out on that stage. By that time the audience was my only friend; those loving, warm, accepting faces were there for me, and I could make a joke and they would laugh. I was never depressed by *The Late Show*. I did not go home and think, Rotten show tonight. I was pleased with it, pleased with myself.

In early March we went to Paris for a week with Melissa and took Billy Sammeth and his sister, hoping a break would help. While we were away, we fought to get Arsenio Hall as a guest host, but Fox refused. We did, however, have a hot lineup of hosts. Now, Fox in its inexperience was even more certain it could do better without me.

I was hoping in Paris we could repeat the good times of the past, the therapy we all desperately needed. But the trip was a flop. Edgar spent evenings in the hotel, and Billy, running a fever, spent days in bed. I was getting desperate calls from Los Angeles—Ron Vandor was trying to get rid of our head writer.

When we returned to Los Angeles, Billy told us he could not continue and was going to disappear for at least a month. Now I was alone, pulling that wagon all by myself.

Edgar was walking and sounding and acting like an old man. There was no force in his voice, no energy. His spirit was dying. He was becoming grouchy—suddenly wanting nobody in the dressing room. His stomach was acting up, his foot ached with gout, and the gout medicine made the heart medicine react badly, and vice versa. He was back to taking a sleeping pill at night. His hiatal hernia flared up painfully. He was terrified of AIDS from the blood transfusions during the heart attack. He had morning, afternoon, and evening pills. He took Tylenol constantly. His blood pressure was high.

I had to do something about the fact that my husband was in major trouble. Actually we were both in trouble, both shipwrecked and in the water, I holding on to the log with one hand, fingernails slipping, and holding Edgar afloat with the other hand. I knew I should let him go and pull myself to safety, but I could not let him sink.

After the heart attack Edgar had tried several psychiatrists, and settled on one he liked. But I was doubtful that he went regularly and talked honestly. Now, in this Fox crisis, I said, "You've got to talk to this man about your problems, tell him the pain you're in. There's no point in going if you play games with him." He agreed.

A few weeks later I called the psychiatrist and asked if Edgar was actually going. Was he admitting to being depressed, talking about his terrible childhood?—"I think he hated his mother." The doctor brushed me off, saying, "Don't you worry. Just don't you worry." Then he added, "He's a wonderful man, and we have delightful conversations about books and South Africa." Despite doctor-patient confidentiality, it smelled too jolly to me, and I begged Edgar to go to somebody else. He refused.

Every time he got upset, I expected another heart attack. In the night I listened to his breathing, expecting to call the paramedics at any moment. I involved myself in fights with Fox that I only half understood and half cared about because I did not want him so upset. I carried our flag into battle, afraid that if he did, he might drop dead.

I, too, was crazed, but controlled my desperation by focusing solely on the show, as though I had blinders on, taking no time for fun, never getting on the phone with Kenny Solms or Treva Silverman and laughing—just working and watching my back, just getting through each day. I became short-tempered; when Melissa called from college, I would say, "Missy, I can't talk to you now." When she got chicken pox, that was the first time I did not fly to her when she was in trouble.

Each day I had to appear cheerful and confident. I had to hear everybody's troubles and be above the office politics, had to buck up my husband. My house was no solace. When I came home exhausted, on my pillow would be a note: "Call Peter Dekom immediately." The next morning when I arrived at Fox, there would be Ron Vandor, angry, saying, "You shouldn't have asked

Barry Manilow if he ever used drugs. He won't come back." I began to eat, began to get fat.

There was nobody to talk to.

On Friday, March 20, a routine meeting was scheduled with Jamie Kellner to talk things over—without Barry—and discuss whom to hire as the new producer to replace Bruce McKay. I expected it to be a woman named JoAnn Goldberg, whom Fox had had me interview in New York. Going into the meeting, Edgar and I believed everything would work out. We would be fine if we could just hang on till April when the Fox prime-time shows were to go on the air. When those shows got low ratings, Fox would realize that our numbers were better than they thought. So we wanted no confrontation—just tell us what you want and we'll do it.

The day was dark and dismal, no sun, and I was in full makeup for the show. I sat on a couch and Edgar and Jamie were in easy chairs. The minute we were seated, Jamie, ice-cold, said, "McKay is out as of today, you will no longer have any artistic control, and Ron Vandor will be your producer."

It was like the guillotine. I finally lost it. I cried out, "You can't. You just can't. Vandor doesn't know what he's doing." I was begging—"Get anybody. Just not Vandor." Jamie insisted it would be Vandor. I told him that I would never work under Vandor, and Fox should just pay me off. Jamie answered, "No, you're in breach."

Suddenly Barry walked in, and Edgar's whole body tensed, his face hard and red. I swear they had planned it all—like the French court with Diller listening from behind a screen. He never sat down. He had not come in for a dialogue. In a controlled fury he began pacing behind Jamie, saying he was sick of all the problems, saying we were a failure, and they owed it to the affiliates and the advertisers to rescue the show.

I felt so wronged. I told him the truth—"We're a winner on your network, Goddammit. You can't put me on stations nobody can find and expect me to compete. It's a good show. What do you want from us?"

Barry watched me, emotionless. Then he turned his attention

to Edgar. In one terse sentence he stripped Edgar of all his duties as executive producer and banned him from the set. In that instant the show and our future were balanced on the point of a needle. Then Edgar and I catapulted ourselves into destruction.

"You're a tinhorn dictator," Edgar said. "I don't need this. I'm a rich man."

Barry Diller said, "Go fuck yourself."

Had this been a silent movie, there would have been music swelling and a close-up of my face. What will she choose? Her husband? Or her career? I should have told Edgar to shut up. I should have grabbed Barry, should have said, "Edgar's out of control. Let me talk to you. Help me. I'll do whatever you want. Just keep us on."

Automatically, without thinking, I chose my husband. And I would do it again. There was a marriage there of twenty-two years. I believe that marriage is a total commitment, that once you say "yes" to somebody, that is it—and I had received the same commitment from my husband. That was one thing I doubt Fox ever understood—that the bottom line of my behavior and marriage was loyalty. There is so little of it in life. It is the only thing you have left when everything else between two people is snipped away. You take the words "love" and "affection" and "devotion" and what they really add up to is "loyalty."

We walked out of the meeting with Edgar's dignity and our marriage intact. But from that moment on we were dead. They were setting up the new show with Barry Sand. The Iago-ettes were thrilled. They thought they were going to be television pioneers.

In the car going back to the office, Edgar was railing at the world and exultant—"That son of a bitch. Somebody finally told him off." He thought he would go down in Hollywood history, and was furious at me for not joining in. "Don't you know what you've done?" I told him. "You've just pulled down the temple." I was out of my mind. Twenty-two years of building had gone up in flames. My husband—the businessman who always understood what was happening every moment—had lost all touch with reality. He was thinking only of himself. If I was alone before, now

I was really alone—and with no place to go, no emergency plan to fall back on.

I doubled over, convulsed with stomach cramps. I had never felt such pain, like knives shredding my stomach. At the studio I could barely walk. In my dressing room I realized I could not continue. Edgar called Peter Dekom, who told us the Fox people would not believe that I was sick unless I used their doctor for an examination. When he came to the house, he took one look and told me to stay in bed for a week. I was finally breaking down.

But I could not stay in bed. Edgar was lying next to me in the darkened bedroom staring at the ceiling, too depressed to move. Even with the cramps I had to get up, start looking for a way out. Maybe I should still tell them I would be their puppet, be handed my monologue and go out and do the show. But the show would die without the stamp of my identity. And I had made my choice.

Then Peter Dekom called to say that Fox had relented enough to hire JoAnn Goldberg as producer, and she would be at my house that Sunday for a meeting. In my paranoia toward Fox I dreaded JoAnn. I assumed she would be Fox's girl and therefore an enemy, but her professionalism, her open-mindedness at the meeting, made me think there was hope. I went into the studio on Monday, still with cramps. I knew if I stayed away, Fox would do something terrible, use my absence as proof of breach of contract.

The staff was outraged at the way Edgar and Bruce were being treated. When Courtney Conte was told by Fox to stop speaking to Edgar, he refused. A petition to keep Bruce was circulated, and when JoAnn arrived for her first production meeting, everybody in the room was dressed in black.

But JoAnn calmed the waters. When I did not get any more calls from Fox executives, I thought, By God, we've come through. During the next six weeks she ran the show extremely well. She had a kindness that let us accept her. She understood the politics and made Edgar feel included, let him sit with her at the console during the show and save a little face. They liked each other. I actually convinced myself that everything was going to be okay.

People were stopping me in stores, on the sidewalk, to tell me the show was terrific. I relaxed, and the ratings began to go up; we were averaging around 3.2 and higher in the twelve cities, and nationally we were back to our December numbers. At Fox's Los Angeles station the ratings had increased 167 percent over the previous February. Even the press was beginning to come around. *The Hollywood Reporter* wrote, "Translated into dollars and cents . . . Rivers sells."

JoAnn liked and respected Jamie, who was friendly and reasonable. After four weeks, however, Jamie left on a prolonged trip to New York, and Kevin Wendle took over his responsibilities. Ron Vandor was quickly reassigned to another job, and Kevin became JoAnn's liaison with Fox. Almost immediately a newspaper story ran an item: "Our loose-lipped but highly placed sources tell that Joan Rivers is going to be off the air in ninety days." JoAnn, pointing out guests would now be even harder to book, asked for a newspaper ad refuting it. Kevin refused.

He began to find ways to complicate JoAnn's life. I had been making jokes during the show about Fox being cheap, and Kevin passed the word that I was not allowed to say "Fox" on the air. "You must be joking," JoAnn told him and called Jamie in New York to point out that all comics beat up on their parent, that Carson was always making remarks about the NBC commissary. Then Kevin demanded we cancel a guest who was appearing on a show scheduled opposite one of Fox's new series. He fought and fought before agreeing to a small raise for our stage manager— who was essential and threatening to quit. The music budget was cut by $1,750 a week—just when we were increasing the music.

Without telling me, Fox sent a letter to my protection service canceling my guards. Kevin called JoAnn and asked, "How did she take it?"

JoAnn said, "Fine."

"What's going on?" he asked.

"Everything's just fine."

On April 6 Fox introduced its first prime-time shows with a press party, even paying to have the huge HOLLYWOOD sign in the hills altered to FOXWOOD. Once again, I was not invited. I had to be there to contradict the rumors that the show was being canceled.

My public-relations man, Richard Grant, talked to the Fox people, and they said I could come—but not Edgar. The photographers swarmed around me, and every question was, "Is your
show going to be canceled?" Imagine how I felt having my picture taken that night, smiling for the cameras with Jamie Kellner
and Barry Diller.

Edgar wanted me to boycott the party out of pride. He was
unable to say, "Do what you need to do to save the show. I'm
bowing out." He was taking pills now to sleep and pills to wake
up and pills to keep alive. Still, he insisted on coming to the studio
and sitting on the couch in my office while I worked. I discussed
business matters in the car as always, but I did not know how to
give him back his pride. It was clear to me now that his job was
his pride. I tried to detach from his anguish to preserve my
remaining emotional reserves.

On April 20 *Redbook* magazine withdrew a cover story on me
because of rumors the show was being canceled. That night we
got a 4.4 rating in the twelve major cities. Fox's new shows in
prime time, which should have drawn twice my viewing audience, later only got 3's and low 4's. Indeed, their first prime-time
show, *Mr. President,* starring George C. Scott, had ratings in the
2's. So, as I had known all along, with their station lineup, my
show was doing fine after all. But even if Fox finally understood,
it was too late.

At the end of April there was a short gossip item in *People*
magazine quoting "one insider" as saying, "She's not as nitpicky
or as bitchy as she was before," and that Edgar "sits forlornly on
the couch . . . which would be sad if he hadn't been so nasty." We
thought we knew its source—Jeff Yarborough, who was a stringer
reporter for *People* in Los Angeles and a very good friend of
Barry Diller.

I asked Fox to send the magazine a letter denying the story,
and it refused. But *People* magazine had hit my one vulnerable
button when it hurt Edgar. On the air I did a takeoff on it and
ended by saying, "What does it matter about *People*? I just read
it on the toilet," and tossed the magazine over my shoulder. Like
everything else, that monologue had been combed through and

approved by the Fox lawyers. But the next day Fox ordered me to apologize publicly to *People*.

I refused. So Fox wrote its own letter, which was published—"We feel it is important that you know that those remarks were Miss Rivers' alone and were neither approved nor endorsed by Fox Broadcasting Company. We apologize on behalf of Fox for the tone of those remarks and for any implication of a general lack of standards in your magazine's reporting." They were now publicly humiliating me, cutting all ties. The relationship was finished.

We were fired as of Friday, May 15. Peter Dekom called us at home. Amazing as it seems, I still could not believe it had actually happened. JoAnn had run a smooth ship; the ratings were going up. I felt like a woman being divorced, signing away the house and still thinking, He'll come back and say he's sorry.

The news had to be kept secret until a settlement was made and we could put out a polite joint release. Once it hit the papers, finding guests would be almost impossible. The affiliates were not told. They would read it in the newspaper along with everybody else.

For a week I had to go to the studio to do the show, had to put on a cheerful face and be up. I felt so duplicitous. These were my friends, and this show was their livelihood. Jason Dyl, with AIDS, would be out of a job. Rumors flew. The staff was terrified.

There was a lot of lawyer posturing, Fox saying, "Sue! You'll get nothing." Kevin Wendle came around to Courtney Conte asking for dirt on us to build the network's case. Our lawyers told me I would probably win a lawsuit, but we would be in litigation for three years, Fox would appeal, and there would be more years, costing a million dollars or more in fees. While we waited for the payoff, Fox would have the use of the money it owed me and could write off legal fees as a corporate expense. Every rotten thing the network executives could think of to say about Edgar would be said.

This, finally, was what made me decide to close the door and settle. My husband could not take much more. He was already panicky, calling in teams of lawyers, grasping at straws, agitated, smoking again. I thought if we sued Fox, he would be dead of a heart attack in six months.

We hired Mickey Rudin, a tough, famous lawyer who knew Diller. Even then I thought maybe he would get on the phone and say, "Barry, are you crazy?" and save the show. But what happened the day we met with Rudin was one telephone call to Diller. Mickey said, "If you want to drag it out, we'll drag it out. Now what's the number? . . . That's too low . . . Okay." That was that.

The number was somewhat over $2 million, including damages for defamation and emotional stress. It was a lot of money, and nobody will feel sorry for me. But still I was staggered, devastated. For that money I never would have left Carson and given up the foundation of my life, lost my status, lost fans, been forced to live forever with the perception that my show was a failure.

I thought I had an airtight contract. I thought we had sewed up Fox for $15 million. I thought, no matter what happened, I could live out the rest of my life in comfort. Well, that is not show business. One of my lawyers explained that when contracts are negotiated, the poor performer just wants the deal, wants to perform. The studio knows the whole time that the contract is only paper. If the deal unravels, it would never pay one hundred cents on the dollar. Edgar was smarter than I was. When we were negotiating the original deal, he said, "In case something goes wrong, we want the fifteen million put in escrow." Rupert Murdoch was outraged. "We are honorable men," he said.

The settlement was signed on Thursday, and the news hit the press Friday morning, May 15. When the affiliates read the news, there were angry calls to Fox, which placated them by promising a new, wonderful show they would love. At last Kevin Wendle had a free hand. He took over as executive producer and installed Ron Vandor as producer. They had Courtney Conte fire twenty-four people in one day. They cut back the lighting, fired our superb director, David Grossman, and began taping the show in the afternoon. Their plan—perhaps inspired by the week of my substitute hosts—was different star hosts every night, who theoretically would bring on as guests their star friends.

I still had one farewell performance. I remember it in flashes, the standing ovation when I said I would be back, the tears on the cameraman's face, Pee-wee Herman trashing the set, the pain in Edgar's face, JoAnn, so upset, such a wonderful producer. The Fox executives were so worried what I might do, they had a tape of an old show at the ready and Ron Vandor in the control room poised to put it on the air.

The good memory came the next day—a full-page ad in *Variety*, a letter signed by all those people who worked so hard for the show. On *Late Show* stationery, it read, DEAR JOAN, WE THINK YOU ARE TERRIFIC! WE LOVED WORKING ON THE SHOW WITH YOU AND ARE PROUD TO HAVE BEEN A PART OF IT.

Today, when Barry Diller's name is mentioned, people expect to see fury in me. Instead, I feel a terrible sadness—and that is one final thing that makes no sense. But my intuition always told me—and still tells me—that Barry and I could have been friends and worked well together. After Fox, whenever we met—always by accident—we'd move toward each other for an instant—then, just as quickly, pull back.

Then, two years ago at NATPE, the annual convention for independent stations, I was in the Tribune Corporation booth promoting my new show. Suddenly my mouth dropped open. At the end of a long line of people waiting to meet me stood Barry Diller. Ten minutes later, when he reached me, he took my hand. "I wish you luck," he said.

"I know you do," I said. "I know you do."

16

ooooo

As the days went by, I became more and more angry that I had been forced to choose between my husband and my show. I was furious at myself. In my turmoil of grief—my panic thinking—I was deciding very, very deep in my heart that if Edgar had not been involved, I could have made the show work. I saw myself throwing away everything I had wanted since the day I was conscious in order to save this man's pride. Too, somewhere in myself, I was looking to Edgar to save me—I had always looked to him—and he had failed. I had always been the juvenile in the relationship, and now, suddenly, I was the head of the family who had been given the reins after the horse was dead and told to drag it into the barn.

I felt lost, like a child with nobody to pat me on the head and say, "Just keep pushing, honey. We'll come out of it." What I had always feared was true, was indeed true. I had become my work. When there was no work, I felt as if I did not exist.

Every time I drove out the gate of Bel Air, turning left meant going into town, a failure, turning right meant heading toward someplace in the Midwest, where nobody knew me—gaining a few pounds, wearing no makeup, growing my roots out, and becoming a waitress. It would be easy. People would say, "Boy, you remind me of Joan Rivers," and I would answer, "Yeah, I'm her cousin."

I wanted some time of isolation to be quiet about Fox, to get some distance, to take the edge off the bitterness. Details about the show, now in Kevin Wendle's hands, just stirred up the old anger, increased my grief. But friends and well-meaning staffers kept me informed of events, and a gloating side of me did want to know everything but found no comfort in "I told you so."

While Barry Sand from David Letterman readied his new permanent late-night program, Fox kept *The Late Show* going each night with a different host. The first week included Carole Bayer Sager and Suzanne Somers—who one reviewer said made me look like Ted Koppel. During succeeding weeks Fox had such names as Marla Gibbs, Jackée, Martha Quinn, Estelle Getty, Malcolm-Jamal Warner, Frank Zappa, Joan Lunden, Martin Sheen. The show's ratings slipped to 1.1.

I believe the press thinks in terms of winners and losers, and puts energy and point of view into their stories by glorying with winners and analyzing losers. Overnight they became my champions. In *Newsday* Marvin Kittman wrote, "I still think the Joan Rivers Show . . . would work . . . I still think they will look back with tears in their eyes at Joan's huge ratings."

In August, to keep the time slot alive for Barry Sand, Fox brought in Arsenio Hall for thirteen weeks. During that time, Howard Stern, the flamboyant radio personality, was a guest on the show. He blasted Fox for the firing—on their own network—and Carson for making me appear disloyal. Howard told me his outspokenness about Fox cost him plenty. His support meant a great deal to me then, as it does now.

Arsenio had his own telling experience with Fox. He later recounted, "Never once did any executive come and see me. In fact, I was at the Ivy restaurant in Los Angeles one night when I spotted Rupert Murdoch waiting for his car. I introduced myself, and he started fumbling through his pockets for a ticket. He thought I was with valet parking. I told him, 'No, Mr. Murdoch. I do your show," and he mumbled, 'Nice to meet you.'"

In early August Fox announced *The Wilton North Report,* and
at a press conference, Barry Sand explained that the show would
be like "buttermilk . . . something you may not like at first but
which you grow to love, depend on, as time goes by. . . . Formats
with a host behind a desk and celebrity guests," he said, "wind
up at the bottom of the ocean. At the bottom of the Nielsen
ratings are sitting a lot of talk-show hosts, among them Joan
Rivers. I thought America was ready for something different."

The show debuted in mid-December 1987. It wanted to be a
late-night soft-news magazine version of *Spy* magazine. The reviews were horrendous, affiliates began to cancel. It was pulled
after eleven shows.

A year later Mr. Barry Sand came to see me at the Westbury
Hotel in New York. Now he wanted me to know how much he
would like to be the producer of my new Tribune show, with its
desk and couch and celebrities. "Sit down," I said. "Just throw
those papers off the couch. Can I get you something?" I had to
smile.

Next Fox tried to get Arsenio back, but, I understand, offered less
money than he had received earlier. He signed for his own talk
show with Paramount and the rest is history.

None of the young men who complicated my life are still employed by Fox. Wendle, using his favor with Diller, usurped the
duties of Garth Ancier, who departed to be head of TV programming at Disney. Eventually Wendle himself left Fox. He now
works for Quincy Jones Productions. Ron Vandor is station manager for KADY in Oxnard, California.

I admit to taking some satisfaction from the final comparison
of ratings. In Miami, for example, my *Late Night* averaged 4.3,
Arsenio 1.5, *The Wilton North Report* 1. In Chicago it was 5.8, 3.3,
1.3. In New York, 6.9, 3.6, 2.1. And so forth.

A year after I was canceled, Fox gave up and returned the
late-night slot to the affiliates—losing millions of dollars and five
nighttime hours of programming. They never got that time back
and they've never had a successful nightly show since.

The irony is—as I'm writing this book, Fox has bought a syndicated show starring my friend Dennis Miller. They've sched-

uled him in my old night slot. The double irony is that the syndicator is the Tribune Corporation, which owns my daytime show. So here I am, touring the country to promote Dennis, wishing him well—working indirectly for the Fox network.

After the firing, I was damned if I was going to be destroyed and let the industry be able to say, ". . . and she never recovered." After the train wreck, you just get those casualties out and push the cars back onto the track. I went to work on my career—made appointments, went through my Rolodex starting with *A*. I asked my new agents to negotiate with *Hollywood Squares* and *Hour Magazine.* I lunched almost daily at Le Dome, the restaurant on Sunset Boulevard. Yes it was me at the table with one of my old scripts clothed in a new binder. I was seeing writers, producers, going, looking, trying, putting a thousand little boats in the water hoping one would come back with an offer.

In August 1987 one offer did come through, at least one that allowed us four expense-paid days in England with a five-day vacation in Ireland, where I was going to fulfill a fantasy. Like a child, I looked forward to kissing the Blarney stone.

I appeared on the Barry Humphries show. He is a female impersonator who plays the role of Dame Edna Everage—a national treasure. But I was too strung out to be in control, my timing was off, and next to Barry—who is a friend and wanted me to do well—I looked like an unfunny fool.

This confirmed my sense of failure, my terror that I could no longer make it as a comedienne. My booking agent called with the news that the ticket office in North Tonawanda, New York, where I was performing the next week, was doing no business, and was giving away tickets to fill the hall. I told myself, "As a last resort, I can always go down to Florida and entertain old people in condominiums."

When I made the mistake of worrying aloud to Edgar, "How can I stop my slide?" he told me my act was all wrong.

I was devastated. He had to know the self-doubts that would

start: Am I too old for those jokes? Can I find another persona?
Is this the end? My husband hit at what was sustaining me to that
point. If the act was wrong, I was the reason we were in trouble.

I realized that this man, who had built his life on being my
champion, had turned against me. I had become his Barry Diller.
The frustration, the fear, directed at Fox, had now swung onto
me, and his deep, simmering anger was like a slow-motion bomb.
Even the simplest exchanges became loaded and dangerous.

I was confused by this new, huge black force in our relationship. For the first time, barely able to hold myself together, I
found myself wanting to strike back at him. We had come so far
together, been so good together, had one goal in business, one
thought, one brain. I wanted to break this destructive pattern.

The next morning I went shopping by myself and left Edgar
a note: *Life is so good to us—let's not reach a point where we can't
enjoy it—and enjoy it together. I love you—and need you.*

But Edgar had gone far beyond my reach. He was in a path-
ological world of his own. That afternoon he stood in the lobby
at Claridges and told the manager of the hotel, "I lived here as
a boy. My uncle was Jack Hilton, and I lived with him." Total
fantasy. The next day—with my career apparently finished—he
went to his tailor and was fitted for five suits and ordered a
dozen pairs of handmade shoes. I was scared, scared, scared.

My own fantasy was that on this trip, away from Hollywood and
our troubles, we could heal each other—sleep and relax, have
fun, get well. But in Ireland, Edgar only grew sicker. He hated
the place—and his rage, his terror, his need to control, poisoned
everything we did. Everything was wrong, was ugly. He complained constantly of feeling ill—that his sleeping pill had not
worn off, that his stomach hurt. If this man were sitting in
heaven, he would have criticized the clouds.

Then, on our second night in Dublin, we were invited by the
American ambassador for dinner. Edgar's health was miraculously restored. He was in his element. He was wonderful, my
husband again—brilliant, articulate, charming, warm. During
the meal the ambassador, Margaret Heckler, asked everybody
around the table to tell his thoughts on Ireland. One was a promi-

nent Irish poet, but the most eloquent was Edgar, who quoted
Yeats and then said we felt so welcomed that from now on we
would never hear the word "Ireland" without realizing that it
really means "Our Land." Sitting there, I thought, That's why I
loved you—and suffered a rush of overpowering sadness.

The next day he was back in his misery. A single, small moment
summed up my despair. One evening I paused in the hotel lobby
to hear the piano player perform songs from *The Phantom of the
Opera.* Instantly Edgar was saying, "Come on. Come on. Let's
go." I thought, Is this going to be my life? Now I wasn't even
allowed a second of pleasure. I knew then that he was going
down and taking me with him.

Edgar kept postponing the best day of the trip—the drive to
Blarney Castle to kiss the stone—until it was our last in Ireland.
This was to be my absolute high point, the adventure I had
looked forward to since the trip was planned, the escape from
myself that would have bolstered me for weeks.

Well, I never had that adventure. The night before we were
to go, Edgar woke me up to say he thought he might be bleeding
internally. At 2:30 A.M. I took him to a hospital, where three Irish
nurses clucked over him. He basked in their attention. Feeling
better, he refused to spend the night, and made plans to come
back the next day. Good-bye, Blarney stone. After he was tested,
the doctor came to me and said, "There's nothing wrong."

Moving Edgar by a wheelchair that he requested, we returned
to New York and the Westbury Hotel. I had to leave the next day
for three days on the road—one in upstate New York, one in
Rhode Island, and one in Connecticut. Help was arranged to get
Edgar to the plane and directly to his doctor, Elsie Giorgi in Los
Angeles. Traveling to upstate New York, I was close to tears most
of the day. I had no peace with Edgar or without him.

Two nights later my agent called me in my dressing room.
Fox wanted me to come back and do my show one week a
month. They had finally realized that it had been a success. This
should have been a moment of vindication. A triumph. To my
surprise, I simply felt sad. And amazed. Could Barry not realize
what he had done to Edgar and me? Or maybe show business is

all business. I turned down the offer by setting impossible conditions.

Then came a new hammer blow. That night I telephoned Edgar and asked, "Are you all right? What did the doctor say?" He answered, "I canceled the appointment. I'm feeling fine."

When I heard this, something inside me snapped. I had been trying to be a good wife to a husband who was breaking down, a man riding in wheelchairs through airports with a blanket on his lap, hurrying to get to his doctor. And he had not even troubled to keep his appointment.

In New York on Sunday I had one happy day of relief meeting my two friends Kenneth Battelle and Tommy Corcoran. They said, "Let's play!" So we walked and ate and laughed. Just these few hours of freedom felt like the treatment for a nervous breakdown when they slip you into a warm tub. I felt as if I were twenty-three again.

That evening I had dinner with Tommy, such a dear friend, so funny, always there when I needed him. I poured out all my misery, and he, who had known Edgar and me for thirty years, kept saying, "It can't go on like this. He's got to get serious help."

Monday morning, August 10, I flew to Los Angeles. My day of freedom, of normal, natural pleasure, had put my life with Edgar in perspective, confirmed how sick we both were. I finally acknowledged to myself that our house would henceforth be his kingdom with one subject: me.

As I always did, I telephoned Edgar from the car to say I had landed safely. But this time my deepest feelings finally came to the fore. "Edgar, we've got to get major help because we can't live like this. We're falling apart. We must get help."

Edgar could not believe what I was saying. "We can handle it ourselves," he insisted. But this time I was determined. He told me to come home, and we would talk it over. I said, "You must go into psychotherapy—and both of us will begin marriage counseling."

He rejected therapy, saying the man he was seeing was ridiculous. He kept telling me we could work it out ourselves. I told him, "I don't have the strength to help you. I don't even have enough strength for myself." He said, "I'm not going into any deep therapy."

A wise friend of mine once told me that people only make real changes in their lives when they feel their backs up against the wall. I finally understood what she meant. "You cannot do this to Melissa, to me, to yourself." I told him, "I will not come home until you get help." I drove right past our road and on to the Century Plaza Hotel.

That night I was so frantic, so frightened, that I slept in my clothes. I knew this was my last stand.

The next morning Edgar telephoned to tell me he had reconsidered. He would do as I asked, but first he wanted to go to Philadelphia. Melissa had persuaded him that talking it out with Tom Pileggi would be helpful. I was tremendously relieved. His dearest friend, so totally rational, could insure that Edgar got the help he needed.

On the eleventh Edgar telephoned his estate lawyer and told him he thought he and I might be getting a divorce, and he wanted to change his will, leaving to Melissa his share of our property, which under California law was half of everything we had. The lawyer explained that this was impossible. Nothing could be changed without the agreement of both spouses.

That morning Edgar flew to Philadelphia. He arrived at Tom's construction office with file folders containing records of everything we owned, every piece of silver, every bank account, every insurance policy. During the next three days Edgar made Tom Pileggi go through every paper in every folder in the minutest detail, discussing the values and dispositions. Tom told me later, "My brain felt like five hundred pounds, the pressure was so great. I didn't think I was going to last."

On those same days I was back at work trying to feel good about myself, trying get my life back in gear. I had a lunch on Wednesday with the producers of *Hollywood Squares.* They wanted me to come on the show, but were telling me very nicely I was not going to be the star. Part of me was choking down tears of humiliation. But another part of me was thrilled to be doing

it, thrilled to have somebody want me. I will be grateful to Rick
Rosner and Ernie DiMassa forever. God bless them.

On Wednesday I talked to Edgar several times, arguing now
about what kind of help he should get. His doctor, Elsie Giorgi,
wanted to put him in a hospital psychiatric unit, but he refused,
still terrified of facing himself.

Yet even in the midst of these terrible discussions, there was
a wonderful grace note. Edgar said, "Did you see the new painting that came in? Isn't it great?" I said, "Yes, fabulous. I hung it
in the guest room," and then we were back into our awfulness—
"Edgar, we've got to save ourselves." But now I thought things
would be all right, thought we were still playing the old games
by the old rules: You're wrong—No, you're wrong—Kiss, kiss, see
you Tuesday.

During that talk Edgar said, "I'm so depressed I'm going to kill
myself." Of course I did not take him seriously. I remember
making a flip joke: "Don't do it till Friday, because Thursday I'm
going under anesthesia." And I was in fact going into the hospital
for a minor liposuction operation, which I decided to have done
after the Fox show came to an end. He laughed.

In my family, suicide was an abstract concept. I never thought
anybody would kill himself; there's a lot of talk and a half hour
later you have a good sandwich and life's not so impossible. I
thought Edgar was bottoming out—as I was—and now would get
help, begin a total cure, brain and body. I thought then that he
had tried pressing the usual buttons—"I'm sick. She'll worry
about me"—and suddenly the buttons weren't working, so he
upped the ante. I told my closest friends, and, like me, they all
thought it was another ploy to bring me flying to his side, everything forgotten—and with my capacity for guilt, he'd keep me
locked to him forever.

Even his own psychiatrist, who was speaking to him by phone
in Philadelphia, told me he didn't think Edgar was in danger.
None of us thought Edgar was that kind of man. We all thought
he was too much of a control freak, had too much pride to say,
"I've lost," was too rational for suicide—which he used to call "a

permanent solution to temporary problems." Nobody wanted to believe it.

Edgar made the same suicide threat to Tom Pileggi, but Tom was smarter than all of us. He immediately called me, wanting to check Edgar into a Philadelphia hospital. Edgar refused. "I won't do anything foolish," he told Tom.

Alarmed, Melissa and I went in person to see Edgar's psychiatrist, who said he thought Edgar was not as unhappy as we did, said he was in a regular depression and would not do anything drastic. But we should get him back to Los Angeles. Finally Edgar agreed to fly back on Friday and check into a hospital. Tom arranged for the security man to check his hotel room every hour all night in the meantime.

Tom believed deep down that Edgar was not serious. He considered Edgar too full of ambition to want to end his life; he was a man, in Tom's words, "who lived life, who wanted to achieve everything, be everything, own everything." That night as they parted, Edgar again promised not to do anything foolish.

No one person knew all the signals that had been accumulating, and only in retrospect do I see the pattern. Weeks before we left for England, he must have considered suicide as an option. One of our staff stole wine and money, and I found out later that Edgar claimed his stock of tranquilizers and sleeping pills had been taken and made the doctor duplicate them all.

On the weekend after we returned, while I was still East, he summoned our accountant, Michael Karlin, to the house to discuss some items, but was really only interested in being certain the life insurance and estate planning were in perfect order.

On the other hand, nearly a week later, he telephoned Dorothy and asked her to arrange limousines to take him to the Philadelphia airport on Friday and pick him up in Los Angeles. He had a doctor waiting to take him to the Cedars-Sinai hospital to check him physically before he went into therapy. He asked Dorothy to arrange for the accountant to see him at the house at 9:00 A.M. Saturday and have a limo to take him to the hospital at 10:00. Also one of Gavin DeBecker's guards should be posted at his hospital-room door. He must have been as confused as the rest of us.

On Thursday afternoon Edgar phoned Melissa, told her he was coming home on Friday, and promised her he would do no harm to himself. He was in Tom Pileggi's Warrington, Pennsylvania, office. Tom, worn out by Edgar, had decided to join his family at their house on the Jersey shore. He and Edgar had agreed to meet the next day for breakfast. Edgar promised again not to do anything foolish, and Tom told me later, "I believed him. I thought he would never lie to me." When Edgar asked Tom to call off the hourly security checks at the hotel and give him a good night's sleep, Tom agreed.

As Tom escorted his friend from his office to the limousine, Edgar picked up a nickel and two pennies off the sidewalk and said, "Look, I've thrown a seven." Edgar put the coins back into his own pocket, hugged and kissed Tom, and got into the car. The driver took him into Philadelphia to a barber shop, where the barber shaved off his beard. On his way back to the hotel Edgar had the driver stop while he bought a small recorder and three blank tapes.

From the hotel he telephoned Dorothy at home to ask whether she had reconfirmed his flights and the limos. It was typical, routine behavior for Edgar. Melissa called Edgar at the hotel at about eight o'clock and was relieved that he sounded fine—and did not call him back because she knew he had to get up early to catch a plane home.

Now we know that in the hotel room after dinner Edgar tape-recorded three messages—one to me, one to Melissa, and one to Tom. As he recorded Tom's message at ten-thirty, Tom himself, acting on a premonition, called to ask, "Are you okay?" Edgar said, "I'm fine. I'll see you for breakfast." He promised again not to do anything foolish. His psychiatrist telephoned from Los Angeles, and Edgar confirmed that he was returning the next day for extensive therapy.

He put the tapes into three hotel envelopes. In other envelopes he left tips for the restaurant maître d', the luggage boy, the maid. He addressed a manila envelope to *Joan Rivers,* then crumpled it and threw it under the desk. On another he wrote *Joan Rosenberg.* In it he put business papers and instructions. In Melissa's envelope he put his Rolex watch, which she had always admired, and his gold money clip, the only keepsake he had from his mother. He marked each envelope with three kisses, *X X X*.

He placed these envelopes on a small rack at the end of the bed, along with a note indicating where they should be sent. At the bottom of the note he wrote, *Mr. Pileggi will arrange to get three suitcases to the above address in Los Angeles.* A second note neatly listed the people to be notified of his death, including all his doctors with their office and home telephone numbers. At the top of both notes he wrote *Aug 13, 1987 Midnight.* He meticulously packed his bags and unlocked the door. Against the bedside lamp he leaned an unframed picture of me and one of Melissa.

Then he swallowed the bottles of Valium and Librium he had been saving. Next, completing the combination he knew had killed the columnist Dorothy Kilgallen, he removed the miniature scotch and brandy bottles from the courtesy bar and methodically drank them from a tumbler.

17

ooooo

The reality of death is very hard to absorb. Melissa told me she did not believe her father was dead. *I* did not believe her father was dead. Yet, in the midst of all the pain, the symbols of the past brought a kind of comfort. I kept Edgar's office desk untouched, the files of investments, the family pictures, the border of name cards under the edge of the blotter, his copy of my schedule book kept up to date. The top of his bureau was sacrosanct. Melissa, too, wanted to keep Edgar alive through his imprint, make shrines of his areas. She felt that no one should ever sit in his chair, and nothing should ever be taken from his closets. She told me, "I could make lunch every day and put it on his desk. I would love that.

"I've accepted the fact that he is not around," she added, "but every time I get off a plane or walk into a restaurant, I look for him." In early September I took her back to college at the University of Pennsylvania, within blocks of the Philadelphia hotel where Edgar had committed suicide.

This trip was extremely difficult; both of us were still grieving, and I didn't want to let her go. Still, I was trying to be upbeat until the car pulled up in front of a row of dilapidated mansions half a block from the McDonald's where the police arrested a man who had been burying women in his basement. Students had been destroying this house for the past fifteen years. We climbed three broken steps onto a porch where the furniture was old automobile seats. Inside, there was nothing but a broken-down table where one leg was missing.

Melissa's room was a hovel. There was no closet, just racks and hooks. The common bathroom was—well, better to wear rubber pants. When my daughter turned to me and said, "Isn't it great, Mother?" I said, "Melissa, I'm glad your father's dead. If he saw this, he would kill himself again."

We laughed. It was our first healing moment.

My mourning process pretty well fit the classic pattern. For three months I was, for all intents and purposes, insane. Week after week, I was racked by wild highs and deep, deep lows—hyperactive, crazed, too angry, too much the life of the party. I would be hit by crying jags out of nowhere and people would stand by helplessly as I sobbed. Melissa told me I was like a top spinning out of control.

Everything that had been my normal routine probed my loss, stirred up my pain. Mentally I was operating on sixteen nutty levels at once. I now understand what had seemed a bizarre experience in 1985, when I visited Steve Lawrence and Eydie Gorme after their son Michael died suddenly. His death changed Steve and Eydie's life forever; they are still grieving for him. That day Eydie was sitting on a couch looking 185 years old, surrounded by people weeping. We put our arms around each other and had a quiet moment together. During our conversation her eyes strayed to my collar, and out of nowhere she asked me, "Where did you get that necklace?" The next day her secretary called to get the name of the store. I was in shock. But that's how cuckoo you can get in grief.

Like Eydie, I was a feather in the wind. I had always been a survivor and a coper, but now I was frightened because I could not deal with the house, the people, the situations, my daughter, and the decisions that come each day in life—and most of all, I could not handle myself.

Every part of my life, no matter how minor, overwhelmed me. I did not know how to work the burglar alarm or the VCR. I did not know where to find the key to the freezer, did not know which key fitted the car. I was nibbling all day long, chocolates, pasta, cookies.

But I cleverly figured out a solution to the overeating. I went into the bathroom, put my finger with its pretty little $4.50 nail down my throat, and threw everything up. Afterward, I felt thin, my stomach flat, okay again in my clothes, and thrilled that I would not be a fat slob, that I had found a way to literally have my cake and eat it, too.

I did that once every ten days, and it felt so good that I upped the vomiting to once a week, denying to myself that this was sick behavior. I thought, What a great way to diet. Then, after telling myself I would only do it once a week, I decided it was okay to do it twice a week, then three times a week. That went on for two months until one day I found myself in a public toilet vomiting my head off. Dear God, I thought, I'm in trouble. I finally admitted to myself that this was an addiction, that I was bulimic. I needed months before I finally stopped—with help from my therapist, who explained that I felt helpless about everything in my life, and this was the one area of control left to me.

And I *was* helpless everywhere else in my life. When I met with my agent, he said there was little interest in me around the country. I asked, "What about Pittsburgh?" "They're not interested." "What about Puerto Rico?" "No." Nobody wanted a loser.

My accountant explained that most of my money, including the Fox settlement, was tied up in real estate. I must cut my huge overhead immediately. But how could I? Let the gardener go? Francisco had been with me for ten years, and I knew his mother and his wife. His daughter was ill and his boy hoped to go to college next year. Fire Sabrina Lott, my lovely secretary? She who worked three jobs, had just signed up for night college, was a girl who lived by herself and supported her mother and sent money to her sister in Baltimore? All the staff were extended family. How could I say to them, "Tough-o. Too bad."

My accountant also warned that I might have to sell the house, sell the one stable thing in our lives, sell the exciting part of our marriage—the conquering, becoming a star, coming home in our laurel wreaths—sell Melissa in Halloween costumes and birthday parties and six kids in sleeping bags on the floor. The house and my memories were my roots now. I clung to what I had. Selling the house, my trophy, cutting my standard of living, would mean I had given up.

Edgar's role in our partnership had now fallen to me. One day four contracts with Caesars Palace, sixty pages each, waited on Edgar's desk. The lawyer's note asked me to read them carefully, because they were taking perks away from me and he wanted my comments. My comment was, "I don't know what the hell I'm reading." I felt I was fifteen and back in trigonometry and couldn't get it. I was lost and frightened when faced with "Read. Sign. Co-sign."

But you cannot let anybody know you are ignorant because you are dealing in huge sums. I was being told, "That bank transfer goes there, and this one goes to that, and this is this, and we've grandfathered that, and that's why you're okay, but you still owe the bank." How the hell could I know what was going on, know whether somebody was slipping thousands of dollars into his pockets? Every time I signed something, I felt I was signing away my rooms and my food. I was furious at Edgar for leaving me buried under this mess and so totally untrusting.

The fears churning in my head kept me up at night. Should we sell the house? Or get a smaller one? Should we move to New York? What staff must I let go? Can I go back to work? Will the insurance companies find a way to not pay? Will Tom Pileggi continue to be my friend? What will all this do to Melissa? Is it my fault? What will become of us? I wrote that question again and again in my diary: "What will become of us?"

One day my frustration and helplessness exploded. I kicked his desk and almost broke my toe.

Looking back, I see that the inevitable anger after suicide was, in fact, my best friend. It kept me from falling back into self-pity, kept the adrenaline pumping, energized me to lash out at the grief and sweet memories that can unhealthily hold you back from a new life. Anger helped me over the first giant hurdle after Edgar's death, removing his possessions, his imprint, our shrine, from the house—a first step into a new life.

This process started with a major breakthrough. In the office trying to concentrate on a bank statement, I was furious that I was running eighteen hours a day doing Edgar's chores, not doing my job, which was creating new jokes and bringing in money. I said to myself, "Enough with keeping his desk as a memorial," and sat down in his chair and pulled out the name cards stuck in the side of his blotter and tossed them out. Each day there was one less folder with his handwriting on it, one less sharpened pencil. I felt like a rebellious little girl defying a parent, the way I did when I went into my mother's living room, which was off-limits except when there were guests. Sitting in Edgar's chair, I was surprised that my feet touched the floor.

Yet one does go on maintaining shrines as a sort of tribute. I kept the desk drawers undisturbed, even when the desk itself later went into storage.

One afternoon I was rearranging the garage and stumbled upon Edgar's collection of free carry-on bags from airlines no longer in existence, his ancient luggage shot to hell, all the useless things he had collected, all his hedges against want. This is ridiculous, I thought, and soon Jacob, my houseman, and I were hauling everything out.

When it was all down in the garbage, guilt—which seems to go hand-in-hand with rage at these moments—made me ask Jacob to bring it all back. As long as his possessions remained in place, Edgar was not dead.

I kept his pajamas hanging on the closet door for a long, long time, kept his shirts and ties in place, the shoes lined up waiting for him. But slowly his things took on the invisible dusting of age. Edgar's books were increasingly out-of-date. On the piano were pictures of people he had never met, pictures of Melissa in a dress he had never seen. The newspaper kept on his desk was yellowing. The pajamas were no longer fresh and crisp. When they finally seemed like souvenirs, I gave away most of his clothes to charity.

• • •

I now realize that I did not have to force myself so much to make changes. That simple passage of time wears down the cutting edge of sorrow.

We had a new guard dog and blackly joked that if Edgar ever came up the driveway, the dog would bite him. But what had been a joke suddenly became a macabre possibility. One night we heard Spike barking upstairs. When I went up, nothing was there, but still he went on barking, until I had to bodily carry him away. This performance became almost routine. Meanwhile, every night at ten of seven, Edgar's alarm clock would ring, and nobody could shut it off. We would turn up the temperature on the air conditioner and come back to find it down to ice-cold, the way Edgar liked it.

Then one day Kathleen White, our bookkeeper, casually mentioned, "I was pouring coffee, and Mr. Rosenberg walked through the kitchen dressed in his pink shirt and beige pants." A few days later Marcia Tysseling, my assistant, announced she saw Edgar in the same outfit, passing by the doorway on his way upstairs. I was furious. Why hadn't he shown himself to me?

I was also frightened the way a child is scared of ghosts, but at the same time I thought how wonderful it would be to see him. I do not entirely believe in psychics; if they could reach the dead and foretell the future, we would all be doing just fine. But I do believe that spirits can come back, and just in case, I called a psychic I had met during the Fox show. She told me to carry a tape recorder, and if Edgar appeared, it would pick up his voice. I carried that recorder with me for days.

More psychics kept calling me with bulletins from the beyond. One said she had spoken with Edgar, and he was happy. One phoned from Houston to say she was a channeler and her spirit, Benton, had messages for me: Edgar was filled with joy on a higher plane, but I was going to get sick unless she came to California and allowed him to fill me up with his energy. This was all funny, yet given my precarious emotional state, I was becoming alarmed.

An Australian psychic I had once met phoned me at 2:00 A.M.— at her own expense—and said, "Joan, are you all right? I've been having terrible feelings about you for the past four days." My heart went crazy, pounding, racing. I thought, Because of this stupid woman, I'm going to die—right now. I tried to call her back and then could not get an international line because of Edgar's damn phone system; the operator was saying, "What system are you on?" and I didn't know!

A psychic suggested by a former governess came to the house and said she could put me in touch with my spirit guide. His name was Harpo Marx. Great. A mute comedian! The intermediary with Edgar was a character who did not talk. A friend went to a psychic who told her Edgar was annoyed that I would not let him rest. I wondered, Is everybody crazy?

If Edgar was there, I wanted him to come forward and talk to me or be put to rest. And though I was not a believer in ghosts, I did not want the poor man unhappily wandering the house. I called a Catholic church and asked for an exorcist. When the priest arrived, he had forgotten his holy water. I said, "It doesn't matter—I'm Jewish." He went from room to room with his stole and Bible, saying a little prayer, asking that peace should come back to this man's house. I prayed for peace in Edgar's soul.

While all that was going on, I had to come to terms with being single and self-reliant. In widowhood, your husband is there in your thoughts, in your heart, but he is not there at the kitchen table when things go wrong and decisions have to be made. When you go out socially, he is not at your side. You have nobody to poke in the ribs and say, "Look at that portrait of the hostess; she'll never look like that again."

The first time I went out alone with a couple, I felt as if we were a three-legged table. I worried about talking too much to the husband, not giving enough compliments to the wife. I felt as if I had to perform and be funny to earn my dinner—which I hate to eat in any case—because I was sitting there on sufferance— "Let's take Joan out, the poor thing." I swore, never again.

Widows are like a single-digit number in a double-digit society. So you seek out other single people because with them you are a whole and they are a whole. In early October I flew to New York to meet with two screenwriters who wanted to write a comedy for me. We went for dinner at Elaine's, but when the check came, there was no husband to pick it up —just my two escorts sitting there staring at me. I told myself it was okay to pay because it was business, but I also saw the scene with acid clarity—two witty, young gay men watching the old star pick up the check. I wondered, "Is this what the rest of my life will be?"

Soon after Edgar's death, I began to escape the house, the memories, by going to New York. There I could put grief on a Hold button by playing hard. I could not stand still. I could not finish a crossword puzzle, could not sit through an hour of *Masterpiece Theatre*, could not concentrate on a book. I was manic. I would have lunch with friends, visit a museum, go to an Off-Broadway show.

I took Spike with me everywhere. I've always been an animal person, always loved my dogs—always had big dogs—but I never had this kind of relationship with an animal. Tommy Corcoran named him "Raw Paws" because we were never still.

Spike was given to me by Melissa's governess right after Edgar's heart attack, when Melissa had just gone off to school. He was the runt of the litter—I could hold him in the palm of my hand—and they were going to kill him. She said, "You need someone to love." And I did. He became the one thing that loved me. I look at him and I know what we've been through together: Edgar's heart attack, the horrific days at Fox, when I had no career, through Edgar's suicide, the move to New York. This is the dog who slept with me the night my husband killed himself. He's a piece of history in my life. I love him so much. He's the only one who went through it all—twenty-four hours a day. And God knows what else he'll face.

Underneath my compulsive restlessness, my search for distraction, was panic. The panic that I would never be able to spend an evening alone without the loneliness and sadness filling up the room, the panic of no career, no money, being single, frightened of the effects on my daughter. Melissa knew none of this, only that I was never home at night.

I have learned that everybody grieves in his own way at his own speed. Even Siamese twins will do it differently. I know Melissa wanted me to be happy—but to her, my frenetic playing meant I was just the Merry Widow. When those closest to you do not see conventional signs of sorrow, they feel their own grief invalidated, feel misunderstood and alone. Most important, they feel you do not care.

Most of the time when Melissa visited me, we were loving and good to each other. But I was also very careful not to stir up the resentment I sensed just below the surface.

During the Jewish holidays in early October, I was in New York, and Melissa and I planned to observe the High Holy Days at Temple Emanu-El. Yom Kippur is the holiest day of the Jewish year, the time when you confess your sins and God decides your fate for the next year, the one day we had always gone to temple as a family. Melissa and I went to the 3:45 memorial service specifically so we could rise and stand with the rest of those who had lost someone that year and hear Edgar's name read aloud this one time only.

It was raining, and because of traffic, we arrived ten minutes late. At the door we presented our tickets to the usher, an honorary position for the pillars of the temple, like a deacon of a church. This elderly man, very affluent, a big shot, told us we were late, that every seat was taken, and refused to let us in. I started to plead, "But we have assigned seats which we've paid for. We were caught in traffic." He said, "I've given your seats away."

I knew it was a lie, a power play to show he was unimpressed by a celebrity. Temple Emanu-El was huge, never full. He would have had to be blind, deaf, and dumb not to know we had just lost a husband and father. I thought, This is temple? This is God?

We huddled under the canopy in the pouring rain like two rejected waifs. My daughter just stood there, unable to pay her last respects to her father, devastated, on the brink of tears. I thought, God wants this girl to get through the day. I said, "Let's go shopping."

We went to Polo, where the manager is a friend, and they put us in a private dressing room and brought us white wine, and I went crazy, buying Melissa everything. We did not look at one price tag. Anything she liked—sweaters, shoes. I was spending hundreds and hundreds of dollars I could not afford.

Suddenly, in front of the saleswoman and fitters and manager, seeing myself in that lavish room instead of temple, spending, spending, spending—I began sobbing and could not stop. "Why am I doing this?" I wondered, terrified. "We're going under." I felt as if we were circling the drain.

Even as my daughter put her arms around me, I felt she was thrilled to see me suffering, too.

Melissa was in her own throes of grief. She said she felt numb, detached, watching herself from a distance. She constantly studied Edgar's picture and imagined how he would have solved the problems in her life. She used the suicide as a scapegoat: "If Daddy were alive, I wouldn't be unhappy. If Daddy were alive, I'd be doing better on my exams, the car wouldn't be breaking down." She joked to me, "At least he should come back to life during an exam—Help me out, is Question Seven true?"

She woke each morning feeling there were a thousand pounds on her chest, feeling there was no way she could get out of bed and get her work done. When she tried to read, she finished a page and had no idea what it said. She tormented herself with "what ifs"—what if she had ended her last call from her father with her usual "Good-bye. I love you." Would he have changed his mind? What if she had called him back that night when he was preparing his death? Her one escape was sleeping and sleeping and soothing herself with a dozen showers a day.

Of course, when you are in pain and panic, you do lash out. By November, Melissa and I, perhaps because we trusted each other's love, were using each other to vent anger. We were each other's closest targets—and she knew the truth. While people were saying, "Oh, your mother was the most wonderful wife," she knew that at the end there was no marriage.

Melissa did not know the back story that led up to the suicide, did not realize how ill Edgar had been. She had come in to see the last seven minutes of the movie where the wife is saying, "I'm leaving you unless you go into analysis," and the husband is saying, "Better dead."

Melissa's therapist, to help her work through her grief, was encouraging her to act out whatever she felt at the moment.

When I telephoned Melissa daily so she would know she was not alone, our phone calls sometimes disintegrated into fights, and she would pull the ultimate weapon, blaming me for her father's death.

My psychiatrist was telling me by phone to just be there for her, be very happy that she was venting her feelings. But even the most innocent remarks played on my guilt. Once she said, "I would give up everything, all the money, the house, to spend one minute with Daddy alive." When I told her I planned to sell Edgar's big Mercedes, which neither of us liked to drive, she answered, incredulous, "But it's Daddy's car."

Once while we were talking, Melissa was so furious at me, she threw her phone at a picture, and the glass exploded across the room. Then she called me back to say, "I don't hate you. I was just miserable."

I was so sad that she was being asked to grow up so suddenly. As she put it, "I went to bed one night as a college student, and all of a sudden, the next morning, had to be an adult."

The more time I spent in New York, the more I considered moving there. Hollywood was a company town where nothing mattered except my current low status in the business. If it had been Detroit, I would have been a car painted the wrong color. In California your achievement is the last thing you've done. I had been fired by Fox. I was finished. In New York, my home-town, people let me keep my achievements—Hello, Joan. We've known you for twenty years. Good luck to you. I was walking Spike when a cop jumped out of a car to get my autograph; a garbageman said, "We love you, Joanie"; a delivery boy said, "How you doin'?" and I said, "Surviving," and was surprised to hear the word come from my mouth. God, I thought, I hope it's true.

In New York Tommy Corcoran or Kenneth Battelle were often my companions. They knew I was mulling over a move to New York. To entertain me, Tommy often arranged appointments to see apartments for sale, not really looking, just to distract me more than anything else. One afternoon in late October I went to see a co-op just off Fifth Avenue, and checking the view, I peered across the street and said, "Look at that beautiful Palladian window." The agent said, "That apartment's available, but it's not right for you."

The building turned out to be the mansion of J. P. Morgan's daughter, and the apartment had been her two eighteen-foot-high ballrooms, separated by huge sliding doors. It had been built in 1897 and then expanded in the 1930s, beautiful, opulent, fantasy-fulfilling—sort of Fred and Ginger meet the Sun King. It was now a broken-down warren of cloakrooms, maids' rooms, and musicians' changing rooms, and then vast spaces of no use whatsoever. It had been on the market for two and a half years without one bid, and by now plaster was falling from the walls, the floor was coming up. There was major water damage. Edgar never would have bought it.

I went out to dinner with Kenneth and then looked at it again by moonlight. In the past when I looked at houses for sale, it was as a married woman with a child at home. A room for Melissa, a study for Edgar, a family room—these were important considerations. I bought homes like normal people. Nobody in their right mind would buy this apartment. But I saw instantly how the space could work—the dining room off the front ballroom, a study next to the terrace, my bedroom above.

I love to decorate. I love to create, as we all do. What could be more fun than to take something nobody can visualize and say, "Just you wait, guys, hang in there!" It's like giving birth again. Creating something from nothing. What therapy, to focus on this apartment, to be happy about it every day.

At Ambazac, Edgar was totally involved in the decor, and there were compromises, which was fine, natural. But this apartment would be the first place that would be totally mine. It would be my cave, safe, a place nobody could invade or take away from me.

I would put in all the special comforts I'd always dreamed about. Growing up, one of my worst memories was the bathrooms in Larchmont. They were freezing! It was my father's immigrant mentality—go put on a sweater if you're cold. Today, the marble floor in my bathroom is heated.

I always wanted a fireplace in the bedroom. I always wanted

a bedroom that was totally romantic—all white lace and pale satin—and I have one!

I always wanted peach walls in the dining room. Everybody looks great at night in a peach room, with candles, and silks. Women look just sensational. Now, the Elephant Man could come to dinner at my home and you'd have to think, "Well, maybe he's not so bad after all."

And I would have books and books and books and books. Nothing is more wonderful. And needlepoint everywhere. I started doing needlepoint when I started writing scripts. While my collaborator would wield the pen, I would wield the needle. My apartment is filled with the comfort of pillows—and the joy of knowing I created them.

I love people who know what they like and live the fantasy. Just do it. Malcolm Forbes bought a château and lived in a château, in the tradition of a château—with all the original furniture from Brittany. You went there and there were seven ladies-in-waiting—"May I do this for you . . . that for you?" Incredible. And John Kluge. He once showed me around his yacht. "Take a look," he said, "this bathtub, a hundred thousand dollars." Scored out of marble, one piece! Even Donald Trump, God bless him, with or without money sure manages to have a good time!

The more my sensible advisers told me I could not afford this apartment, the more I wanted it.

Making this rubble into something fabulous would be a new focus for me, the first statement that I was now able to run my own life. Never mind that I was ice-cold and had no bookings. This would become the incentive to rebuild my career because I would have to work extra hard to pay it off. It would be my Phoenix.

18

ooooo

In mid-October I returned to the part of my life that, more than anything else, is me. I returned to the stage, the one place I felt I still *belonged.*

My first performance at Caesars Palace was going to be the moment of truth, the test of whether I could walk onto a stage and not break down. Whether audiences would think the wife of a suicide was funny.

In the dressing room before the show, I was almost shaking with fright. There would be thirteen hundred people in the showroom, a sellout, all come to see the freak act. Would they accept me? Would they laugh? I banned all friends from the audience, anyone who would remind me of who I was—so in my head I would be just a funny lady with no past, trying to see if even one suicide joke would work.

Getting ready, I perversely refused to wash my hair—"To hell with them!"—and then changed my dress four times to look good and slapped a diamond pin on my shoulder. I did not want to be glitzy show business. I wanted to be classy, wanted a minute and a half of dignity onstage before I said "shit."

When I walked onstage, the audience stood up, and the orchestra applauded by rapping their violin bows on the music stands. But I was still very shaky, and the musicians knew it. Without being asked, they remained behind the curtain, ready to go on and play if I could not cut it. I was so touched by their support.

Onstage I went right at the suicide. I wanted the audience to see I was able to deal with it and so should they—and not have them sitting there through the whole act waiting for it to come up. I steeled myself for the first joke: "My whole life has been so horrendous this year—as many of you may know—because of my husband's suicide and being fired by Fox. Thank God my husband left in his will that I should cremate him and then scatter his ashes in Neiman-Marcus. That way he knew he would see me five times a week."

When I had their laughter and their relief, I knew the show was going to be okay. Thank God. I discovered, however, that my audience no longer wanted to see me as a sexual woman. They wanted me to be their sister who had lost her husband and has no boyfriend. One night a man up front called out, "I'd sure like to sleep with you," and the audience gasped.

When I tried new jokes about dating men, the audience became very quiet. Here's an example: "I don't think I'm good in bed. I said to this guy, 'Why don't you call out my name when we're making love?' and he said to me, 'I don't want to wake you up.'" Silence. They were embarrassed, so I changed it: "I don't think I'm good in bed. I once said to my husband, 'Why don't you call out my name . . .'" Same joke. Roaring laughter. Fascinating.

I knew by now that mourning is an emotional roller coaster, but I did think I was leveling out—and then, out of nowhere, I was hit again. Ironically it was the day before Thanksgiving that a friend called to read me an article she had just seen in an advance copy of *Gentleman's Quarterly*. It was horrifying.

Illustrated with a savage caricature, it was written in the first person by somebody who signed himself "Bert Hacker." A pseudonym. "I have known Joan Rivers for more than twenty years," he began, "since the day when she used to crack up small clubs and dinner parties, before anyone knew her name."

Hacker went on to say that he had met me by chance after the

Fox firing, and I practically forced him to have dinner "right then and there." He described me tearing into Edgar and confiding that I had told Edgar to "stay out of my life." When Hacker politely defended Edgar, he had me telling nasty jokes—"Really, when I think of the way he makes me crazy, I really wonder if they didn't execute the wrong Rosenbergs."

After Edgar's death, Hacker was supposedly summoned by Billy Sammeth to attend our *shivah*. Depicting himself as the only kind person in a bizarrely ostentatious house, he portrayed a scene of utter crassness, with an unspeakably brassy, vulgar Joan Rivers telling savage jokes about Edgar.

At one point Hacker had me on the phone telling my publicist to negotiate for a *People* magazine cover story, and saying, "I've done a lot of crappy stuff for *People* that I didn't want to do. They owe me this one. Who's got a bigger story this week?" I was devastated. You cannot imagine the lies the reading public will believe if they are endorsed by being published in a national magazine. I went over the details of the piece in my mind time after time after time, wishing I could just let it go but emotionally unable to. I had to set the record straight.

Hacker set the date for the dinner we were supposed to have had ten days before the *shivah* began—which was when we were in Ireland. *People* did have an article on the suicide, but the writer, a family friend and my collaborator on this book, came primarily as a mourner. When the *shivah* started, the article was already written, and I refused to pose for pictures, allowing him to choose old ones.

After Thanksgiving I announced a $50 million lawsuit pending a retraction. I also offered $5,000 for the real name of Bert Hacker.

Meanwhile, I was again saved by my career. I was scheduled to depart on December 2 for a tour of Australia, booked before Edgar's death. Just before I left, I learned that Hacker was a Los Angeles free-lance writer named Ben Stein, a former Nixon speechwriter. He had never met me or been inside my house.

Almost immediately *GQ*—which publicly said the piece was only a spoof—began putting out feelers to settle. Ben Stein took the low road. His lawyer telephoned mine and threatened that unless I called off the suit, Stein would release a statement that I was a lesbian and Edgar a homosexual and that I gave him the pills he used to kill himself. My lawyer wrote asking for a letter confirming this phone call, and Stein's lawyer wrote back saying he had misunderstood. I am a little sorry the statement never happened. I looked forward to telling the world that it was Ben Stein's wife who brought me out of the closet.

Stein went on the interview circuit, insisting that what he had done was just emulating the reporting on Watergate by Bob Woodward and Carl Bernstein, and writing under a false name was "in the tradition of Alexander Hamilton and Samuel Johnson." He told Mitchell Fink, a columnist for the *Los Angeles Herald Examiner,* that he taught a course in libel law at Pepperdine College. Fink checked and found it was, in fact, a "cultural course" titled "From Woodstock to Watergate."

My lawyers were getting depositions, and the bills were mounting. I was assured I would win, but I also remembered Wayne Newton's $19 million victory from NBC. It was reduced on appeal to $5 million and he is still in litigation. After a lot of wrangling, Stein sent me a check for my favorite charity, and *GQ* printed a statement which included:

> It was never the intention of either Mr. Stein or GQ to portray Ms. Rivers in a negative manner. Instead, both Mr. Stein and GQ believe that the statements and actions which appeared in the article showed Ms. Rivers using her famous wit to get through a very difficult period. Both Mr. Stein and GQ sincerely regret any inadvertent imputation of negative or inappropriate conduct to Ms. Rivers in connection with her late husband's death. They have no reason whatsoever to believe that Ms. River's grief was anything but sincere, or that she was anything but a devoted wife.
>
> For her part, Ms. Rivers wishes to emphasize that she did not mean to question the integrity of Mr. Stein as a journalist or of GQ as a magazine.

I had made my point to the public.

The three weeks in Australia in December were a flashback to the years before leaving Carson, when I was fresh and hot and writers reviewed my comedy, not me. The Australian audiences were loving, and one review even said I should have a statue built in my honor. At last I felt the dark weight lifting a little, a kind of bittersweet happiness.

With my little group of helper-friends, I went sightseeing through grasslands, ranch lands, holding koala bears, petting kangaroos, spending three magical days in a semitropical rain forest. In the midst of all this natural beauty Bert Hacker and *Gentleman's Quarterly* seemed, at last, far far away.

During the trip my friend Marci Goldberg died. Four months earlier she had been at Edgar's memorial service, so alive, so beautiful, in pain yet denying anything was wrong, such a trouper. For her, no more dreams and plans to fulfill. She had always been there for me, someone I could truly depend on. I had a tremendous sense of fate, everything so much bigger than all of us, snipping off lives. I thought then that forces larger than I took away my career and my husband—and now my friend. At that moment I began to understand that my own courage, mine alone, would have to be enough.

I arrived back at Ambazac on December 23, feeling I had a career on some level in England and Australia. I felt together enough to fly to New York for Christmas with Melissa. In the hotel we had a little tree and presents, which we opened with Tommy Corcoran and Marci Goldberg's daughter, Jessica. Tiny, vital steps like sharing the ritual of opening Christmas presents with friends can bring a new calm, a small sense of self-reliance.

Back in California I had my first dinner party since Edgar's death. Every piece of silver was polished, the house was filled with flowers. I learned again how to handle a car and drove myself out to the airport and back and was ridiculously proud. I went alone to perform at Carlos 'n' Charlie's and forced myself to go alone to parties.

My concentration returned, and I could read again. I had a business lunch with Mel Brooks and represented myself entirely. Now, *I* was worrying about the house, whether the roof was seeping water. With that came pride for my possessions.

I was beginning to master my business life—and found myself becoming much tougher, able to say a flat-out no without palming the job off on somebody else. I was proud of these new sea legs, of my ability to watch costs, check bank statements, to get on the phone to my business people and say, "Wait a second. Maybe we should form a separate corporation."

Though self-consciousness and guilt were never far from the surface, my pleasure was less manic, and it lasted longer. One afternoon Melissa, a college friend of hers, Tommy Corcoran, and I were in the Palm Court of New York's Plaza Hotel. They were laughing and enjoying themselves, and I found myself thinking, Well, at least we have a semblance of a family, when suddenly a friend of Edgar's came over from another table to offer condolences. The thin skin of our fun was broken, and the pain welled through. We were out of there in fifteen minutes.

One of the best things, though, about this period was that my anger at Edgar was beginning to soften. I began having dreams about him. In my dream I would be talking to somebody, and he would show up. No explanations. And I would be furious at him. "You're back?" I screamed at him in the dream, "After what you've done, no apologies?" Perhaps those dreams were part of a purging process, because the pettiness was melting away, the shock finally easing.

Now, I could allow myself to move on, to think more and more of the simpler times between the two of us, our relationship at the beginning. The good things in our life stood separately, unconfused by blame. I was able now to polish the barnacles off my memories of our marriage. A tremendous weight was lifting.

There was still one last area that remained full of fear and uncertainty—romance. I think a widow's two most painful passages beyond her own sorrow are finding a new relationship with her children and dealing with the single men who begin calling for dates.

I enjoy the company of men, yet I was frightened that if men found the real me, they would dislike this person who was not very pretty, not easy to live with, desperately shy, terribly driven, compulsive, a workaholic, a textbook of insecurities. All women are still twenty when it comes to love. Nothing changes. I did go out with a few men but disliked being a *date*, being with somebody but not *with* him. I was not ready for the ritual questions. When a man's hair is pepper-and-salt, asking "Where did you go to school?" feels stupid.

Some men didn't even try to ask questions. All they were interested in was Joan Rivers the celebrity. One time an architect, a Princeton man, invited me to the theater in Pasadena. When I arrived, he had three friends with him who had been told, "Joan Rivers is coming," and a photographer from the local newspaper was waiting. I was a trophy.

On the other hand, I was discovering, too, that no matter how much I wanted to be treated like everybody else, most men outside of show business cannot deal with what Dom DeLuise once told me: "The minute you leave the house, it is all public relations." I began seeing a funny, funny man, Bernard Goldberg, to whom my career was an impediment, an embarrassment. When a *New York Post* photographer wanted to take my picture as we went in to a charity event, he tried to pull me away. Paradoxically I was delighted that he was unimpressed by who I was and simply liked the humorous widow Rosenberg, yet I was hurt that he could not accept my career, never went to see me perform. I told him, "This is part of the package when you untie the bow."

In public I am constantly on display, constantly in a performance mode—tense, having to charm, a little distant, and extremely careful. If a man takes my hand, I pull it away. If he wants to talk deeply in a restaurant, he does not get my undivided attention. Once, while a new acquaintance was telling me about the year he spent watching his wife die of cancer, four people shoved paper in my face asking for autographs. In situations like this, it takes longer to turn people away than to give in and sign.

The public pushes right in, does not see anybody but you. This is difficult for men. Some are furious at the intrusion, and I never see them again. Others join in too much and clown with the fans. Either way, I am embarrassed.

A celebrity is really barred from normal life. Even in private I find it difficult to be spontaneous among the civilians outside of show business. At a dinner party, if I mention a celebrity friend, suddenly guests are asking, "Oh, do you know her?" So you feel isolated. You are coming from a different castle.

Show business is like a giant cousins' club. I can be myself with show-business people because an unwritten celebrity code says we do not talk about each other to civilians. With civilian men who are not yet real friends, I have to be always on guard, careful not to give away real intimacies. If I tell a man that my business manager had a tail and two weeks later we split up, sooner or later that man will be saying at dinner parties, "Did you know Joan Rivers's business manager had a tail?" Fifteen years ago Elizabeth Taylor had a romance with a man named Henry Wynberg. He sold the story to the *Star*—including private pictures.

Now that I'm going out a lot, I'm aware of how some women are treated by their husbands and lovers—the lack of respect. I will not settle for a man who does not appreciate me, does not think he's getting the prize package. The package may be a bit older by then, may take the stairs a bit slower—but unless he thinks he is getting the best in the world, I'm not interested.

19

⦾⦾⦾⦾⦾

My head was churning with the words, "Don't dream but wouldn't it be wonderful if . . . keep smiling; the cameras are on you. . . . God, for once let it happen. . . . No matter what happens, *smile.*" It was June 28, 1990, at the Emmy Award ceremony in the New York Marriott Hotel. I was there, and the screen was flashing the nominees for Best Talk Show Host—Sally Jessy Raphael, Phil Donahue, Oprah Winfrey, The Frugal Gourmet, and Joan Rivers. I had made it back from the dead with *The Joan Rivers Show,* produced by the Tribune Corporation.

Susan Keith from *Loving* opened the envelope. "The winner is, JOAN RIVERS."

The instant was entire, immaculate joy, nothing mingled in it, no fear, no guilt. Total happiness. My feelings were a sheet of shining glass, not a bump, not a mark, not a scratch, clean, pure glass with sunlight streaming through. One of the purest moments in my life.

If I had fallen and broken both legs, I still would have gotten onto that stage. On my way up Donahue kissed me, and later his wife, Marlo Thomas, had tears in her eyes. I know Phil was genuinely pleased I had won—which is very rare in this business.

At the podium I started with a joke: "I always had a fantasy as a child that I'd win one of these, but I never thought I'd be this old when the fantasy came true." I thanked all the Tribune people as honorable, decent men, thanked my amazing staff, my own people, and Melissa. Now I understood why winners thank everybody. You want to share the joy, let it spill onto your friends and loved ones.

I went on, "Two years ago I couldn't get a job in this business. My income dropped to one sixteenth of what it was before I was fired. My husband, as you know, had a breakdown. It's so sad that he's not here because it was my husband, Edgar Rosenberg, who always said you can turn things around. And except for one terrible moment in a hotel room in Philadelphia, when he forgot that, this is really for him, because he was with me from the beginning."

I could not continue. I was crying. Welling up in me was the tragedy of Edgar's whole life, the futility of his suicide. I wanted to tell him, "We're back. We're back, you *idiot.*"

As I made my little speech, I felt an intense empathy with the crowd, a respect in a silence I could almost reach out and touch. I was speaking to my peers, who had all known their own pain, the fear that next year they would not be here. We all share a profession lent to us by businessmen and audiences who can leave us in a day. We had all started out as children reaching for a foggy something we only half recognized, and we had all fought through humiliation and degradation and become household names—an incredible achievement. United by struggle and luck and anxiety, we were a kind of club, and I think when I made it back, they were thinking, Thank God. That could someday be me, too.

Feeling a rush of triumph, I thrust the Emmy above my head— like a Lilliputian Statue of Liberty. At that moment I was the top woman in my profession. There was a rightness to the universe. Hard work had done what I had been taught it should—it had won the award, won the dream. I had proved that I did belong in the business. I had done it twice, twenty-five years apart, against all odds, which meant I could do it again in 2015.

Afterward, clutching my Emmy, I raced out of the hall to a

limo to drive to New Jersey to a private plane for a flight to Las Vegas and Caesars Palace. Along the road we realized we were famished, and we stopped at a McDonald's. I was not going to let go of that Emmy, so I carried it inside, and Miss Top of Her Profession stood in line for her burger, clutching a gold statue.

The turn in my luck that led to the Emmy began in early March of 1988. Still knocking on every possible door, I saw an item in *The New York Times* saying that the producer Manny Azenberg planned a repertory company at Lincoln Center. I called Manny, who had known me as an actress ever since Neil Simon wanted to rewrite *The Odd Couple* for two women, me and Nancy Walker. I told Manny to keep me in mind, and he said he would think about it.

Two weeks later he asked if I was interested in replacing Elizabeth Franz in the role of Kate Jerome, Eugene's mother in Neil Simon's *Broadway Bound.* Even with the Pulitzer Prize that he won for *Lost in Yonkers,* I think Neil Simon is the most underrated playwright in America; the critics always give him backhanded compliments, but he has such depth, such insight into human pain—and he does it with humor. Instantly I told Manny Azenberg I wanted to pursue the part. He said, "Come and look at it and we'll talk."

Suddenly I was terrified. Acting had always been a diamond I carried hidden in my pocket. Now, after all these years, I did not want to reach into that pocket unless everybody was going to say, "Wow, we've got to get sunglasses."

Exhausted by my doubts and anxieties, I traveled to New York to see *Broadway Bound*—and fell asleep during the second act. Fell asleep! So I had missed the mother's big scene where she describes the one magnificent moment of her life, going to a dance where George Raft chose her to whirl with him around the floor. Talk about Freud!

The second time, believe me, I kept my eyes open and saw the part was wonderful. I knew that woman, that poor lady who did everything she thought was right and lost her husband and her boys in the space of three months. That was me in the last scene all alone, polishing the dining-room table where nobody would ever eat again. Polishing that table, I knew the disintegration of a family.

I told Manny I was interested, and he told me I would have to come in and read. That was fine with me. Other people were saying, "Stars don't read for parts." But I knew better. Colin Higgins, the director, once told me that Burt Reynolds, at his height, wanted the part of the Sheriff in *The Best Little Whorehouse in Texas* so badly, he asked to audition.

After four intense days working with Nina Foch in California, I reported in early April to the Minsky Building in New York. I read for Manny and Gene Saks, the director. Neil Simon had told them not to offer the part unless they were 100 percent sure. "We're not looking for a celebrity stunt," he said.

Manny and Gene offered me the part then and there. After twenty-five years, my first love had called me up. I was ecstatic.

I telephoned Melissa to tell her I had the part. She was thrilled for me, glad that I was making my way. I learned later that she had been worried about me, and kept asking friends, "Is my mother all right?" We felt truly bonded, but our relationship was the last unfinished business from the suicide. We still had to work through and close off the blame, the survivors' legacy.

We had compartmentalized in ourselves, created the fond-mother-and-daughter box and the anger box, which was kept closed and shut away. But the compartments sometimes leaked, and suddenly in a phone call, the anger would flash back and forth between us—both of us needing the other, feeling abandoned. Our relationship became more and more unstable, both of us playing out upon each other our hurt and loss.

Our major bone of contention was the house on Ambazac Way. Melissa wanted desperately to keep it—wanted to hold on to the scene of all her childhood memories, of her happiness, her roots—in total, her father. But nowadays she was almost never home and planned after college to move into a place of her own.

I, however, had come to hate Ambazac. It depressed me. It was too large. I felt imprisoned at night behind those locked gates with a patrolling guard. I wanted to leave the house and live in my New York apartment. When my accountant told me I could not afford both places, Melissa and I were at loggerheads. Terrible, hurting things were said by both of us—until we made peace, ventilated our anger in sessions with her therapist.

Then, in a plane to Chicago, I made my decision. I stood at an airport phone and made maybe the hardest call of my life. I told Melissa, "I know the house means so much to you; I will stay in California. I will sell New York." I hung up and cried for an hour.

Later in the day, she called back. "Sell Ambazac," she said. "It doesn't matter. Home is where you are, Mother."

That was our major turning point. The healing began. Forgiveness began. A week later we had some days together in Ambazac, and she slept in my bed, she on my side, I on Edgar's.

My four days of rehearsal with the cast of *Broadway Bound* began in the four days before the opening on June 20. They were very skeptical about me, not happy at all.

Both Linda Lavin, who had created the role, and Elizabeth Franz had used roughly the same movements, same timing, same line readings, both playing the mother as a tough, proud woman who had one shining moment when she danced with George Raft. I played Kate Jerome as a woman beaten down by life. Every day from two o'clock on she had always cooked the dinner and set the table. At the end, polishing that table, she is left with only the memory of her one moment with George Raft.

Kate Jerome was a great part for me because I felt sorry for her and yet admired her, so strong, so proud, so angry. In a way I played the women in my audiences whom I know so well. I played her funny, funny, sad. To play Kate, I tapped into that part of myself that had seen many, many dreams go awry.

In my version of "Method acting" I find a memory that will make me feel the way my character needs to feel. For the George Raft scene I recalled a time that is like a rainbow to me. I was in high school. Six of the most popular boys in the school took me with them on a three-hour drive around Manhattan in one of their father's convertibles. The top was down, the radio was playing, and it was a bright spring day. For the first time in my life I felt pretty and young; everything was ahead of me. You have to savor those moments. The rest of life is just waiting to have them again.

The evening of my first performance Dorothy Melvin stood at the stage door refusing everything. At the Fox opening I had been inundated with flowers and telegrams, so this time I did not set myself up for such hurt. It would have been bad luck. In my dressing room I was very nervous, my hands sweaty, a tingling in my fingers, shooting pains in my legs. Melissa came up from college and cued my lines for me until curtain time. Elizabeth Franz came by and wished me well—a classy woman.

Afterward Manny Azenberg said, "Terrific, terrific. It was all your doing. Don't forget that"—which was lovely. He knew I had received little help onstage from anybody. The cast was cool to me. I was still not one of them.

Manny staggered the invitations to the critics over the next week, so I would not be hit with all the reviews in one night. But the critics liked me, and, relieved, grateful, I felt as though I had escaped a prison. The performance went fairly well, and I received an ovation. They wrote: "Rivers's performance simply amazing"—"Joan is riveting"—"first and foremost an actress"—"unexpectedly stunning." The New York *Daily News* said, "There's no doubt that Rivers is, after many years as a comedienne, still an actress."

Clive Barnes of the *New York Post* went to the theater "not expecting very much." He wrote, "Rivers has always struck me as precisely the kind of vulgar, raucous individual, rude, insinuating, and so much else, that I thoroughly dislike." He then went on to write, "Rivers is beautifully truthful and touching. Her coolly understated acting looked neither contrived nor phony. The shtick-stuck, jokey, elbow nudging naturalism of television had been abandoned and Rivers was indeed Broadway bound. . . . I went to scoff and stayed to admire."

The tickets, which had been twofers, went back up to full price, and the curtain came down ten minutes later at night because people were laughing. The actors had to play again to the balcony. They were amazed when I got applause after my big scene. Their faces were shocked when I got standing ovations and three curtain calls. But they still fought me onstage, trying to take over scenes—and were flabbergasted that I had the stage-craft to hold my own and protect myself.

People do not realize how much craft stand-up comedy re-quires. Making everything sound fresh each night, as though it just entered your head, requires acting. Stand-up is like being in the same play for five years.

One by one the actors stopped fighting me, and we became a terrific cast working together. The first to come around was Adam Philipson, who played my son. I had just finished the George Raft scene with him, and he whispered through the back curtain, "That went *very* nicely." I was so proud to be accepted.

Just walking onto that stage was bliss. I felt like it was *my* set, *my* kitchen. I was not a visitor. I was being let into the castle. Seeing my name on Broadway, being part of that community, was sheer joy. On opening night the whole cast of *M. Butterfly* sent me a signed poster from their show. Walking down Forty-fourth Street, I often met Mandy Patinkin, who starred in *Sunday in the Park with George.* He would ask, "How's it goin'?" and I'd go, "Great, how's it goin'?" "Great." Every cop on the Broad-way beat said hi. When I went to Sardi's, they gave me the actors' menu—half-price to show people.

I went to a cocktail party and stood with Michael Crawford, who was in *The Phantom of the Opera* when the phantom was *the Phantom,* and we talked about sustaining a mood when you feel ill onstage, and how one keeps going—the two of us talking actor to actor.

Broadway Bound saved my life. I was joyful about my work again. It made me remember why I was in the business. I saw, too, that I could hold people without making them laugh. In comedy people come primed to laugh, and making that hap-pen is a high—but I had forgotten the even bigger high that comes from creating a character, an emotional environment that moves an entire audience. That is what theater is to me, a whole room in the grip of a single feeling and letting that feel-ing wash over you.

Edgar once said to me, "We'll get you a dramatic part on Broadway, and then you'll do your act the same night and show you can do everything." So each night after *Broadway Bound* I put on those beads and necklaces and went to Michael's Pub and hit them over the head with Leona Helmsley and Imelda Marcos jokes. I was going into debt about seven thousand dollars every week I was in the play, so the club money was welcome. But more, for me the act was like going to the gym. I was working out like an athlete.

We closed after a Sunday matinee on September 25, 1988. The theater was going to be taken over by another play, and the producers considered moving to another theater, but cutting the set down became too expensive. They wanted me to extend through January 1, but I had to go to Las Vegas for two weeks just to make money. I was miserable. During the scene where Kate says good-bye to her two boys, I usually hugged each of them. But I was scared that if I touched them, I'd cry. I just stood there, stiff, and they had to hug me—and then I did cry. On the last day, I found the correct performance.

The cast of a Broadway show becomes your family, your social life. We work on the weekends; public holidays are not our holidays. We must have our own Thanksgiving. The feeling is very close-knit, very tight. Anyone who ever went to summer camp knows about this—the heartbreak of absolute loss when the season is over.

Positive events seem to beget good things. I was offered a made-for-cable movie by HBO. I had the apartment now and was deep in its restoration. And my house couple, Jacob and Inger Bjerre, who had stayed on to see me through all my troubles, agreed to rearrange their lives again and settle me in New York. A life of my own was taking shape again. My comedy bookings increased, and audiences in Las Vegas once more filled the showroom. I believe people like to see their icons humanized by suffering. Elizabeth Taylor fell off the wagon, got back on, fell off, got back on again, and now she is more beloved than ever. Because my life had gone through so many upheavals, people learned to have an affection for me not possible before. If in their eyes I could survive, then they could survive, too. By getting through one day at a time. By blustering and wearing blinders. By riding through the bad stuff and staying busy and never stopping.

I thought often of my Aunt Alice, who was married to a bank vice president and had an affair with the famous impresario Sol Hurok. My uncle, protecting his child and his career, said nothing, but quietly disinherited her. When he died, she found herself sitting alone in a Park Avenue apartment, a penniless woman of fifty-four who had never worked in her life.

"I'm too old to sell hats in Macy's, thank you very much," she said, and rented out rooms to Russian refugees—you would open a closet, and there would be somebody cooking eggs. She opened an art gallery and did just fine. My mother was just as strong. On no money she kept her family afloat with style, got her girls into good colleges, and lived in Larchmont until she died.

The next step in my salvation really began one night onstage during *Broadway Bound* when I thought, This is terrific, but I miss interviewing people. The next day my agent called with an offer from the Tribune Corporation to host a syndicated daytime talk show. If he had called a day earlier, I would have said, "I'm finished with that. I'm an actress. Look at me, I'm wearing jeans and a pea jacket. Can't you tell?"

When I met the Tribune people, I liked them. They were midwesterners, seemed up-front about everything, nice, straight-shooting guys who said, "We like you and want to do business with you." But I needed a long time to really believe that. I had my lawyer check everything and confirm everything in writing. I even called Geraldo Rivera—whose show is syndicated by the Tribune Corporation—and asked him what I should do. Geraldo raved about them, which was lovely considering he would no longer be their only child.

I arrived angry at the creative meetings to choose the director, the staff, design the set. I remember sitting with my hands clenched under the table, and my first words were always, "What's the matter?" They would say, "Nothing's the matter." I would say, "I want the set beige," and they said, "Fine." I was dumbfounded. We were all on the same side.

I knew the budget inside and out—it started out at $130,000 a week. These people had no subtext. When they came to me and said, "This is what we want," that was what they wanted, no more, no less. When I said, "This is what I want," they usually said, "Let's try it."

When I said, "There's no way we can pull in what we need at this price," they would say, "Then increase the budget"—and we still ended with an economical show. They did not come to me with every single problem, only the ones that couldn't be solved without me. The producer handled everything else, which is as it should be.

When we went on the air on September 5, 1989, I never knew that the president and vice presidents of Tribune were in the control room during the first half-dozen shows. They said, "Leave her alone. She doesn't need us second-guessing her." Because of the Fox experience, when they did not come near me, I thought they were disappointed and angry.

In those first months, still wounded from Fox, I was scared to ask for things that had been such huge issues, like a car and a personal guard. But without my asking, they quietly gave them to me. More important, they gave me respect and returned to me my self-respect as a talk-show host.

Being happy alone, not dreading another long night of anxiety and fear and remorse, was the last goal to be reached. As late as 1989 I still did anything to kill an evening. Publicists have lists of celebrities, and I accepted every party invitation. Cartier is having an opening? I'll be there. A book party at the Madison Avenue Bookshop? Here I am.

I went out several times as Malcolm Forbes's date, once to the eighty-ninth birthday party he gave for Mrs. Douglas MacArthur, a charming lady who to me is a real piece of history. I spent the Fourth of July on Donald Trump's yacht, which was like an ocean liner. For about 150 people fifteen chefs made quail eggs Benedict, goat-cheese lasagna, rack of lamb, four kinds of lobster salad, twenty-five kinds of hors d'oeuvres, thirty-seven hot and cold dishes, and a scale model of the yacht sculpted in chocolate. I sat next to Diandra Douglas, Mrs. Michael Douglas, who asked me,

"What do you think of the decoration on this yacht?" I said, "I don't know you well enough to tell you."

I found that recovery from grief takes place not in the head but in the gut. I think your body, not your head, knows what you need to survive. I think you should let your instincts tell you what to do, and ignore all those people so full of advice on how to behave.

Because of the hectic pace, when I did get home, I was happy to be there. Gradually solitude became something to be desired. The social whirl had worn out my need to be in constant motion. I settled into an old life that felt like a new life. Now I found myself returning to early friends from my struggle years. And friends who were peripheral to my marriage became important in my new life.

I had known Kenneth Battelle professionally for twenty-three years and did not realize there was a close, close connection there, waiting to happen. Kenneth is the voice of reason in my life, my Jiminy Cricket who has no time for my neurotic worrying. I wear his friendship as an ornament because he gives it to so few people.

During that year some of the changes in my world were extremely painful. Dear, funny Billy Sammeth, my friend and manager, decided not to come to New York with me. For some people California will always be home. But I was lucky. I had Dorothy Melvin to take over brilliantly. And no one has been so loyal, so caring. She's grown to be a sister to me.

Jason Dyl, who had given me the confidence that I could look good, who had lifted me onto the International Best Dressed list, was being taken by AIDS. In an era when you do not live and die with your kin, the list of people with AIDS who were among my extended family was getting longer and longer. In their thirties and forties, they were like a picture in which one face after another disappears. When Lucille Ball died, I could handle that. She went out with flags flying after a great life. She had money, family, recognition. To die approaching eighty is not tragic. To die at forty is.

I haven't had the opportunity to say good-bye to many people. Not my mother. Not Edgar. So it was truly restorative for me to

be able to help Jason. I had the chance to act out my love for him.
I think God should give everybody the chance to say good-bye,
to close and seal those doors, because who you love is what life
is all about, being there for people.

Throughout that year my daughter began finding peace by
giving help. She counseled a friend whose mother decided to
take her own life by stopping treatment for cancer. She advised
another friend who had been holding his father's hand as his
father died of a stroke.

By 1988, when she came up to New York on weekends, we
could start confiding again. Just as I had sat on the rim of my
mother's tub gossiping with her, now Melissa sat with me as I took
a bath.

We still had rough times, but I was less vulnerable to guilt. I
understood at last that no one killed Edgar. Edgar killed Edgar.
He had the choice to change our relationship, to evolve through
therapy. He decided he would rather be dead. I could now tell
Melissa, "If you really still think I killed Daddy, that is your
problem now, and you must go back into therapy."

She in turn was coming to see that she could love her father
and still love me, too.

I have always understood that the grief process takes two years,
and I think that is right. Melissa's graduation from the University
of Pennsylvania was the last gasp of my mourning—two ceremo-
nial rites of passage that finally laid Edgar to rest.

Watching the graduation ceremony, I was thrilled by the pomp
and circumstance, the professors and the Ph.D.'s, the graduating
class filing in dressed in their robes. Over that sea of robes I
spotted Melissa, so pretty and full of life, so popular with her
peers. When she proceeded to the stage in cap and gown and
accepted her diploma, I felt this moment was the jewel in my
crown. I had done something right. Edgar had done something
right.

My last day in Philadelphia, I went alone with a priest to the
hotel suite where Edgar killed himself. I wanted to see where he
had spent the last days of his life. In the bedroom Spike jumped
onto the bed and went right to what would have been Edgar's
side and snuggled against the pillow as he always did. That's nice,

I thought, like stroking Edgar. While the priest prayed, I looked at the bedside table where my picture had stood beside Melissa's and at the phone that he had reached for, and I stood on the spot where he had fallen. I prayed that the unhappiness that had become such a part of him could evaporate.

I left Philadelphia knowing that the human spirit is indomitable. But you must be honest with yourself and know what you want—and leave self-pity in the drawer. You must, with love, put your own needs and serenity first, because within the human spirit beats an independent, peaceful heart if you can just set it free.

Today I wake up happy with who I am and where I am. I think now I can face anything. I have learned to rely on myself, to know I can get through whatever faces me each day when I open the door. *That* is freedom.

And my happiness is my daughter, who is pretty and smart and laughing—and who is my friend. True friendship comes from surviving together, and Melissa and I have *some* backlog of "Look what we've come through."

What will I be doing in five years? I'm not worried. I'd love to be single in my great apartment—or married to a wonderful man. I'd love to be still doing my television show. But nothing is secure in show business. Maybe by the time you read this, my show will have been canceled. It's happened to me before, God knows. But the bottom I might hit would be nowhere near as deep. I have become my version of an optimist. If I can't get through one door, I'll go through another door—or I'll *make* a door. Something terrific will come no matter how dark the present.

God always comes up with a third-act twist—and we won't know until we die whether the play was a comedy or a tragedy. So you'd better be prepared for both. That's the exhilaration of being alive. There is always another scene coming out of nowhere. God is the best dramatist.

Index

•••••

ooooo

PHOTOGRAPH CREDITS

Broadway Bound: © copyright 1988, Martha Swope; by the pool at Ambazac: © copyright 1991, Harlequin Enter. Ltd.; Edgar's funeral: *People Weekly* © 1987 Curt Gunther; Melissa Rosenberg, equestrian: © Kenn Duncan; inside atrium at Ambazac: © Harry Benson 1983.

20

21

22

23

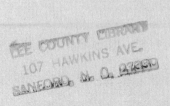

24

25

26

27

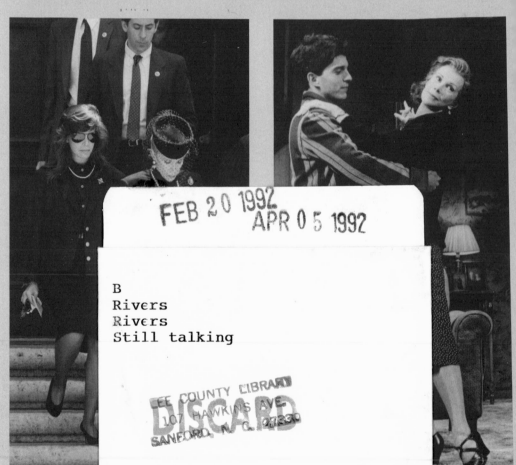

28